CITIZENSHIP IN A FRAGILE WORLD

Studies in Social, Political, and Legal Philosophy
General Editor: James P. Sterba, University of Notre Dame

This series analyzes and evaluates critically the major political, social, and legal ideals, institutions, and practices of our time. The analysis may be historical or problem-centered; the evaluation may focus on theoretical underpinnings or practical implications. Among the recent titles in the series are:

Moral Rights and Political Freedom
  by Tara Smith, University of Texas at Austin
Democracy and Social Injustice
  by Thomas Simon, Illinois State University
Morality and Social Justice: Point/Counterpoint
  by James P. Sterba, University of Notre Dame; Tibor Machan, Auburn University; Alison Jaggar, University of Colorado, Boulder; William Galston, White House Domestic Policy Council; Carol C. Gould, Stevens Institute of Technology; Milton Fisk, Indiana University; and Robert C. Solomon, University of Texas
Faces of Environmental Racism: Confronting Issues of Global Justice
  edited by Laura Westra, University of Windsor, and Peter S. Wenz, Sangamon State University
Plato Rediscovered: Human Value and Social Order
  by T. K. Seung, University of Texas at Austin
Punishment as Societal-Defense
  by Phillip Montague, Western Washington University
Liberty for the Twenty-First Century: Contemporary Libertarian Thought
  edited by Tibor R. Machan, Auburn University, and Douglas B. Rasmussen, St. John's University
Capitalism with a Human Face: The Quest for a Middle Road in Russian Politics
  by William Gay, University of North Carolina at Charlotte, and T. A. Alekseeva, Institute of Philosophy and Moscow State University
In the Company of Others: Perspectives on Community, Family, and Culture
  edited by Nancy E. Snow, Marquette University
Citizenship in a Fragile World
  by Bernard P. Dauenhauer, University of Georgia

CITIZENSHIP IN A FRAGILE WORLD

Bernard P. Dauenhauer

323.6
D238

ROWMAN & LITTLEFIELD PUBLISHERS, INC.

ROWMAN & LITTLEFIELD PUBLISHERS, INC.

Published in the United States of America
by Rowman & Littlefield Publishers, Inc.
4720 Boston Way, Lanham, Maryland 20706

3 Henrietta Street
London WC2E 8LU, England

Copyright © 1996 by Rowman & Littlefield Publishers, Inc.

British Cataloging in Publication Information Available

Library of Congress Cataloging-in-Publication Data
Dauenhauer, Bernard P.
Citizenship in a fragile world/by Bernard P. Dauenhauer.
p. cm.—(Studies in social, political, and legal philosophy)
Includes bibliographical references and index.
1. Citizenship. 2. Democracy. I. Title. II. Series
JF801.D28 1996 323.6 dc20 96-2177 CIP

ISBN 0–8476–8222–6 (cloth : alk. paper)
ISBN 0–8476–8223–4 (pbk. : alk. paper)

Printed in the United States of America

♾ ™ The paper used in this publication meets the minimum requirements of
American National Standard for Information Sciences—Permanence of
Paper for Printed Library Materials, ANSI Z39.48–1984.

Contents

In Memoriam
Bernard P. Dauenhauer, Sr.

Acknowledgments

In the course of writing this book, I have received valuable advice and help from a number of sources that I gladly and gratefully acknowledge. My colleagues, Victoria Davion, Beth Preston, and Clark Wolf have helped me considerably with their thoughtful responses to a number of my ideas. Bernard Crick, whose writings on politics are so admirable, generously provided some crucial guidance. I am especially indebted to Lawrence Biskowski and Joseph Walsh. Not only have they given me acute critiques of many parts of this book. But over a number of years they have been the finest of interlocutors. I deeply appreciate their friendship. An important stimulus to my thought about this topic was a faculty seminar some years ago sponsored by the Carnegie Council on Ethics and International Affairs. It was then that I first met Joel Rosenthal, now its president. I am most thankful for the encouragement he has given me during this project. I am also happy to acknowledge the support for my research that I have received from the University of Georgia Research Foundation.

Chapter 1

Points of Departure

The notion of citizenship has long held a prominent place in Western political thought. Though it has naturally undergone change over time, it always makes some claim to integrate the requirements of justice with those of society or community membership. It "is intimately linked to ideas of individual entitlement on the one hand and of attachment to a particular community on the other."[1]

Recent political developments in various parts of the world have prompted renewed attention to the notion of citizenship and its normative demands. Voter apathy in some states, the resurgence of nationalism in various parts of Europe, and the frequent failures of efforts to protect the environment that rely on the voluntary cooperation of citizens are just some examples of the sorts of matters that call for a fresh examination of what citizenship demands today. "These events have made clear that the health and stability of a modern democracy depends not only on the justice of its 'basic structure' but also on the qualities and attitudes of its citizens."[2] Such health and stability depend on such things as citizens' ability to tolerate and work with those who are quite different from themselves, to exercise self-restraint in their economic demands, to make responsible choices in matters that affect their health, and to participate thoughtfully in the political life of their society. "Without citizens who possess these qualities, democracies become difficult to govern, even unstable."[3]

The objective of this book is to articulate a new normative conception of democratic citizenship, a conception that responds appropriately to these and the other exigencies that democratic politics must deal with today and for the foreseeable future. I argue that the traditional conceptions of citizenship found in mainstream versions of both liberalism and communitarianism are insufficient to respond to

1

these exigencies. These conceptions are likely to remain insufficient because they depend, each in its own way, on an impoverished concept of the needs and capabilities of human beings, who are the practitioners of politics and the patients of its doings. In place of these conceptions, I propose and defend one that I call "complex citizenship." Complex citizenship requires that those who practice it recognize that they have political responsibilities not only to members of their own society but also to humanity as a whole. This latter set of responsibilities is sometimes directed to a particular group of foreigners. For example, citizens can have the duty to support peace-making or peace-keeping efforts in lands ravaged by either civil or interstate war. Complex citizenship requires that its practitioners also concern themselves with the political aspects of a sound approach to preserving the environment. It requires citizens to discharge these responsibilities even if doing so leads them into conflict with the policies of the government of their own state.

Complex citizenship is a notion that faithfully reflects all the politically significant features of the human condition, the condition of political agents. It squarely faces the fact that some people are thoughtful and others are thoughtless, some good and others wicked. It therefore makes an explicit issue of the political competence of citizens. A traditional staple of democratic politics has been the simple, nearly unquestionable assumption that every mentally normal adult citizen is competent to take part in all aspects of political life. Complex citizenship calls for its practitioners to make citizen competence an explicit issue. Responsible politics, on this conception, must both demand competence of its participants and provide sufficient resources so that all members of the society can gain that competence. Further, because it acknowledges that every society has had its thoughtless and wicked members, complex citizenship demands that its practitioners grapple with the practical ineliminability of coercion from political life. The thoughtless and the wicked must be stopped from doing damage either to members of their own society or to people elsewhere. Political thought and practice have the task of finding effective ways to stop them. Part of this task consists of spelling out the normative demands of citizenship.

Of course, no conception of citizenship entails without further ado any particular full-blown set of laws, policies, or institutions. But the conception that I propose and the considerations that warrant its adoption provide the basis for a set of recommendations and cautions that those who are charged with framing and implementing them should heed.

Like every serious political proposal, my argument begins in medias res. It rests on a complex set of antecedents that cannot, by their very nature, be definitively established. And I address it to the present audience that has as its task acting politically in a way that will prove in the future to have been sensible and decent. My argument for the concept of complex citizenship thus amounts to an exercise of what Aristotle called deliberative rhetoric. It is a discourse that seeks to determine how a society should understand and conduct itself so that it achieves a good future.[4] Such arguments are obviously always contestable. But the evidence for some of them can be compelling. I trust that my argument is one of these.

Let me begin my argument by making explicit four crucially important considerations on which it rests. Two of these considerations are drawn from the history of democracy's emergence as the form of government that best respects the human dignity of those who live under it. They amount to questions about whether citizenship is fundamentally an office or a status, and what the basic location or site of citizenship is. The other two considerations are drawn from reflections on the distinctive exigencies of our era that motivate a reconceptualization of citizenship. One of these considerations is the pervasive and increasing internationalization of so many parts of human life. The second is the emergence of a significant threat to the human habitability of the earth.

Taken together, these four considerations provide a rough sketch for how one should think anew about the normative dimensions of citizenship today. On the one hand, they warn against accepting a conception of citizenship that fails to acknowledge that the long tradition of thought about citizenship contains much that deserves preservation. On the other, they reveal that a conception of citizenship that takes as its domain of applicability only a particular state or commonwealth is insufficient for the material and cultural conditions that political life today must respond to.

Consider first what the tradition of thought about citizenship teaches us. In the history of the West since the Greeks, by and large, the title *citizen* has been prized and to be a good citizen has been grounds for praise. Citizenship and its appropriate exercise matter significantly not only to the citizen but also to those with whom he or she interacts, whether they be fellow citizens or not. But throughout this history, and particularly in times of widespread ferment, both how one comes to be a citizen and what makes one a good citizen have been matters of dispute. These disputes, unsurprisingly, have led to changes over time in the conceptions of what citizenship consists of and what one should expect of citizens.

Prized and praised as it is, state citizenship, like politics itself, is an artifact, dependent for its possibility on a population favored with appropriate material and cultural resources. Among these resources are such items as a dependable supply of the necessities for physical survival, diverse interests and aspirations, diverse technical skills, an education that enables at least a sizeable portion of the population to think abstractly and thereby to have the capacity to entertain alternative courses of communal action, and a widespread agreement on the propriety of resolving social problems by legal means. But no stock of such resources is of itself sufficient for citizenship. Indispensable for citizenship is a widely shared will to exercise it.[5] Though its exercise will of course be episodic, the shared will indispensable for citizenship must be habitual and settled. It cannot be constantly open to wholesale reappraisal even if the ways in which it is exercised are always open to criticism and revision. The settled character of the will is, of course, not absolute. But neither can it be nothing more than a brief stasis amid a more fundamental flux.

Nonetheless, the capacity for citizenship can never become a definitive attainment. The threat of losing this capacity is ineliminable. No individual or small group can guarantee a sufficiently inclusive shared will to make citizenship possible. Nor can we guarantee that the stock of necessary resources will always be available. Citizenship is thus always contingent, always more or less fragile. It is always possible that the capacity for citizenship may cease to exist.

Actual citizenship is always made up of two parts. One part is the legal ascription of citizenship. This ascription brings its recipients under a rule that both confers entitlements and immunities and imposes obligations. In doing so, legal ascription always introduces distinctions among people over and above those occurring by virtue of "accidents of birth," that is, by virtue of "any circumstance in a person's congenital condition not based on principles of just distribution such as desert or guilt."[6] One is a citizen because he or she has received commitments and become subject to obligations that others do not have.

The other part of citizenship consists in its exercise. One exercises citizenship in acting on the basis of these commitments and obligations. And part of the exercise of citizenship is defending this set of commitments against those who threaten it, whether the threat comes from within the community or from without and whether the threat is deliberately hostile. Of course, much argument within democracies concerns just what is a threat and what defenses against such threats are consistent with democracy. But this argument aside, the legal ascription and the exercise of citizenship exemplify the Aristotelian notion that citizenship consists in a state of being ruled that is no less a ruling.

In addition, actual citizenship constitutes a circumscribed society that effectively rules some people out by the way it rules the other people in. This society is meant to be stable and permanent, one whose members belong to it for life, through hard times as well as good times. And the society itself is "conceived as existing perpetuity: it produces and reproduces itself and its institutions and culture over generations and there is no time at which it is expected to wind up its affairs."[7] Citizenship thus requires the members of the society to be loyal to that society and its objectives.

Some people, it is true, have received multiple ascriptions of citizenship. But should conflict among the associated claims occur, these people are expected to declare their loyalty to one set. This unique loyalty is regularly called patriotism.

Notions of citizenship tied to particular societies have, however, always had their critics. Every political society claims that the ascriptions of citizenship that it makes and the distinctions it thereby draws between its citizens and others are just. But, as is well known, there have been persistent and deep disagreements within the Western tradition about the rational bases and content of justice. Since citizenship is inextricably tied to justice, disagreements about justice bear on the claims of citizenship as well. Who is or should be a citizen and who not? What are proper entitlements, immunities, and obligations to attach to citizenship and what are improper ones?

Roughly speaking, in the Western tradition there have been two main lines of thought about citizenship and the justice it claims as its underpinning. Both of these lines of thought continue to have strong proponents. I will argue that, for a conception of citizenship appropriate to our era, neither line can be either dismissed or wholly subordinated to the other.

One of these lines of thought, articulated by Plato and more subtly by Aristotle, claims that human beings are social by nature. Sociality ties us to other people in a variety of ways. Without these ties, one could not be completely human. Political ties, including that of citizenship, are among the most fundamental bonds that link us to one another. They have their ultimate roots in the very nature of human existence itself.

The other principal line of thought about citizenship and justice is well represented by Thomas Hobbes, John Locke, and Immanuel Kant, each in his own fashion. For them, all political ties spring from prudential judgments that each of us somehow makes about how we can gain protection against what threatens us and thereby find opportunities to satisfy our wants. Political commitments, then, are strategic agreements that we enter into with one another that are ultimately aimed at overcoming some obstacle to our satisfying our own individual purposes. They are not ingredient in the human condition itself. We could conceivably be fully developed without them.

As a consequence of these two lines of thought, as Michael Walzer points out, today

> we have . . . two different understandings of what it means to be a citizen. The first describes citizenship as an office, a responsibility, a burden proudly assumed; the second describes citizenship as a status, an entitlement, a right or set of rights passively enjoyed. The first makes citizenship the core of our life, the second make it its outer frame.[8]

Resolving the conflict between these two interpretations of citizenship requires a reconsideration of how one understands human beings, the political agents. I argue that a proper interpretation of what it is to be human has to acknowledge an equiprimordial commonality and individuality in our makeup. Only in concert with others do we find the wherewithal to recognize and express our individuality. On the other hand, only by virtue of the distinctive features that constitute each of us as an individual can the commonality distinctive of human existence be the variegated historical reality that it is.[9]

The conception of complex citizenship that I will propose fully takes into account my interpretation of human existence. It also has the merit of allowing one to salvage the insights that animate these two main Western traditions of thought about citizenship. Admittedly, the concept of complex citizenship is not wholly devoid of ambiguity. But its ambiguity faithfully reflects the ambiguity that is irremovable from everything political.

The Western tradition of thought about citizenship also contains a second controversy of great import. Its question is: Is one first and foremost a citizen of a particular body politic? Or is one primordially a citizen of the world? Proponents of the primacy of world citizenship have always been in evidence. But historically the far more practically influential view has been that a citizen's primary political concern ought to be the well-being of his or her home state. Giving the home state's well-being primacy has generally been regarded as not merely proper but also usually necessary if the citizen's political activity is to have a solid chance to be efficacious.

Concern for the well-being of one's home state does not restrict one to exclusively domestic concerns. Obviously, part of this concern will be a concern to keep the home state secure against foreign dangers. But it may also include helping to make available to foreigners cultural resources developed in the home state.

This latter effort can, of course, be either misguided or evil. One need only recall the perversity and arrogance that gave rise to the notion of the "white man's burden." Perhaps less perversity but surely some arrogance has been at play in some efforts to "make the world safe for democracy."

Nonetheless, sharing cultural resources is not necessarily either perverse or arrogant. I argue that a properly conceived citizenship today must neither dismiss nor trivialize the claims of either the state or the international community on those who would be good citizens. But state citizenship, or so I argue in Chapter 2, remains the foundation on which appropriate international political action must be based.

Both major strands of the Western tradition of thought about citizenship have naturally influenced reflection about what is the most appropriate kind of government. The upshot of this reflection is the widespread agreement that today and for the foreseeable future every morally defensible political regime must either make a properly conceived citizenship available to all of its citizens or be working toward this objective. Only a regime that is in some recognizable sense democratic satisfies this criterion. I subscribe to this view. Differences in material and cultural conditions may call for different forms of democracy. But to possess moral legitimacy today, a government must be democratic in both form and practice.[10] Only a recognizably democratic state can satisfy the demands of political justice.

This view has found expression in some of the resolutions of the United Nations. As J. E. S. Fawcett has pointed out,

[t]o the traditional criteria for the recognition of a regime as a new State must now be added the requirement that it shall not be based upon a systematic denial in its territory of certain civil and political rights,

including in particular the right of every citizen to participate in the government of his country directly or through representatives elected by regular, equal and secret suffrage.[11]

One can draw from the widespread acknowledgment of democracy's value what I will call the "democratic postulate." According to this postulate, (a) every qualified person has the right to participate in the governance of society to which he or she belongs, (b) every person has an interminable right to opportunities to achieve the requisite qualifications, and (c) every person has a set of legally specified rights that both limit the scope of governmental power and afford protection against arbitrary uses of the power that the government does possess. Though this postulate, like democracy itself, is rather indeterminate, it nonetheless serves as a basic criterion for assessing political thought and action.[12]

At the very least, it follows from this postulate that democratic states must promote as well as they can the spread of democracy to nondemocratic lands. Their citizens must press their authorities to acknowledge this obligation and act to discharge it. There is good reason for David Held to argue that for democracy to be secure in states where it is already established, it must be spread throughout the globe.[13] A substantial part of my overall investigation here is to determine what else one should educe from this democratic postulate.[14]

Reflection on the history of the concept of citizenship, however, whether taken alone or supplemented with the democratic postulate, would not necessarily impel one to look for a new conception of citizenship. Adherents of both liberalism and communitarianism also recognize the democratic postulate. And one can reasonably read the history of the traditional concept of citizenship as a story of tensions and their resolution that could continue to unfold according to its own internal dialectic. The running debates among liberals, civic republicans, and other communitarians might appear to be such a story.

The impetus to seek a new conception of citizenship comes from the complications to this story of citizenship that have come into play in our own era. These are the multifaceted phenomena of internationalization and the not-unrelated threat to the human habitability of the earth. Whether we wish it or not, we must live in a world that has been "made interdependent by communications, travel, technology, economic life, common threats to our environment, and the standing danger of nuclear destruction."[15] No part of politics, and hence no conception or institution of citizenship that ignores these defining features of our era, is defensible. It is these new features that give urgency to a reconception of citizenship.[16] In the absence of these features, one would have reason to dismiss out of hand the conception of complex citizenship that I propose. But in their presence, one can reasonably dismiss it only by proposing an alternative that fully takes them into account.

Consider in somewhat more detail the many faces of internationalization. Not the least of these faces is the internationalization of so much of economic life. Today, economic isolation is absurd. No economic activity of any significant size or scope can avoid having ramifications extending well beyond the borders of the state in which it takes place. To disregard this fact is to leave oneself unequipped to respond either to the opportunities or to the risks that this new situation presents. Today, more than ever before, strong economies can help weak ones improve. But they also have a greater capacity to harm them. And further, no economy is so strong that it can guarantee its own continued strength.

Indissociable from the internationalization of economic life is the internationalization of communication and transportation. What A does or says, B not only can but often unavoidably will come to know about and hence feel the effects of. For good or ill much of what was once the business of only some is now the business of all.

The widely available means of communication and transportation have had important consequences for population migrations, consequences that raise thorny political issues, both practical and conceptual. Of course, there have always been migrations, and migrations have always posed political problems. But today, these problems have grown dramatically in both size and complexity. Today it is harder than ever for many states to control their borders and the conditions under which migrants enter or leave them. It is harder to keep track of the immigrants who do enter them, and it is harder to control the flow of money across borders. The motivations and opportunities for emigrating grow apace. The tasks of formulating and implementing migration policy have thus become extraordinarily complex and unwieldy. The upshot of these centripetal forces is, as Hannah Arendt saw with prescience, "in our own world . . . each man is as much an inhabitant of the earth as he is an inhabitant of his country."[17]

These centripetal forces not withstanding, the context of political life today is complicated by the centrifugal pressures of separatism and nationalism that are in evidence in so many parts of the world. These pressures, often exerted in the name of a democratic principle of self-determination, work at cross-purposes to the pressure for greater international integration such as those involved in the formation of the European Union. The result of these often competing pressures is frequent sharp conflict and, all too often, armed hostilities.[18]

Besides more or less traditional armed conflicts, today's world is one in which terrorism is a constant danger. Few states, if any, can make themselves wholly secure from terrorists. It is a practical impossibility for a genuinely democratic state to do so. To achieve the cooperation necessary to minimize the threat of terrorism, states can no longer insist on their sovereignty in anything like the Hobbesian sense. They must enter into agreements and practices that allow other states or international bodies to make demands on them that they recognize as legitimate.

The multiplicity and depth of the problems that beset our world are such that they will inevitably transform all aspects of human life in the relatively near future. They are such that they lead some to wonder whether democracy as we know it can withstand these profound transformations. Robert Heilbroner, for example, asks:

> Can demographic explosions be halted without recourse to severe, even repressive population policies? Can multinational dislocations be brought under control without radically altering the relationship between business and government? Can an allocation of carbon emission rights be instituted or enforced without military force? Can the imperatives of capitalism be permitted to endanger the very continuity of the Western World (not to mention the underdeveloped continents . . .)? And if not, what socioeconomic system would replace it?[19]

This set of problems poses a threat not just to democratic forms of politics but to the human habitability of the earth itself. Today, one would be hard pressed to deny that there is a serious threat that we ourselves pose to the habitability of the earth. In former times, including the times in which democratic forms of government were developed, there was no evidence that the survival of the human species was in any serious way subject to threat by what people might do. Now, not only does this evidence exist, it even points to the likelihood of uninhabitability unless we change the ways we employ the earth's resources. There is, of course, the well-recognized threat of species-annihilating warfare, the most dramatic but perhaps not the most dangerous threat. But even without war, our now-customary way of living poses no less a danger. As Hans Jonas has said, it is

the peaceful and constructive use of worldwide technological power, a use in which all of us collaborate as captive beneficiaries through rising production, consumption, and sheer population growth . . . that poses threats much harder to counter.[20]

A statement sponsored by the Union of Concerned Scientists, called "World Scientists' Warning to Humanity," vividly spells out these threats. Ozone depletion and air pollution already cause widespread harm to forests, crops, and people. Water resources have been so heedlessly exploited that serious shortages have already developed in some eighty countries. There is severe destructive pressure on the oceans that endangers the supply of food fish. Current agricultural and animal husbandry practices have led to a serious degradation of large parts of the earth's vegetated surface. Both rain forests and dry forests are being destroyed at a terrifying rate. By the year 2100 as many as one-third of the present living species will be annihilated if present trends continue. The potential risks of global warming are huge. Unrestrained population growth threatens to engulf any efforts to bring about a sustainable future.

In view of these dangers, this statement concludes:

Our massive tampering with the world's interdependent web of life . . . could trigger widespread adverse effects, including unpredictable collapses of critical biological systems whose interactions and dynamics we only imperfectly understand. Uncertainty over the extent of these effects cannot excuse complacency or delay in facing the threats.[21]

To respond to these changes, this statement calls for a quick, thoroughgoing change in the way we live. Without such a change, we will bring on vast human misery and will irreparably mutilate the planet. And so:

No more than one or a few decades remain before the chance to avert the threats we now confront will be lost and the prospects for humanity immeasurably diminished. . . . A new ethic is required—a new attitude toward discharging our responsibility for caring for ourselves and for the earth. . . . This ethic must motivate a great movement, convincing reluctant leaders and reluctant governments and reluctant peoples themselves to effect the needed changes.[22]

Nearly a decade before this warning, Jonas had articulated the core principle of this new ethic. He recognized that in terms of biological evolution, the human species is destined willy-nilly to come to an end sometime, and in terms of individual people, each of us may reasonably risk his or her own life for some worthwhile purpose. But none of us has the right to jeopardize, by decisions that we make or actions that we perform, the continued existence of humanity. Accordingly, public policy and our own conduct is obligated to honor the following fundamental categorical imperative.

"Act so that the effects of your action are compatible with the permanence of genuine human life"; or expressed negatively: "Act so that the effects of your own action are not destructive of the future possibility of such life"; or simply: "Do not compromise the conditions for an indefinite continuation of humanity on earth"; or again turned positive: "In your present choices, include the future wholeness of Man among the objects of your will."[23]

Jonas's imperative can be reasonably interpreted as requiring the following: (a) engaging in species-threatening warfare is forbidden; (b) in living one's life, one should use renewable resources only in ways that are compatible with their renewal; (c) one should use nonrenewable resources only in ways that serve some rationally defensible purpose. Determining the precise meaning of these three requirements is an open-ended task. One therefore needs experts to provide ongoing estimates of just what these requirements amount to in practice.

Though there are some who would reject the Jonas imperative under any interpretation, it is hard to see how they could rightly reject it under my interpretation. To reject my interpretation, one would have to both acknowledge that there are some persons who could have full human lives and still hold that consuming resources they would need, even without one needing them oneself, is perfectly permissible. How one would defend such a position on any nonegoistic grounds eludes me. And egoism, I presume, is an insufficient base for a stable, humane politics.

I accept the conclusions of the "World Scientists' Warning" and I acknowledge what I will hereafter call the Jonas imperative as I here interpret it as the fundamental norm that all responsible politics must work to satisfy. The scientists' warning and his imperative, when taken together with the complex set of factors that make up what I will hereafter refer to simply as the internationalization of human life, are the two new considerations that urgently demand a reconceptualization of citizenship. No conception of citizenship that fails to respond effectively to these demands is any longer sound. The conception that I propose finds its warrant in very large part in the fact that it does hold promise of taking these demands fully into account while remaining recognizably democratic. In particular, the urgency of these two new considerations makes it imperative to address the issue of citizens' competence to take part in political decision making.

Without detracting from the grimness of the dangers we now face, though, we should not fail to notice that the internationalization of contemporary life does not exclusively portend disaster. It also gives rise to large opportunities to bring about goods of many different sorts. It brings new educational and cultural opportunities and new opportunities to help people in need.[24] It also allows us to hope that the rapid spread of ecological degradation can be rapidly halted and even reversed. Without internationalization there would be far fewer opportunities of this sort. And among these opportunities for good are those for fresh, vigorous exercises of responsible democratic citizenship.[25]

In sum, then, the four considerations that underpin the new conception of citizenship that I will propose are that (a) the history of the concept of citizenship cannot rightly be ignored in any sensible attempt to rethink it, (b) any acceptable conception of citizenship must observe the requirements of the democratic postulate, (c) today, a responsible conception must take into account the internationalization of human life, and (d) it must take into account the Jonas imperative. To develop a conception of citizenship that successfully deals with these four considerations, I will take advantage, on the one hand, of the substantial resources that Aristotle's practical philosophy contains. On the other, I will make use of leads that Arendt, Maurice Merleau-Ponty, Paul Ricoeur, and other present thinkers provide. What all these thinkers have in common is a keen awareness of the contingency and fragility of everything political. In both political thought and political practice, one cannot reasonably stand pat. One must proceed with innovations, but proceed cautiously.

I develop the case for my conception of citizenship in the following way. Because this conception aims to contribute to a long and rich debate about the meaning of citizenship, I devote chapter 2, to a critique of prominent present views concerning the nature of democratic politics, the notions of citizenship that these views embody, and the presuppositions concerning the constitutive features of human existence on which these views rest. The two most prevalent positions are those of democratic liberalism and communitarianism. Within liberalism, there are those who defend it as the appropriate form of politics for particular states. Other democratic liberal theorists promote a political cosmopolitanism of some sort. Communitarians stand in opposition to both of these forms of liberalism.

In making my critique of these positions, I draw attention to something of their historical antecedents, point out some of their weaknesses, and indicate which of their features one can and should salvage to help construct a new, better conception of citizenship. My discussion of these positions is, of course, by no means thoroughgoing and detailed. In it I aim to show only the need and the room for a new conception.

In chapter 3, I begin to articulate my own proposal. Because citizenship, like all of politics, is an artifact, how one understands what it is or can be is not disconnected from how one understands the artificer, the political agent.[26] My first task, therefore, is to spell out in some detail an interpretation of what it is to be a human being. This interpretation is by no means comprehensive, but it is sufficiently full that it allows one to make sense of the problems and opportunities that political life offers.

The interpretation of human existence that I present focuses on our capacity for action. Action is not creation ex nihilo, but it does bring about something genuinely new. The agent thus is rooted in a historical context but is not wholly determined by it. Agents then, as Aristotle saw, are both "bodily," inasmuch as they are the outcome of causal orders, and yet are "thoughtly," inasmuch as they can inaugurate something that is distinctively their own. With the help of Arendt, Merleau-Ponty, and Ricoeur, among others, I spell out the implications of this "human condition" for what human interaction can and should be.

In chapter 4 I present an account of the domain of politics. In this account the domain of politics is indissociable from the domains of economics and ethics but nonetheless enjoys a relative autonomy from them. It has its own characteristic issues and its own criteria for assessing how these issues are addressed.

These criteria never permit one to let efficiency be the unchallenged standard for determining how we live together. But neither do they permit one to organize society according to principles that would supposedly lead it back to some utopian state of innocence or definitive redemption. Politics, therefore, is thoroughly historical, knowing nothing of a primal origin or a definitive conclusion. Its criteria emphasize that political action must always concern itself both with making room for citizens to exercise initiative in the various domains of life and with ensuring that the society will perdure indefinitely. These objectives are regularly in tension with each other. The task for politics is to preserve this tension. It must never allow one of these objectives wholly to dominate it.

My interpretation of human existence and the conception of politics that I propose, when taken together, lay out the field within which one should formulate a normative conception of citizenship. They do not serve as premises from which one can straightforwardly deduce such a conception. Rather, they show one paths to pursue and pitfalls to avoid.

In chapter 5, I begin to develop my conception of citizenship by reflecting on the characteristics that good democratic citizenship has regularly been thought to demand. William Galston's work proves helpful here. My reflection shows the strength of this traditional conception. But it also reveals the limitations of its validity for an era of internationalization. Even though the traditional conception of good citizenship was developed in the course of reflecting on political life within a particular state, the fact that no state can any longer ignore its dependencies on peoples elsewhere forces one to reconsider what good citizenship demands today.

In chapter 6, I articulate the principal features of the new conception of citizenship that I propose. To do so, I bring the democratic postulate, the Jonas imperative as I interpret it, and the recognition of the fact of internationalization to bear on the traditional conception of citizenship. Doing so brings to light the need for a new approach to dealing with those of today's political issues that threaten the human habitability of the earth. Properly to determine how to address these issues, one should adopt a distinctive way of assessing the risks of proposed courses of political and economic activity. The way that I advocate is a modified version of classical casuistry. The basic principle of this new casuistry is that, when weighing alternative policies of courses of action, one should adopt the one that is least likely to undercut habitability. One should adopt the principle of what classical casuists called probabiliorism.

To make probabiliorism an effective standard and at the same time to preserve a democratic form of government, one must deal seriously with the question of citizen competence. Citizen competence has two distinct components. On the one hand, it consists in the recognition and appreciation of the factual conditions that are to be dealt with. On the other, it consists in the political judgment needed to fashion or to endorse policies that are both efficacious and democratic. Good citizenship today demands that one admit the importance of acting with this competence. When competence is taken seriously, then one has to revise significantly how one understands the traditional characteristics of good citizenship.

Both to show in more detail what my conception of citizenship amounts to and to provide further reasons for one to accept it, I apply it to two large and persistent issues that democratic societies today must address. In chapter 7, I apply it to the issue of education to and for competent citizenship. My objective in this chapter is not to set forth a fully articulated educational program. Rather, it is simply to indicate the sorts of steps that the democratic postulate allows one to take to promote citizen competence. In promoting this competence, the state can and should recognize the stages of development that children go through on their way to adulthood. Doing so, it will respect their bodiliness as well as their thoughtliness. The upshot of my reflection on education is a position that is distinct from both the liberal view espoused by someone like Amy Gutmann and the sort of view that appears to be implicit in communitarianism.

In chapter 8, I sketchily set forth some of the important conclusions concerning dealing with foreigners that my conception of citizenship supports. Because of internationalization, today, every state, democratic or otherwise, has good reason to adopt policies and practices for dealing with other states and peoples that contribute to their common well-being. Individual citizens ought to regard supporting such policies and practices as part of their citizenly duty. Among the more important of these policies are those that govern immigration and naturalization. My conception of citizenship provides substantial guidance for discerning the appropriate norms that these policies and practices should honor.

A brief conclusion brings this book to a close. It recapitulates the main features of the case that I make for my conception of complex citizenship, it summarizes the most salient implications of this conception for political practice today, and it sketches a defense against two obvious challenges that are likely to be raised against my proposals.

Chapter 2

The Twentieth-Century Debate about Citizenship

The twentieth century has seen vigorous debate about the meaning and normative implications of democratic citizenship. In large measure, the debate has taken place between proponents of some version of democratic liberalism on the one hand and proponents of some version of communitarianism on the other. This debate has shed light both on the bases of their respective positions and on some of their practical implications. It has also made evident that, for all their strengths, neither position is free of substantial difficulties. The conception of citizenship that I propose is an alternative to both of these sorts of views. In it I seek to preserve some of the strengths that each of them possesses while providing a remedy for their respective shortcomings.

To set the stage for my proposal, in this chapter I outline and offer a brief critique of one prominent version of each of these two sorts of views. I take John Rawls as the representative of liberalism and Charles Taylor as the representative of communitarianism. I also consider Jurgen Habermas's position. His Kantianism gives him an affinity with Rawls, but he rightly regards his position as something of a third way between liberalism and communitarianism. My critical remarks are not detailed. They are meant to do no more than point out respects in which these three positions fail to satisfy the exigencies of political life today. In so doing, these remarks give definition to the main issues that any satisfactory conception of citizenship must address.[1]

Before taking up these three positions, though, I should acknowledge that the defensibility of the institution of state citizenship itself, however conceived, has long been subject to attack. Though the condition of possessing citizenship and living according to its norms has historically enjoyed a predominantly favorable assessment in the West, it has never been without its critics. These critics have argued for some version of what one might call world citizenship as an alternative to state citizenship. And, at least since Kant, some have contended that the demands that state citizenship makes on people are incompatible with a proper concept of individual autonomy.[2]

In his famous account of what he calls the "paradox of patriotism," Reinhold Niebuhr gives contemporary voice to the most typical sorts of objections to state citizenship that critics have raised over the centuries. He says:

> The paradox is that patriotism transmutes individual unselfishness into national egoism. Loyalty to the nation is a high form of altruism when compared with lesser loyalties and more parochial interests. It therefore becomes the vehicle of all the altruistic impulses and expresses itself, on occasion, with such fervor that the critical attitude of the individual toward the nation and its enterprises is almost completely destroyed. The unqualified character of this devotion is the very basis of the nation's power and of the freedom to use the power without moral restraint. Thus the unselfishness of individuals makes for the selfishness of nations.[3]

Niebuhr here points to three related but distinct concerns that state citizenship generates. First, and most obviously, Niebuhr calls attention to the fact that every state, by reason of its particularity, has as the intended beneficiaries of its functions only a segment of the human community. How can one defend in moral terms participation in a society that systematically both restricts membership and discriminates in its operation in favor of its members? This is the universalizability objection. Second, Niebuhr raises the problem of the potential loss of individual autonomy by the person who gives to the state the sort of loyalty it calls for. How can one defend the deliberate surrender of autonomy? This is the autonomy objection. Finally, Niebuhr expresses concern that individuals who give their loyalty to the state fail to exercise sufficient critical judgment about the state and its programs and institutions. I call this the wisdom objection.[4]

These three sorts of objections to state citizenship have led thinkers throughout the centuries to propose instead some form of world citizenship, but there are solid reasons, both conceptual and practical, to reject this alternative. Hannah Arendt has concisely articulated some of them. She acknowledges that the history of states, and the institutions of citizenship connected with them, is hardly one that deserves unmitigated approval. But she denies that a global state with a citizenry coextensive with the human population is a sensible alternative. A world government, she fears, would promote a homogenization that would likely lead to worse horrors than any perpetrated in the name of particular states. Nobody, Arendt says,

> can be a citizen of the world as he is a citizen of his country. . . . No matter what form a world government with centralized power over the whole globe might assume, the very notion of one sovereign force ruling the whole earth, holding the monopoly of all means of violence, unchecked and uncontrolled by other sovereign powers, is not only a forbidding nightmare of tyranny, it would be the end of all political life as we know it.[5]

She argues further that political concepts presuppose a plurality of persons and mutual limitations. Citizens are always citizens among fellow citizens of some particular state. A state, in turn, is always one among many states. Hence, a citizen's rights and responsibilities are determined and limited by both his or her fellow citizens and the territorial boundaries of their state. Thus "the establishment of one sovereign world state, far from being the prerequisite for world citizenship, would be the end of all citizenship. It would not be the climax of world politics, but quite literally its end."[6]

Even if one rejects Arendt's argument, there remains the fact that today and for the foreseeable future no world state is feasible. As Paul Kennedy has pointed out, a state remains the principal locus of its members' loyalty and of the authority they recognize. Only states contain a system for formulating political policies and a command system for implementing them. Only states have the standing to make international agreements about ecological and military matters. And no other institution has the capacity that states have to prepare people to deal with impending large-scale economic and demographic changes.[7]

In addition, when justice calls for the redistribution of benefits and burdens, the state is the only presently available agency that can effect it.[8] For the foreseeable future, then, it is through the exercise of state citizenship that individual people can participate effectively in shaping the conditions in which they and their fellow human beings are to live.

Even if the idea of world citizenship is to be dismissed, however, the objections to state citizenship that provided motivation for some people to espouse it remain influential. One can usefully read present-day theories of both democratic liberalism and communitarianism as ways of responding to one or more of these criticisms. One can also with good reason see much of postmodern political criticism as a rebuttal of one or more of these cosmopolitan objections.

Let me begin my consideration of prominent contemporary conceptions of state citizenship with a sketch of democratic liberalism. There is, of course, no orthodox doctrine to which all democratic liberals subscribe.[9] But in general, liberalism emphasizes the individuality of each person and endorses a politics that provides constitutionally guaranteed equal rights to each citizen to pursue goals and aspirations of his or her own choosing. The liberal state is to remain neutral about these choices. Its task is

> to protect basic individual liberties, not to make its citizens virtuous or to impose upon them any particular or substantive conception of the good life. . . . [I]f the state enforces the basic civil and political liberties, it will leave individuals free, within broad limits, to pursue their own conceptions of the good and will preclude itself from imposing upon them any one particular conception of the good or of virtue.[10]

Liberals by no means deny that no one can live a fully human life without some rich set of relations and ties to other people. But they assume that individuals can and are entitled to distance themselves, should they so choose, from any of the specific affiliations or social roles to which they have been socially or culturally assigned. In the liberal conception, a person has the capacities to reflect, assess, and choose his or her own goods. Political liberalism insists on the right of each person to exercise these capacities and to have the resources necessary to do so.[11] By emphasizing the right of each person to exercise these capacities and to be citizens of constitutional states that guarantee this right, liberals in effect respond to all three of the objections to state citizenship that have motivated some thinkers to promote the notion of world citizenship. The liberal citizen happens to belong to some particular state, but in principle citizenship in that state is what citizenship in every state should be.

John Rawls has articulated a particularly well-developed conception of what democratic citizenship demands. Considering his view has two special advantages for my purposes. First, Rawls makes a weaker claim for his conception of liberalism than many other liberals make for theirs. Whereas they regularly claim that democratic liberalism is ingredient in a comprehensive moral doctrine, in his later work Rawls makes it explicit that his conception of political liberalism, though compatible with some comprehensive moral doctrines, neither is part of them nor presupposes them.[12] The criticism I will make of his position will therefore, mutatis mutandis, apply to liberal doctrines that make stronger claims than he does.

Because I claim that responsible citizenship today must take into account the international character of so much contemporary political practice, there is a second advantage to my concentrating here on Rawls's version of liberalism. He and others have explicitly discussed the international implications of his position. Considering those implications both in their own right and in comparison with Jurgen Habermas's version of cosmopolitanism will help prepare the way for the conception of citizenship that I propose.

Political liberalism, Rawls points out, has its historical roots in the Protestant Reformation and the subsequent sixteenth- and seventeenth-century controversies about religious toleration, freedom of conscience, and freedom of thought. These controversies gave rise to a pluralistic society made up of people who disagree among themselves about what constitutes the genuine and comprehensive good for human beings. Political liberalism developed as a theory of how such people could live together in a reasonably harmonious, stable society that remained pluralistic. Thus,

> the problem of political liberalism is: How is it possible that there may exist over time a stable and just society of free and equal citizens profoundly divided by reasonable religious, philosophical, and moral doctrines? This is a problem of political justice, not a problem about the highest good.[13]

In general, the liberal response to this problem involves some version of three rough but crucial ideas. First, liberals stand for at least modest egalitarianism. They favor redistributions of resources in order to reduce the great inequalities among people. Second, they regard as inviolable a set of individual rights to liberty, such as freedom of expression and of religion, freedom from discrimination based on race, gender, or ethnic membership, and legal due process. Third, liberals emphasize tolerance in matters of personal morality.[14]

Rawls takes as his central task the development of a conception of justice that responds to "that impasse in our recent political history shown in the lack of agreement on the way basic institutions are to be arranged if they are to conform to the freedom and equality of citizens as persons."[15] To do so, he seeks to answer two large questions, namely, (a) what the structure of the government and the political process should be, and (b) what the basic rights and liberties are that legislative majorities should respect. Political liberalism admits that there are important nonpolitical values, but it abstains from adopting any particular view of what they are. By so abstaining, political liberalism hopes for the support of all citizen, whatever reasonable comprehensive religious, philosophical, or moral doctrines they happen to hold.[16] It hopes to be the point at which these comprehensive doctrines overlap, to be the outcome of an "overlapping consensus."[17]

Two assumptions lie at the base of Rawls's argument, namely, (a) that the political society in question is closed and (b) that all normal adult human beings have two basic moral powers.

A closed political society is a self-contained, self-sustaining society. "Its members enter it only by birth and leave it only by death. This allows us to speak of them as born into a society where they will lead a complete life."[18] A closed society, furthermore, is one that is "conceived as existing in perpetuity; it produces and reproduces itself and its institutions and culture over generations and there is no time at which it is expected to wind up its affairs."[19]

Rawls's second basic assumption is that all normal adults have a capacity for a sense of justice and each of them has a capacity to form, revise, and rationally pursue a conception of his or her own rational advantage or good.[20] Persons for whom political liberalism makes sense "do not think of themselves as indissolubly tied to any particular final end, or family of such ends, but regard themselves as always capable of appraising and revising their aims in the light of reasonable considerations."[21] Having these powers and holding this view make persons equal and able to be fully cooperating members of society.

Working with these two assumptions, Rawls reaches his political conception of justice with its famous two principles. They are

> a. Each person has an equal right to a fully adequate scheme of equal basic liberties which is compatible with a similar scheme of liberties for all. b. Social and economic inequalities are to satisfy two conditions. First, they must be attached to offices and positions open to all under conditions of fair equality of opportunity; and second, they must be of greatest benefit to the least advantaged members of society.[22]

The conception of justice that embodies these two principles marks off a range of moral and political goods and values that citizens can reasonably seek. This demarcation unavoidably excludes the pursuit of some reasonable values, for there is no system of social institutions that can accommodate the pursuit of all possible reasonable values.[23] Further, within the range of acceptable goods, justice also blocks society from making any particular set of them its official goods. Hence, in a politically liberal society the right has priority over the good.

To implement the requirements of justice, Rawls calls for a sharp distinction between exercises of public reason and those of the multitude of nonpublic reasons. The work of public reason is to specify both the content of the two basic principles of justice and the guidelines for determining what evidence is relevant and what ways of reasoning are appropriate for dealing with political issues.

Nonpublic reason is the sort of reason that people exercise when they act not as citizens but as members of some voluntary association or organization. Through exercises of nonpublic reason, people determine which goods they will cherish and which goals they will pursue. Within a democratic state there is only one public reason, but there is room for many nonpublic ones.[24]

Rawls's political liberalism requires citizens to use only public reason when deliberating about (a) "constitutional essentials," that is, the structures of government and political processes, as well as (b) the equal rights and liberties that regulate basic matters of distributive justice, such as equality of opportunity and "the social bases of self-respect."[25] That is, citizens are generally to confine themselves in these deliberations to invoking only liberal political values. The absence of such a restriction in pluralistic societies, Rawls argues, would open the way for deep social discord and political instability.[26]

Rawls grants that when there is a profound division within society about constitutional essentials, it need not be inappropriate to supplement appeals to political values with appeals to more comprehensive schemes of values. Thus it was not necessarily inappropriate for nineteenth-century slavery abolitionists and twentieth-century civil rights advocates in the United States, such as the Reverend Martin Luther King, Jr., to invoke religious as well as political values to promote their cause. Doing so did not violate the ideal of public reason, Rawls says,

> provided that they thought or on reflection would have thought (as they certainly could have thought) that the comprehensive reasons they appealed to were required to give sufficient strength to the political conception to be subsequently realized.[27]

The invocation was not unreasonable, *given the prevailing historical conditions*, because these religious beliefs "fully support constitutional values and accord with public reason."[28] These advocates could, therefore, invoke these beliefs "*for the sake of* the ideal of public reason."[29]

In sum, Rawls's response to the pluralism concerning values that has emerged in the West since the Protestant Reformation calls for citizens to establish and respect a public or political realm that is strong enough to provide both stability to society and ample opportunity for each of its citizens to pursue his or her individual objectives. To achieve these results, citizens are to observe the sharp distinction between the public and the nonpublic exercise of reason and, especially in matters concerning constitutional essentials and questions of basic justice, always to give decisive weight to the outcome of exercises of purely public reason. In so doing, it is important to emphasize, they do not achieve a mere modus vivendi, a mere strategic arrangement that makes do in the absence of any agreement based on principle.[30] Rather, they construct a rational and reasonable political society based on principles to which they all subscribe.

Rawls has recently indicated how he thinks his position can be extended to show what justice among states requires. He calls the outcome of this development "the law of peoples." The law of peoples is a "political conception of right and justice that applies to the principles and norms of international law and practice."[31] For the law of peoples to be feasible, the standards and principles proposed for it must "prove acceptable to the considered and reflective opinion of people and their governments."[32]

To show how he would extend his liberal conception of justice to relations among peoples and states, Rawls distinguishes between societies that are well-ordered and those that are not. A well-ordered society is, first, peaceful and not expansionist. Second, its legal system has legitimacy in the eyes of its own people. Third, it honors basic human rights.[33] The basic human rights are rights to (a) security and the means of subsistence; (b) freedom from slavery, forced occupations, and serfdom; (c) personal property; (d) formal equality in the application of laws; and (e) emigration.[34] These rights, Rawls says, do not depend on any particular philosophical conception of human nature. Rather, they "express a minimum standard of well-ordered political institutions for all peoples who belong to a just political society of peoples."[35]

Well-ordered political societies may be either liberal or hierarchical.

To extend Rawls's position to include relations among well-ordered liberal states is nonproblematic. But to show that a liberal conception of political justice is not merely historical or Western and applicable only to societies that have liberal political cultures and institutions, he has to show that it is enforceable by at least some nonliberal societies as well.[36] And so, he argues that this conception can and should be adopted by well-ordered hierarchical societies for governing their relations with other liberal or well-ordered hierarchical societies.

Hierarchical societies are often religious in nature and make no separation between church and state. But they can be well ordered if they possess the three characteristics of well-ordered societies mentioned above.[37] Such societies will have an appropriate consultation hierarchy that provides opportunities for different voices to be heard and for dissent to find expression. Though persons in well-ordered hierarchical societies are not considered free and equal citizens, they are considered "responsible members of society who can recognize their moral duties and obligations and play their part in social life."[38] It is both rational and reasonable, Rawls holds, for well-ordered hierarchical states to adopt a liberal conception of justice to regulate their relations with other well-ordered states, both liberal and hierarchical.

The development of the liberal conception of political justice that is applicable to well-ordered societies in their relations with one another and, in the case of liberal societies, in their domestic institutions is the achievement of ideal theory. There are, however, societies that are not well ordered. Indeed, Rawls grants that at any particular time there may be no well-ordered political societies.[39] To deal with societies that are not well ordered, one needs a nonideal theory that "asks how the ideal conception of a society of well-ordered peoples might be achieved, or at least worked toward, generally in gradual steps."[40]

Nonideal theory presupposes ideal theory because without ideal theory the questions that nonideal theory raises cannot be answered. The questions raised by nonideal theory are "questions of transition." In any given case, "they start from where a society is and seek effective ways permitted by the law of peoples to move the society some distance toward the goal."[41]

There are two kinds of societies that are not well ordered. One is the kind that is governed by an outlaw regime. The other is the kind that is so handicapped by unfavorable social, economic, or historical conditions that it is impossible, or nearly so, for it to become well ordered. In dealing with outlaw regimes, well-ordered societies can do no more than establish a modus vivendi and defend their own integrity. In dealing with societies handicapped by unfavorable conditions, well-ordered societies should offer as much help as they can to make it possible for these handicapped societies also to become well ordered.[42]

The law of peoples does not call for the establishment of a world government, but it does allow for the formation of various sorts of cooperative associations, such as the United Nations and the European Union. These associations can serve as a kind of "federative center and public forum" for the formation and expression of the common opinions and interests of well-ordered states.[43] They may also have the authority to deal with violations of the conditions for well-orderedness. That is,

> some of these organizations (like the United Nations) may have the authority to condemn domestic institutions that violate human rights, and in certain severe cases to punish them by imposing economic sanctions, or even military intervention. The scope of these powers is all peoples' and covers their domestic affairs.[44]

Through his development of his doctrine of the law of peoples, then, Rawls has given his liberal democratic theory of political society a cosmopolitan reach. He does so, however, without calling for the elimination of all hierarchical societies regardless of their well-orderedness.[45] In so doing, he in effect answers the world citizen's claim that state citizenship runs afoul of the universalizability objection. He also provides a strong reply to the claim that state citizenship infringes on personal autonomy. Finally, he effectively disposes of the wisdom objection by showing that the worry it expresses can be handled procedurally. Rawls provides these rejoinders without having to call for a global homogenization that would countenance only liberal political societies.

In stark opposition to Rawls and liberals in general stand the communitarians. Communitarians object both to the liberal conception of what a human person is and to the political doctrine that reflects this conception. They deny that the person is first and foremost an independent individual who finds himself or herself situated in a particular group of other people with some or all of whom he or she happens to have a number of strong ties. Rather, for communitarians, among these ties there are some that are constitutive of the person's very identity. Without them, one could make no sense of oneself. Hence, human beings are not radically individualized and the particularization that a person receives from the group to which he or she is constitutively related is not wholly a matter of choice, nor is it a limitation or handicap to be surmounted. It is a condition without which a person cannot live a fully human life, a life with a full-fledged personal identity.[46]

For present purposes I will concentrate on the version of communitarianism that Charles Taylor has argued for. It is less radically opposed to liberalism than are some other versions and is in that respect a "weaker" version. The criticisms that I will make of it will apply at least as much to the "stronger" versions of communitarianism.[47]

Taylor works out his version of communitarianism primarily in opposition to the sorts of liberalism espoused by North American liberals such as Rawls, Ronald Dworkin, Bruce Ackerman, and George Kateb. These liberals, Taylor argues, adopt a wrongheaded methodological individualism even if they may not base a full-fledged social ontology on it. They take it, at least for methodological purposes,

> that in (a) the order of explanation, you can and ought to account for social actions, structures, and conditions, in terms of properties of constituent individuals; and in (b) the order of deliberation, you can and ought to account for social goods in terms of concatenations of individual goods.[48]

These assumptions lead liberals to regard society as an association of individuals, each of whom is entitled to have a life plan based on his or her own conception of a worthwhile or good life. Political society's proper function is to facilitate the formation and implementation of these plans as best it can in accord with an appropriate principle of equality.[49]

Taylor regards the liberal view as fundamentally mistaken about the dynamics of the successfully functioning society. This view is mistaken not only about the members of society but also about the goods that they esteem and seek. Besides strictly individual goods and convergent goods, people also want common goods.

Convergent goods can be achieved only collectively, for example, a fire department, a police force, a military defense. But these goods can be enjoyed by an individual without any intrinsic dependence on anyone else. Liberal social theory has no difficulty in dealing with convergent goods. Common goods, however, are another matter. These are goods that we can enjoy only by sharing with one or more others. Mutual friendship is a common good; so are genuine dialogues about matters dear to the interlocutors.

Taylor argues that if there are common goods that are irreducible to convergent goods, then the human being for whom these goods are good must be so constituted that the capacity to share in them is part of his or her fundamental makeup. That is, if a human life without common goods is thereby blocked from finding the fulfillment it naturally seeks, then there are solid grounds to claim that human beings are so constituted that these are necessary, not merely contingent, goods for them. If this is so, then liberalism, or any other political doctrine that is strongly individualistic, is fatally flawed.

Attention to the array of goods that people pursue brings to light basic features of what it is to be human. An essential feature of human agency, Taylor argues, is the capacity to evaluate one's own desires. The relevant evaluation is not merely one that amounts to a preference ranking. It is rather an evaluation that makes distinctions of qualitative worth among desires. That is, it is an evaluation of what is worthy of being desired and, hence, of being chosen, whether one prefers it or not. Evaluations of this sort are strong evaluations, in contrast to weak evaluations that express mere preferences. Strong evaluations have as their topic not merely the outcomes of our desires but also the quality of our motivation and the modes of life that these desires manifest.[50]

Strong evaluations are essential ingredients in the self-interpretation that characterizes all conscious human life. They are the judgments that people make about what is really important. Taylor therefore concludes: "To be human is to be already engaged in living an answer to the question [about what is important], an interpretation of oneself and one's aspirations."[51] Or again: "To ask what a person is, in abstraction from his or her self-interpretations, is to ask a fundamentally misguided question, one to which there couldn't in principle be an answer."[52]

All interpretations, including self-interpretations, presuppose a language in which the interpretation can be at least partially articulated. Every language exists only within a language community and is always bound up with other modes of expression such as gesture and art. It follows, then, that human life is fundamentally dialogical in character.[53] A self or person can be a self only among other selves. It can never describe or interpret itself, or be interpreted by another, without reference to the other selves with whom it lives. Thus, "I am a self only in relation to certain interlocutors. . . . A self exists only within . . . 'webs of interlocution.' "[54]

The community within which one is constituted a self is, in crucial respects, always a local rather than the global community. It has its own particular history. The narratives that articulate its history provide the context for the formation of each self's own life story. Inescapably, in the final analysis, one understands himself or herself in narrative form.[55]

Given this view of the self, Taylor argues that liberalism and its underlying individualism fly in the face of essential constituents of what it is to be human. The consequences of liberalism's failure to appreciate the communal dimension of human existence are apparent in the recent history of modern democratic societies.

In one version of liberal democratic theory, the point of the society and political life in it is to satisfy its members' individual needs, desires, and purposes. Society, with its structures and institutions, is simply an instrument to this end. Utilitarianism is the clearest expression of this version. But, Taylor says, "utilitarian man whose loyalty to his society would be contingent only on the satisfaction it secured for him is a species virtually without members."[56]

In search of more solid grounds for identifying with one's society, much of modern democratic theory has turned away from the utilitarian model of society as a mere instrument for promoting and coordinating individual interests. It has instead advocated a doctrine of equality and absolute freedom. In this view, we would give our allegiance to our society precisely because it is our own creation, a manifestation of what is most significant in human existence, namely, freedom itself. It guarantees our right to exercise this freedom.

This more Kantian approach, however, has its own fatal flaw. Absolute freedom cannot sufficiently acknowledge significant differences among people. It requires homogeneity. But, Taylor claims,

differentiation of some fairly essential kinds are (sic) ineradicable. . . . Men cannot simply identify themselves as men, but they define themselves more immediately by their partial community, cultural, linguistic, confessional, etc. Modern democracy is therefore in a bind.[57]

The effort to promote the homogenization that absolute freedom requires, in Taylor's view, actually increases, in minority groups, their alienation from and resentment against society, for it undermines the communities in which these groups had found their identities. In reaction against this homogenization, militant nationalism has come to prominence in our world. Shaken loose from their traditional communities by the ideology of equality and total participation, people tend to seek their identities in either a militant nationalism or some totalitarian ideology. But both of these alternatives aim to crush individuality and diversity. They would necessarily reduce some peoples to the silence of radical alienation by the very fact of providing so homogeneous a focus for others.[58] Ironically, homogenization issues in fragmentation.[59]

Taylor thus concludes,

> one of the great needs of the modern democratic polity is to recover a sense of significant differentiation, so that its partial communities, be they geographical, or cultural, or occupational, can become again important centers of concern and activity for their members in a way that connects them to the whole.[60]

Communitarianism is the political theory that gives expression to this need and the conception of human beings that shows this need to be ineradicable.

For Taylor, communitarianism ignores neither the demands of utility nor those of rights that the liberal emphasizes. But it recognizes not only that the demands of one of these may conflict with those of the other, but even further that the demands of the citizen republic may require the subordination of both of these sorts of demands. In Taylor's words:

> The citizen republic requires a certain sense of community, and what is needed to foster this may go against the demands of maximum utility. Or it may threaten to enter into conflict with some of the rights of minorities. And there is a standing divergence between the demands of international equality and those of democratic self-rule in advanced Western societies. Democratic electorates in these societies will probably never agree to the amount of redistribution consistent with redressing the past wrongs of imperialism or meeting in full the present requirements of universal human solidarity.[61]

It follows that if normative political thought gives any single-consideration procedure unqualified priority, then it cannot fully respect the diversity of goods. In the final analysis, if the claims of either rights or utility are to have effective weight, there must be a durable society to sustain them. Insisting on either of them at the price of ruining the very society on which they depend for their efficacy is incoherent.[62]

The communitarianism that Taylor endorses has at its core a patriotism that consists in identification with a historical community founded on a set of values. Some of these values are specific to the particular community rather than universal. Taylor admits that there can be a patriotism in unfree societies, for example, societies resting on racial or blood ties that develop despotic or authoritarian forms of rule. But Taylor's communitarianism has freedom understood as participatory self-rule as part of its core. Citizen dignity consists primarily in the capacity of the society's members to share in self-rule. Patriotism consists in devoting oneself to the practice and preservation of this self-rule.

Communitarian patriotism, Taylor says, falls between friendship or family feeling, on the one hand, and altruistic devotion to just any other human being whomsoever, on the other. Altruism inclines one to act for the good of anyone anywhere. Family feeling links one to a very specific small group of people. Patriotism, by contrast, involves joining others in a particular common political undertaking. As Taylor says:

> My patriotic allegiance does not bind me to individual people in [a] familial way. I may not know most of my compatriots, and may not particularly want them as friends when I do meet them. But particularity enters in because my bond to these people passes through our participation in a common political entity.[63]

In this way, though every functioning political society requires sacrifice and discipline from its citizens, the republican community is one in which the citizen's relation to government is normally not adversarial. Neither is it one in which the citizen seeks to make government subservient to his or her own purposes or to those of some segment of society to which he or she happens to belong. Full participation in self-rule, rather, consists in the capacity to be involved, at least some of the time, in forming a ruling consensus. "To rule and be ruled in turn," Taylor says, "means that at least some of the time the governors can be 'us,' not always 'them.' "[64]

In the end, Taylor argues that his version of communitarianism is not so much opposed to liberal democracy as a different model of it than is usually presented. As the present Quebecois movement in Canada exemplifies, Taylor says, there can be a society that is liberal, inasmuch as it accords to minorities the unassailable rights that are fundamental to the liberal tradition, namely, rights to life, liberty, due process, free speech, and free practice of religion, but is nonetheless not merely procedural. On the other hand, though, in Taylor's model there would be important privileges or immunities that, for strong reasons of public policy and to foster or preserve historically established common goods, can be restricted or revoked. Societies that fit Taylor's model weigh the importance of some forms of uniform treatment against that of cultural survival. Sometimes they opt for the latter. "They are thus in the end not procedural models of liberalism, but are grounded very much on judgment about what makes a good life—judgments in which the integrity of cultures has an important place."[65] Such societies, Taylor proposes, are more practical than procedural ones for tomorrow's world.

Many communitarians have ignored the sorts of criticisms of state citizenship that have animated proponents of a world citizenship. Explicitly or by implication, they take such criticism to be fundamentally misconceived. Taylor, though, does offer a response to two of them. His endorsement of universal fundamental human rights responds to the universalizability concern. And his opposition to democratic homogenization amounts to support for some self-rule that recognizes group autonomy, if not individual autonomy. Finally, one might take his support for political practices that foster the preservation of traditional common goods to entail that citizens be educated to participate in these practices. Such education would make for politically competent citizens and thus would in effect reply to the world citizen's wisdom objection.

To get beyond the limitations and defects he finds in both liberal and communitarian conceptions of democracy, Jurgen Habermas has developed what he calls a discourse ethics theory of democracy and deliberative politics. For liberals, the democratic process consists exclusively in the form of compromises among competing interests. For communitarians, democratic will formation takes place in discourse that relies on the particular cultural consensus its citizens share. Discourse theory draws on both of these views. The democratic procedure that discourse theory calls for grounds a presumption that the outcomes of deliberations achieve reasonable and fair results. Such deliberations allow participants to weave together pragmatic considerations, their own understanding of themselves, and their recognition of the demands for justice. Thus:

> According to this proceduralist view, practical reason withdraws from universal human rights, or from the concrete ethical substance of a specific community, into the rules of discourse and forms of argumenta-

tion. In the final analysis, the normative content arises from the very structure of communicative actions.[66]

With communitarianism, discourse theory recognizes the importance of citizen interaction in the formation of political opinion and choice. But it does not, as communitarianism is prone to do, relegate constitutional provisions to a secondary status. With liberalism, this theory insists on adherence to constitutional principles in the institutionalization of the communicative forms for political deliberation and decision making. "Discourse theory," Habermas says, "has the success of deliberative politics depend not on a collectively acting citizenry but on the institutionalization of the corresponding procedures and conditions of communication."[67]

The point of departure for Habermas's theory is the arguments that crop up in the course of the life of a social group about the norms that should regulate it. If these arguments are to be conducted rationally, that is, if they have as their objective the achievement of genuine consensus, then the participants in the argument must do all that they can to observe the requirements of discourse ethics.[68]

For Habermas, we would fall into a "performative contradiction" if we attempted to engage in argumentation that sought to validate our claims concerning moral and political rights and obligations unless we tried to ensure that

(1) all voices in any way relevant get a hearing, (2) the best arguments available to us given our present state of knowledge are brought to bear, and (3) only the unforced force of the better argument determines the "yes" and "no" responses of the participants.[69]

Accordingly, one who enters into such argumentation is required under pain of performative contradiction to do all that he or she can to ensure that his or her contribution is meaningful, true, and appropriate to the issue and that it expresses what he or she sincerely believes.

This discourse ethics presupposes the idea of a communication community that is unlimited by either time or place. The arguments that actually occur, of course, always take place in some spatiotemporally limited context among some specific people. But the aim of such arguments that deal with the validity of norms of conduct is to arrive at judgments based on all available evidence. These judgments claim to be worthy of universal assent and thus deserve to be called true.

These judgments always have as their subject matter some localized "lifeworld" practices and beliefs about norms. The aim of the argumentation belonging to discourse ethics is to arrive at normative claims that on the one hand have validity unrestricted by their localization and on the other hand are applicable to and transformative of the local interest. The evidence for any of these claims is never exhaustive, hence, the claims are fallible and historical. But all testing of claims must proceed through the sort of argumentation that discourse ethics demands.[70]

Among the most prominent consequences of Habermas's notion of discourse ethics is a theory of democracy that calls for a "political public sphere" in which there is "a discursive formation of opinion and will on the part of a public composed of the citizens of a state."[71] Discourse in the public sphere concerns itself not only with matters of political principle, matters that generally have a moral dimension. It also concerns both politically relevant empirical matters and questions having to do not with justice but with the good life. Among these latter are those that "have to do with ethical-political self-image, be it of a whole society, be it of some subcultures."[72]

It is the task of law to establish and maintain the public space in which this sort of political discourse is to take place. In this way a state's laws make themselves subject to the requirements of discourse ethics. Legislative programs and actions are to proceed within the parameters of debate set by this ethics. Thus, properly constituted legal procedures in principle

> demand the complete inclusion of all parties that might be affected, their equality, free and easy interaction, no restriction of topics and topical contributions, the possibility of reversing the outcomes, etc. In this context the legal procedures serve to uphold within an empirically existing community of communication the spatial, temporal, and substantive constraints on choices that are operative within a presumed ideal one.[73]

The constitution of every modern Western state, according to Habermas, in effect acknowledges the requirements of discourse ethics. They do so inasmuch as they embody the postulates of universal democracy and human rights as constitutional principles.[74] These postulates serve as norms against which all articulations of any particular national identity are to be judged. In Habermas's words:

> The abstract idea of the universalization of democracy and human rights forms the hard substance through which the rays of national tradition—the language, literature, and history of one's own nation—are refracted.[75]

This abstract idea embodies "the occidental understanding of freedom, responsibility, and self-determination."[76]

For Habermas, then, one's first and foremost political responsibility is to be a citizen of the occident, with its intrinsic commitment to global universal democracy and human rights. One's commitment to a particular political society should finally rest on its being part of the occident by virtue of its having made the occidental constitutional principles its own.[77] Occidental cosmopolitanism, therefore, serves as the final court of appeal for determining the rational defensibility of espousing or perpetuating the traditions of any particular national group or body politic. State citizenship, for Habermas, has its validity just insofar as it is compatible with the requirements of cosmopolitanism, and cosmopolitanism is the sort of politics that discourse ethics validates.

Indeed, Habermas looks forward to the development of a democratic cosmopolitanism into a kind of world citizenship that promotes and accepts a worldwide form of political communication. Because states have already lost some sovereignty, world citizenship, he says, "is no longer merely a phantom, though we are still far from achieving it. State citizenship and world citizenship form a continuum which already shows itself, at least, in outline form."[78]

Habermas's version of cosmopolitanism is strikingly different from a Rawlsian society of societies that honor the law of peoples. Rawls develops his concept of the law of peoples by extending the principles of justice constructed for a particular liberal society to other well-ordered societies, even if they are hierarchical rather than liberal. But for Habermas the legitimacy of the political order of any particular society depends on its compatibility with the universalistic principles of democratic constitutionalism, for these principles embody the demands of discourse ethics. Habermasian cosmopolitanism is thus in some respects stronger than its Rawlsian counterpart. It allows for a rejoinder to the world citizen's universalizability and autonomy objections to state citizenship that is at least as strong as Rawls's view can support, and its proceduralism makes it just as effective for disposing of the wisdom objection.[79]

Rawls's liberalism, Habermas's discourse theory, and Taylor's communitarianism all emphasize something of great value for political thought that is appropriate for today's exigencies and those of the foreseeable future. Each of them has something substantial to contribute to a defensible conception of citizenship. But none of them is sufficient as it stands. Each has disabling weaknesses that do not appear to be remediable by the internal resources available to it.

For my purposes, I need only briefly point out here some prominent flaws in their positions. The alternative conception of citizenship that I develop and defend in the next chapters amounts to an extended critique of them and, by extension, of stronger versions of liberalism and communitarianism. In the course of developing my conception, I make use of elements salvaged from them. Hence my conception is by no means wholly discontinuous from them. But, as I will make clear, neither is it merely an amalgam of bits and pieces extracted from them.

Let me make one prefatory remark here about the criticisms I make of these three positions. Every normative conception of citizenship is or should be action guiding. It makes claims about how citizens should both see and conduct themselves. Or, from another standpoint, it should aim to guide the formation and operation of institutions concerned with citizenship and its exercise. Conceptions of citizenship are therefore future oriented. They and the evidence adduced in their support amount to contributions to what Aristotle called political or deliberative rhetoric.[80] They are contributions to deliberations about how we should judge and act now and in the foreseeable future. All deliberative rhetoric is therefore pervaded by contingency and historicality. It is embedded in both a history-already-made and a history-to-be-made. The assessment of rhetorical arguments must always take into account what would happen if they were acted on. My criticisms of Rawls's, Taylor's, and Habermas's positions at bottom challenge their capacity to serve as guides for good political action.

There are two basic criticisms to which these three positions are subject. First, each in its own way fails to give due weight to the historical character of everything political, including, of course, citizenship. Second, and not wholly unrelated to the first, none of them adequately addresses either the internationalization of life today or the conditions that give the Jonas imperative its pertinence.

Rawls and Habermas both defend theories that are both ideal and proceduralist. It will simplify matters if I deal with Taylor first and then turn to them.

At first blush, it may seem strange to accuse Taylor or any other communitarian of failing to give due weight to the historicality of political life. Insistence on tradition is a trademark of communitarians, but, at least in Taylor's version, there is excessive emphasis on the past and too little attention to the new conditions with which politics must cope. Taylor lays heavy stress on the individual's roots in local community. He speaks with approval, for example, of Quebec governments that take it as "axiomatic" that it is their duty to preserve Quebec-French language and culture. These governments refuse to be neutral between those citizens who want to perpetuate their ancestral culture and those for whom this preservation is not a primary concern. Taylor approves of the governments that adopt policies that "actively seek to *create* members of the community . . . in assuring that future generations continue to identify as French-speakers."[81]

In Taylor's view there is nothing idiosyncratic about the Quebecois' efforts. Canadian Indian tribes have similar objectives as do many other tribal, ethnic, or cultural groups throughout the world. These objectives, for Taylor, are sound.[82]

In so emphasizing one's ties to the local community, Taylor unduly slights the centripetal forces that today link local communities to one another in ways that are dramatically changing all of them. Beyond some very general remarks about federations of local communities in which the particularity of each community would be respected, Taylor says very little that is applicable to the new, multifaceted phenomenon of internationalization. Nor is it clear that the basic tenets of his, or any, version of communitarianism could provide the support necessary to make it applicable to today's world.[83] Until Taylor or someone else shows how the communitarianism he espouses can effectively and nontyrannically deal with large-scale international political issues, his position, whatever its merits, will remain inadequate for responsible politics.

It is true that Taylor recognizes the validity of universal human rights. He has also admitted that a democratic order that is basically procedural may be the right order for pluralistic political societies.[84] But he has not shown how the principles of communitarianism provide grounds for doing so. It is doubtful that he, or anyone, could.

In at least one essay Taylor has suggested that one might well hope for and seek a theory of democratic politics that breaks free from the impasse that the liberal-communitarian debate has apparently reached.[85] Perhaps he himself has provided a crucial clue about how to do so with his doctrine of strong evaluation to which I referred above. Strong evaluations are always made by individuals. The evaluator, of course, draws upon his or her communal background. But he or she is not determined by it. I will make use of this clue in fashioning my alternative conception of citizenship.

Let me turn now to the proceduralists. Consider first Rawls's position. Rawls emphasizes in *Political Liberalism* that the version of

38 Chapter Two

liberalism he holds is a response to the pluralism of moral and political values that has become a permanent feature of life in the West since the Protestant Reformation. Since his version is a response to a problem that developed at a certain point in history, he does not claim a radical ahistorical validity for political liberalism in any form, not even his own. But he does take this pluralism to be a permanent feature of any political society that is genuinely democratic. And so, he believes, not only can one work out an ideal liberal theory, but he in fact has successfully done so.

There are, however, strong grounds for holding that his position is seriously flawed. Some of its major flaws are consequences of his search for an ideal theory that is supposed to serve as the standard against which the conclusions reached by nonideal theory and the practice following thereon are to be assessed. Despite his admission that his ideal theory is an answer to a question that came to the fore with the Reformation, he fails to draw the full consequences of the bonds that tie it, like all political theory, to history. This failure leads him to claim too much for his ideal theory. This, in turn, undercuts a number of the conclusions that he reaches concerning both domestic and international politics.

The very distinction that Rawls makes between ideal and nonideal theory betrays the insufficiency of Rawls's grasp of the historicality of everything political, theory as well as practice. His distinction requires him to subject political matters, which are always historical, to philosophical principles that are purportedly universal and, in the end, ahistorical. But as Michael Walzer has pointed out, there is an important difference between philosophical knowing, which is universalist and singular, and political knowing, which is particular and plural. Political knowledge answers questions such as, "What is the appropriate structure for our particular community?" and "What is the meaning and objective of this particular association?" It is highly unlikely that such questions have a unique right answer. And even if they have right—that is, good—answers, it is not at all unlikely that there will be as many of them as there are associations and governments.[86] Further, what is at one time a good political answer is hardly likely to be always good. Indeed, it may become positively bad. Hence efforts to find some single best ideal theory that can be rightly used as the basic action-guiding norm for political practice are misguided.

It is true that a particular community can and should try to improve itself through a self-criticism that does draw on philosophical truths.

But its members would rightly object to an application of such truths that would simply override their traditions, conventions, and expectations. People value not just the outcome of their shared political experience. They also esteem the particular process they live through to achieve the outcome. To engage in this historical process is part of what it is to practice democracy. Walzer thus rightly concludes:

> Any historical community whose members shape their own institutions and laws will necessarily produce a particular and not a universal way of life. That particularity can be overcome only from the outside and only by repressing internal political processes.[87]

Such a repression would be unwarranted and hardly democratic.

One can also criticize other key Rawlsian distinctions on grounds of their insufficient recognition of the historicality of everything political. Take, for example, the strong distinction that Rawls makes between procedural matters, which are matters of justice, and substantive matters, matters concerning the goods that the members of a political society pursue. This distinction lies at the base of his claim that in liberal democratic political life the just or the right ought always to hold unequivocal priority over the good.

Actual political life, however, in its historical specificity, does not warrant this sharp distinction, nor does it allow one to give procedural matters unequivocal priority. First, as Walzer has said, "no procedural arrangement can be developed except by some substantive argument, and every substantive argument (in political philosophy) issues also in some procedural arrangement."[88] Further, Rawls's distinction overlooks the historical dialectic that can and should inform our dealings with both substantive and procedural matters. Sensible people adopt procedures with an eye to the goods that they are expected to promote or the ills that they are expected to forestall. They discard or amend procedures that fail these expectations. And the attainable goods and forestallable ills vary over time. They vary with changes in such factors as the kind of technology that is available. Both the society's set of procedures and the set of goods that these procedures permit or forbid the society's members to pursue thus ought always to be open to criticism in the light of each other and of the material and cultural resources on which the society can draw for its political life. Rawls's failure to acknowledge this interminable critique is a serious defect in his theory.

A quite similar criticism is applicable to Rawls's strong distinction between exercises of public reason and those of nonpublic reason. Insistence on this distinction would unduly circumscribe what reasons people can properly invoke in their participation in political processes.[89] To see the excessive constraints that this distinction would call for, recall Rawls's remarks about the permissibility of Dr. Martin Luther King's invocation of religious reasons for promoting civil rights for blacks in the United States. For Rawls, the propriety of such an invocation hinged on its usefulness in providing auxiliary support for a position that rested fundamentally on exclusively secular grounds.

There is no good reason to think that Dr. King and his religious supporters would accept Rawls's contention that one could rightly invoke religious reasons only for the sake of public reason. To accept such a constraint would be tantamount to admitting that their religious beliefs have no independent capacity to legitimate their political activity. To yield to Rawls's demand that basically religious arguments should be subjugated to the norms of discourse prescribed by political liberalism would be to require the religious citizen to truncate the full articulation of his or her reasons for supporting or opposing political practices or institutions. It would in many instances effectively "preclude her—the *particular* person she is—from engaging in moral discourse with other members of society."[90] Of course, religion is not the only nonpublic matter that many people find pertinent to determining their political activity. Linguistic and cultural heritages are also often pertinent. Rawls's sharp distinction between public and nonpublic reason, like his distinction between procedural and substantive political matters, thus betrays the inadequacy of his grasp of politics' ineliminable historicality.

The weakness of Rawls's appreciation of politics' historicality not only tells against taking his position as sufficient to guide domestic democratic political practice. It also makes it nearly impotent to guide the action of democratic states and their citizens in international political matters. Two closely related sets of considerations make this impotence clear. One set concerns Rawls's ideal theoretical conception of the political society as a self-contained, self-sustaining society. The second concerns his conception of a well-ordered society.

Consider first his conception of the political society as closed. If there ever has been a closed political society, now and for the foreseeable future such a society is nearly unimaginable. Mid-twentieth-century North Korea and Albania may have tried to be closed, but neither of them was democratic and neither has been able to maintain its closure. Rather, what history shows is that any political society that deserves to be called a state has always faced issues of population migration, secession, federation, and annexation. Each of these and other related issues always arise in some historically specific way. When they arise even for a state that has adopted what Rawls calls the constitutional essentials constitutive of a democratic society, how they are to be dealt with always involves giving heavy weight to the exigencies of the particular moment as well as to the particular history and future prospects of the people concerned. No set of universal liberties or rights can be sufficient to guide the action that addresses these concrete situations.[91] And further, regardless of how a state responds to one of these situations, it can never properly presume that this response will be appropriate for all subsequent similar situations.

Consider now Rawls's conception of a well-ordered society. To be well ordered it must be nonexpansionist. Such a society may not be absolutely unachievable. Perhaps some very small island states can be well ordered in Rawls's sense. But can any large industrialized state today be in all respects nonexpansionist? Even if it eschews territorial expansion, can it be in all economic and cultural respects nonexpansionist? Given the internationalized in which we now live, perhaps not even the most Draconian regime could prevent all cultural and economic expansions. And yet, it is just such expansions that are largely the stuff of international politics today and for the foreseeable future. Rawls's criterion of well-orderedness, along with his concept of an ideal society as closed, precludes his theory from being action guiding in any robust sense.

Rawls's quest for an ideal theory has apparently led him to overlook the fact that agents, in acting, very often cannot avoid impinging somehow on some patients. At the very least, A's action modifies the context in which B, the patient of A's deed, can subsequently act.[92] This is certainly the case in political action. Rawls's quest has also led him to overlook the fact that the evidence in favor of anything political is never all in. That is, the evidence is never definitive. This twofold failure blinds him to the political merits of modi vivendi.

For Rawls, a modus vivendi is no more than the outcome of political bargaining among persons or groups whose interests conflict but who are motivated to avoid battling each other. Such a modus vivendi is, he holds, insufficiently stable for a political society, particularly a liberal society, because the competitors remain "ready to pursue their own goals at the expense of the other, and should conditions change they may do so."[93]

But there can be quite stable modi vivendi. Competing groups can reasonably commit themselves to maintain a modus vivendi that they establish. They can come to see that in both domestic and international politics, given the enduring fact of pluralism, bargaining or negotiating is the most appropriate way to handle their conflicts. No particular negotiation fully settles matters, but a readiness to negotiate can be a permanent commitment. Negotiations can yield relatively stable agreements on some matters, which agreements serve to facilitate further negotiations, but for no agreement is the evidence of its reasonableness ever definitive. And no agreement about anything political can wholly eliminate the impingement of A's actions on B.

In sum, Rawls's impoverished appreciation of the historicality of everything political blinds him to the importance of the fact that every society, and the politics practiced in it, is always in medias res, in midstream.[94] Individual members and particular groups within the society are always engaged in a deliberative process about what to do next. They are not, nor should they be, in search of timelessly valid political norms or outcomes. And what holds for politics within each nontyrannical society holds also for international politics. Political deliberation and decision always rest on a history already made and are aimed toward a history-to-be-made.

Let me turn now to Habermas's version of proceduralist theory. Inasmuch as his theory is ideal and makes a strong distinction between procedure and substance, it is subject to some of the same lines of criticism that Walzer makes against Rawls.[95] On the one hand, inasmuch as Habermas's discourse ethics presupposes the idea of an ideal communication community unlimited by time and space, it has an ahistorical utopian conception at its heart. On the other hand, his strong distinction between procedure and substance is no less problematic than Rawls's is.[96]

There is, however, at least one important matter that separates Habermas and Rawls. The public sphere that Habermas envisions has weaker constraints on what can count as appropriate discourse in it. For Habermas, the public sphere is the arena in which disagreements about the rational legitimacy of a particular community's received practices and norms is thrashed out. The content in dispute always shows the particular history of the society in which it emerges, and the consensus that the argument seeks to produce is fallible and hence always open to review and revision. So there is room for the interlocutors in the dispute to articulate without inhibition whatever evidence—religious, cultural, ethnic, and so on—they believe makes intelligible or supports their respective claims. In this respect, Habermas's position is less ahistorical than is Rawls's and is closer to the position that I defend later in this work.[97]

Nonetheless, at the end of the day, Habermas attenuates the thoroughgoing historicality of politics. Particular ways of life must be made subject to the "abstract idea of the universalization of democracy and human rights." Apparently, for Habermas there is no correlative need to entertain the revisability of this abstract idea in the light of particular ways of life and their specific histories. Democratic constitutionalism, embodying the demands of discourse ethics, is the definitive norm against which Habermas would have one judge the political institutions of every society. If a state is to achieve rational legitimacy, it must either be or become a constitutional democracy.

There are at least two reasons to reject this Habermasian cosmopolitanism as the basic guide for political judgment and action. First, for citizens of a constitutional democracy in today's politically pluralistic world to adopt such a position would bode ill for the possibility of good faith negotiations with nondemocracies, even about matters such as the planet's habitability, in which they have a common stake. At the very least, these citizens should recognize that no extant constitutional democracy has demonstrated its ability to guard effectively against ecological exploitation and degradation. And it is hard to imagine that any set of procedural norms alone could do so. In any event, the contingency of everything political runs counter to any claim for the definitive superiority of any form of political order.

The second reason for rejecting Habermasian cosmopolitanism is closely related to the first. Habermas claims that all argument about practices and norms necessarily aims at consensus. If the term "argument" is defined weakly enough, that may be so, but not all communicative activity aims at agreement. Sometimes, it seeks only to make the bones of contention more precise. Other times, it aims simply to clarify its own position. At still other times, its aim is to reinforce the conviction of those who already hold the position it espouses.[98]

In short, not all political communicative activity aims at finding what I would call "first-order" constitutional provisions that everyone can and should accept. At most, it aims to foster, maintain, or extend a "second-order" consensus to continue the communicative activity. But this is just to say that this second-order consensus amounts to a commitment to maintain with one's fellows at least a modus vivendi.

To maintain a genuine modus vivendi that is more that mere tolerance is arguably not the highest of reasonable political aspirations, but it is an indispensable minimum for any genuinely responsible politics. As I noted above, all politics transpires in medias res. It always consists in playing the hand that one is dealt, a hand, however, that has no beginning and no end but is continually in the process of being dealt.

Ideal theories always abstract from the messy contingencies that are constitutive features of all actual political practice. It is only through such abstractions that they can articulate their ideals. But these ideals, belittling as they do the worth of modi vivendi, threaten to make their ideal best the enemy of the realistically achievable good. They therefore threaten genuine politics with principles that belong to a domain extrinsic to politics. They fail to recognize the conflicts of values with which responsible concrete political practice always has to deal.[99] If rigorously insisted on, these principles would make it practically impossible to justify any concrete extended sequence of political judgments or actions.[100] Contrary to the implications of ideal theory, a concrete judgment or action that does not square with the theory can do more than merely escape blame by reason of some set of circumstances that provides it an excuse. It can, as I argue in chapter 4, deserve positive praise precisely because it responds so well to those circumstances.

The second fundamental criticism that I have of Taylor, Rawls, and Habermas is that none of their theories takes into account the present conditions that give the Jonas imperative its importance. All three of them either fail to notice or simply give no weight to the threats to the habitability of the earth. And none of them asks in any significant way about the competence of democratic citizens to deal with these threats.

Each of them draws attention in general terms to the importance of education for responsible citizenship. But none of them deals with the problem posed by the fact that so many otherwise normal people fail to become even moderately knowledgeable about issues of central importance for responsible political practice today. Leaving criminals aside, one still finds in every state, democratic or otherwise, rampant ignorance and thoughtlessness about political matters of vital concern to everyone. This ignorance and thoughtlessness is today a serious danger not only to the freedom of particular people and states but to human life itself.

For reasons both understandable and perhaps once good, democratic theorists of all stripes have generally presumed that normal adult citizens all possessed both the technical or factual competence and the political competence to participate in all the vital questions that confronted their respective societies. Indeed, this presumption has regularly been held, even if not explicitly, to be an unassailable principle of democracy. Today, or so I argue below, one must recognize that in all too many cases there is more than enough evidence to rebut it. A politics that is fully responsible in today's circumstances will have to institutionalize ways to both promote citizen competence and protect itself against citizens who fail to achieve it.

In his discussion of the worldwide ecological crisis in the September 1989 special issue of *Scientific American* entitled "Managing Planet Earth," William Ruckelshaus succinctly indicated the depths of today's problem of citizen competence.[101] What, he asks, can move peoples and states to restrict growth and development to the limits set by ecological imperatives? Nothing short, he concludes, of bringing people to recognize that they have a vital interest in such restriction will do.

To bring about his recognition, Ruckelshaus says, requires three things:

> First, a clear set of values consistent with a consciousness of sustainability must be articulated by leaders in both the public and the private sectors. Next, motivations need to be established that will support the values. Finally, institutions must be developed that will effectively apply the motivations. *The first is relatively easy, the second much harder and the third perhaps hardest of all.*[102]

To save the environment, it is most urgent that these three conditions be achieved in the world's industrialized democracies. But it is also in these democracies that achieving these changes while remaining democratic is unusually difficult. If democracies are to overcome these difficulties and thereby lead the way to a sustainable use of the world's resources, Ruckelshaus concludes, "we shall have to redefine our concepts of political and economic feasibility."[103]

It is evident, I take it, that neither the proceduralist democracy that Rawls proposes nor Habermas's constitutional democracy nor Taylor's communitarianism, their respective virtues notwithstanding, is sufficient to meet the environmental challenges that Ruckelshaus discusses or the other major challenges posed by internationalism. None of the three, therefore, is in a position to spell out a conception of the rights and responsibilities that are appropriate for democratic citizenship today. My aim in this work is to contribute to the discourse needed to formulate such a conception.

Isaiah Berlin has said: "The ideas of every philosopher concerned with human affairs in the end rest on his conception of what man is and can be."[104] To lay the proper groundwork for the conception of citizenship that I propose, I make explicit in the next chapter my conception of human beings, the political actors. Then, in chapter 4, I spell out the principal features of the domain of politics. To do so, I make use of a number of important insights that I take over from the liberal and communitarian traditions.

Chapter 3

The Political Agent

As I pointed out in chapter 2, the debates about citizenship between liberals and communitarians on the one hand and between proponents of state-centered conceptions of politics and cosmopolitans on the other have been vigorous. In the case of the liberal-communitarian debate, some scholars have suggested that the debate in its standard form is intractable.[1] This apparent intractability leads one to suspect that each of these camps has hold of some important part of what responsible political practice demands but that it also either wholly misses or badly slights some other important part.

There is, furthermore, good reason to think that both the strengths and the weaknesses of each group of competitors are closely tied to a specific view, either expressed or implied, about what people are and can aspire to become. The set of norms and aspirations that one finds it reasonable to advocate is not wholly detachable from his or her understanding of the constitutive features of human existence. One's view of these features may not entail just one set of endorsable political practices, but it does define the field of plausible ones.[2]

A persuasive case for proposed political actions or practices should include two sets of considerations. On the one hand, it should provide a plausible account of how the proposed conduct can bring about the beneficial outcome it is meant to achieve. On the other hand, it must either offer or endorse an account of what it is to be human that allows one to see that these purposes or objectives fall within the scope of human capabilities.[3]

To satisfy this latter requirement and thus to lay the groundwork for the conception of citizenship that I will present, I want now to propose a conception of human existence that is instructed by both liberals and communitarians but differs from them in important respects. Neither liberals nor communitarians, I claimed in chapter 2, did full justice to the complexity and the historical character of everything human. With the conception I propose, I provide a remedy for the defects of their positions.

A satisfactory conception of the human beings who are political agents must allow us to make sense of the broad range of conduct that the historical record displays. This record shows a persistent tension between the individual and the communal dimensions of all aspects of human life, political and otherwise. Sometimes this tension gives rise to conflicts and antagonisms and sometimes to convergences and collaborations.

The record of history thus shows us in every age and every land examples of thoughtfulness, generosity, and courage. Some individual people in every era manage to accomplish something new, fresh, and excellent. Their achievements, whether artistic, scientific, moral, or political, may only infrequently be earth shaking, but even relatively minor achievements improve their lives and times. Recalling them today can still quicken our own.

This same historical record, though, also shows us that people are regularly flawed in either mind or will. They are often ignorant, thoughtless, or lazy. And there is no shortage of examples of meanness, greed, and vindictiveness. People, therefore, never cease to need education and inducements to learn. Neither do they ever cease to need some "apparatus of restraints and correctives, internal and external."[4]

An appropriate account of what it is to be human thus has to enable us to make sense of both virtue and vice, of both nobility and baseness, and of everything lying between these poles. But to underpin a political proposal such as mine concerning citizenship, the conception need not be comprehensive. It need not, for example, try to settle such metaphysical issues as the nature of minds and bodies and their relationship to one another. For political matters, it is enough if the account gives us a coherent way to make sense of the prominent forms of human conduct.

On my reading, the historical record of human sayings, doings, and makings provides compelling evidence for construing human existence as basically an interrogatory project. This project is literally ambivalent. On the one hand, the human person is drawn to or interrogated by the surrounding world and responds to it. On the other hand, every human response can with good sense be read as interrogatory whether the responder recognizes it or not. Every response can be expressed in something like the following way: "Given that the world confronts me as it does, my doing, saying, or making X makes sense, doesn't it?" So construed, human beings are fundamentally explorers, wayfarers. They are, as long as they live, in the game of interrogation.

To develop and defend this construal, I draw heavily on the work of Hannah Arendt, Maurice Merleau-Ponty, and Paul Ricoeur, all of whom owe a debt to Martin Heidegger. For Heidegger, human existence "is ontically distinguished by the fact that in its very Being, that Being is an *issue* for it."[5] Merleau-Ponty explicitly argues that human beings exist as so many interrogations addressed to a world that, though it does not speak, itself exists in the interrogative mode.[6] The work of all of these present-day thinkers has ties to Aristotle's practical philosophy.[7]

In the *Politics*, especially in book 3, Aristotle emphasizes that human beings are neither gods nor beasts. They all are both bodily and thoughtly. Among the many ordinary people, there are indeed some extraordinarily gifted and accomplished ones and some handicapped or wicked ones. But no one is merely bodily or exclusively thoughtly. All of them bear resemblances to both gods and beasts.

These two dimensions of human existence, the bodily and the thoughtly, and their thoroughgoing temporal character both make possible and set limits to what people can do and think. Political life fully displays these two constituents of the human condition. People can be free, but not absolutely free. If they are to practice responsible politics, they

> must not live as beasts who seek only pleasures of the moment . . . but they must accept obligations from the past and responsibility for the future. They must recognize the debts that their predecessors have incurred . . . and they must exercise their ability to deliberate and to choose, or to look beyond their immediate appetites.[8]

Everyone, the exceptional people and the ordinary ones, ought to heed these demands. And among the most important implications of this human condition is that in sound politics, no citizen either rules or is ruled completely. They both rule and are ruled "in turn."[9]

To say that human beings are bodily and thus not gods is not merely to say that they are physical and are physically bound to the material world. They are also bodily inasmuch as they are under the sway of habits. Some of these habits are routine ways of bodily activity, others are routine ways of talking about and arranging things, and still others are routine ways of taking note of and assessing things. In short, they are bodily inasmuch as they have a past that they cannot set at naught.

On the other hand, to say that human beings are thoughtly and thus not beasts is to say that they are not merely the product of their past. They are thoughtly inasmuch as they can reflect on their own bodiliness and its habitual comportment to its surrounding world. They are thoughtly to the extent that they can judge both their own comportment and that of others, and they are thoughtly inasmuch as they can imagine and weigh the merits of alternatives to the ties they have to other people and to the world. Without ever shedding their circumstances or ridding themselves of their past—indeed precisely by contending with them—they can and do rework their situation and thereby give it distinctive stampings of their own. These stampings are often short-lived but some are long lasting. Though some stampings are surely for the worse, others are no less surely for the better. Accordingly, if politics is to take seriously both dimensions of the human condition, it must concern itself with the human capacity for bringing about changes, sometimes allowing, sometimes urging, and sometimes blocking its exercise. But it must also not pretend that people can rid themselves of their bodiliness.

To fill out this Aristotelian insight, I want at this point to draw attention to some recent reflections on the salient constituents of all human sayings, doings, and makings, political or otherwise. For convenience, I will speak of all these human performances as actions. Doing so risks obscuring Arendt's important and proper distinction between action and fabrication. In fabrication, I use some things as means to an end. And I can fabricate alone. In action, by contrast, there is no strong distinction between means and ends. And I can only act in the presence of others who are also capable of action.[10] But if the reader keeps her distinction in mind, my usage will not lead to confusion.

Every action has as its stimulus some need or desire, and it acquires its unique specification through a choice. Deliberation prepares the ground for choice. And choice can give rise to commitments that influence subsequent deliberations and choices.

Consider first the stimuli to action, namely need and desire. Both needs and desires are lacks, but there are striking differences between the sorts of lacks that they are. Throughout the history of thought people have reflected on these differences. Properly distinguishing between needs and desires is a permanent task. For good politics it is a crucial one.

"Questions about human needs," Michael Ignatieff points out, "are questions about human obligations. To ask what our needs are is to ask not just which of our desires are strongest and most urgent, but which of our desires gives us an entitlement to the resources of others."[11] The desires that people have are innumerable and incalculable. It would be fatuous to claim that they give rise to duties to see that they are satisfied. But needs, by definition, have to do with what is essential for a person to function normally. If people cannot satisfy their needs by themselves, then they have a claim on others' help to do so.

Unlike desires, which are variable and transient and which differentiate us from one another, needs are what we share with others. In defining needs we define what we have in common with others but "not by what we have, but by what we are missing."[12]

There are, however, two distinct sorts of needs. There are natural needs such as hunger and thirst that everyone has and that they are all entitled to have recognized and satisfied. Natural needs make us "feel a common and shared identity in the basic fraternity of hunger, thirst, cold, exhaustion, loneliness, or sexual passion. The possibility of human solidarity rests on the idea of natural human identity."[13] This is an identity of the naturally needy.

Besides natural needs, people also have social needs. But unlike natural needs, social needs give rise to differences among people. They divide humanity into those who share bonds that make them members of the same family, religion, or political society and those who are foreigners or strangers. We have corresponding social duties to our fellow members that we do not have to strangers. Unlike our natural needs, which are universal, our social needs and the obligations tied to them are specified by our particular culture, locale, and historical period.

Far from being secondary because they are contingent, however, our social needs generally strike us as being no less fundamental to who we are than our natural needs are. Though all our natural needs are apparently bodily needs, we experience them in socially different ways. As Ignatieff says,

even the natural identity of my body seems marked by social difference. The identity between such hunger as I have ever known and the hunger of the street people of Calcutta is a purely linguistic one. My common natural identity of need, therefore, is narrowed by the limits of my social experience here in this tiny zone of safety known as the developed world.[14]

Social needs are so weighty that they tend to block our recognition of the duties we have to help strangers satisfy their natural needs. As history shows, people regularly have thought of themselves primarily as members of families and particular social, tribal, and racial groups. What matter most to them have been the things they share with their fellow members. They have regularly disregarded strangers and what makes them their equals. Indeed, they have often prized just what differentiates them and theirs from the rest of humanity. As Ignatieff points out, the new language of universal human rights with corresponding duties has made only slight headway against the claims of ethnic, cultural, and social difference. The reason for this slim progress is that

> we think of ourselves not as human beings first, but as sons and daughters, fathers and mothers, tribesmen, and neighbors. It is this dense web of relations and the meanings which they give to life that satisfies the needs which really matter to us.[15]

Nonetheless, none of us has to justify demanding what he or she genuinely needs. We are all entitled to have both our natural and social needs satisfied simply by reason of being who we are. Needs are thus egalitarian. All the relevant individual persons have the same ones and are equally entitled to have them satisfied.

On the other hand, honors and awards are things we have to earn. Different people earn rights to different things. Some people earn rights that others do not have by becoming learned. Others do so by winning elective office. These rights are not linked to fundamental needs, but they do beget duties to recognize them. And, as history shows, these earned rights are a practical necessity for any durable society. Without the distinctions that earned rights introduce, there could be no hierarchical order among people, no defensible ruling. Hence without them there could be no genuine politics.[16]

Though we know of no actual people who have had no social needs whatsoever, every particular social need is historical and contingent. Each of them is open to contestation and it survives only as long as it has enough support to withstand challenges. In effect, a concrete social need survives only as long as people recognize it as a need for some desirable and achievable good. This good is something that one could conceivably live without but that people take to be constitutive of a good life for them. Particular social needs thus come to be, endure, and pass away by virtue of debates about the need for what one desires. It makes no sense to debate whether people have a natural need to have their thirst quenched, but it does make sense to debate about, for example, the social need of a child to be reared by its biological mother or to receive a specific sort of schooling.

Natural needs do not conflict with one another. In principle, at least, they can all be satisfied. Social needs within the same society ideally should not conflict either. But in practice it is not infrequent that some of them may become so contested that insisting on the obligations connected with them runs counter to some other generally accepted social need. Examples of these conflicts abound in pluralistic democracies. Mere desires, by contrast, are naturally prone to clash.

If we reflect on the complex network of natural and social needs as well as desires, we see the multiple ties we have to what is other than us. We have ties to other people. Some of them are close to us and some of them are strangers. We have ties to previous generations and to coming ones. We also have ties to the material and cultural world. Everything to which we have ties, each in its own way, addresses us, makes some claim on us, and presents itself as open to our response. We have the needs and desires that we do not only because of the way we are. We have them also because of the way the world is.

Talk about needs and desires is, in Aristotelian terms, always talk about the bodily part of human beings. We can react emotionally and empathetically to the needs and desires of others only because we are bodily, and our own needs and desires can also affect us as they do only for the same reason. But needs and desires do not move us only bodily. They engage our thoughtliness as well. By virtue of our thoughtliness we can do more than merely react to needs and desires. We can respond to them with our own initiatives. Human initiative, of course, depends on bodiliness for its very possibility but is not wholly reducible to mere physical motion.

The action that we take in response to needs and desires has three basic forms. We speak, we do—for example, we dance and play—and we make things. All of these forms of action display our recognition of needs and desires, our assessment of them, and our effort to satisfy them. In these forms of action we display deliberation and choice about needs and desires. In them we find exhibited those traits that distinguish human beings from other sorts of entities. These are the traits that both make politics possible and show its inescapable finitude. For present purposes, it is useful to dwell a bit here on these three forms of action.

Consider first the act of speaking. There is no speaking without material such as mouths, vocal chords, and air, nor is there speaking without a received language with its grammar, vocabulary, and conventions of usage. Speaking thus depends on the speaker's embeddedness in a material and cultural world. But there is no speaking without a speaker who is trying to make sense. Utterances provoked by neural stimulation are obviously possible, but they are not full-fledged enunciations. Unlike enunciations, mere utterances are not subject to criticism. It makes no sense to assess them as true or false or as appropriate or inappropriate. They simply occur.

Full-fledged enunciations, genuine speaking, thus manifest multiple orders of causality. The speaker's bodily speech apparatus is tied to the order of physical causality. The language he or she receives belongs to the order of social causality. But the speaker's effort to make sense shows him or her to be capable of making truth claims and commitments to live by them. This capacity to make sense and to commit oneself belongs to a distinct order of causality, one that Ricoeur calls intentional causality.[17]

Speaking is a form of doing. All doing displays these three orders of causality and their inextricability from one another if there is to be genuine doing at all. All doings are events, but not all events are doings. Every event has a precipitating physical cause or set of causes to which it can be ascribed as an effect. Sometimes the precipitating cause of an event is a person. Sometimes it is not. Falling logs as well as persons can crush wildflowers and kill mice. But events are actions only if, besides being ascribable to some physical cause, they, on the one hand, display a socially established pattern of behavior and, on the other hand, can be imputed to an agent as something he or she is uniquely responsible for initiating and executing.

Doings and sayings are thus the sorts of events about which it makes sense to make what Charles Taylor has called strong evaluations.[18] Strong evaluations are fundamentally different from subjective reactions of liking or disliking. They make claims about the truth, goodness, beauty, or appropriateness of particular sayings and doings. And they refer not only to what happened but also to the agent who brought it about.[19]

Makings, like sayings and doings, also display these three orders of causality. Makings act directly on the material world and transform it. Through what we make we can give some permanence to sayings and doings. We can make documents and monuments that record or commemorate them. Over and above the things that we make to preserve sayings and doings, we can also make instruments to help us satisfy our needs and desires. And we can fashion institutions that promote and support socially established patterns for further sayings, doings, and makings. Through these three forms of action, then, we respond to the material and cultural world into which we were born, change it somehow, and hand it over at death to our successors. This is a world that includes art, science, religion, and politics, all fundamental ways in which people have responded to the needs and desires that the material world and our bodiliness have given rise to.

Arendt, Merleau-Ponty, and Ricoeur help to fill out the account of human agency in ways that are directly pertinent to making sense of political practice. When I reflect on my particular sayings, doings, and makings, I find that none of them contains its own full meaning and efficacy. A saying or doing without a making that records or commemorates it is ephemeral. A making without a saying communicates little if anything. All of my actions, whatever their form, gain clarity and efficacy by receiving supplements not only from other actions of mine but also from the actions of others.

Nonetheless, whenever I act, in any form, I unavoidably impinge on others. What I choose and do necessarily affects what some other people can subsequently choose and do. These impingements can be, and not infrequently are, beneficial to them in some respects. But Arendt rightly points out that our actions always cost some people something, always trespass on them and theirs and thus prompt them to react in ways they otherwise would not have. Similarly, every action inserts itself into a material and cultural world that antedates it. Lying beyond the total control of the agent, the world does not permit him or her fully to determine the outcome of the action. Hence, there is no pure action. Action is always amalgamated with what the agents cannot control. When agents act, they are therefore themselves patients.

All action, then, is necessarily interaction. As Arendt says,

> since action acts upon beings who are capable of their own actions, reaction, apart from being a response, is always a new action that strikes out on its own and affects others. Thus action and reaction among men never move in a closed circle and can never be reliably confined to the two partners.[20]

Because no action is pure and all action is interaction, neither ascriptions of causes nor imputations of responsibility on the one hand and praise or blame on the other are straightforward. No one is wholly responsible for what he or she does, and nothing that one does is absolutely praiseworthy or blameworthy. But, nonetheless, we find ourselves impelled to make strong evaluations, evaluations that fix responsibility for actions and specify their worth. We thus find ourselves in an awkward position, a position that led Merleau-Ponty to say:

> But what if our actions were neither necessary in the sense of natural necessity nor free in the sense of decision *ex nihilo*? In particular, what if in the social order no one were innocent and no one absolutely guilty? What if it were the very essence of history to impute to us responsibilities which are never entirely ours? What if all freedom is a decision in a situation which is not chosen but is assumed all the same? We would then be in the painful situation of never being able to condemn with a good conscience, although it is inevitable that we exercise condemnation.[21]

And yet, enmeshed as we are in a world not of our own devising with others who are beyond our control, we can and often do recognize and reflect on our own distinctiveness. We find that it is precisely by exercising the thoughtliness that constitutes each of us as the individual that he or she is that we can appreciate the depth and complexities of the ties that bind us to others and to our common world. We likewise find that we need and want our uniqueness to be recognized. Even the most thoughtless among us rebel against having their individuality ignored or denied.

Part of the uniqueness that each of us prizes about ourselves consists in our responses to both our own needs, wants, and previous choices and those of others. Another part consists in the judgments each of us makes both about these responses of our own and about the responses and judgments that others make about these matters. Each of us wants what he or she does and says to be acknowledged as his or her own and taken seriously.

In short, as G. W. F. Hegel saw, in and through our interaction with one another we engage in a mutual struggle for recognition.[22] On the one hand, we want recognition of our basic humanity, a humanity that is in principle no less worthy of respect than anyone else's. We want recognition that we are no less entitled than anyone else to receive satisfaction of both our natural and our social needs. On the other hand, each of us wants no less to have his or her own particular talents and achievements recognized precisely as his or her own. We want these two sorts of recognition both for ourselves and for those whom we most cherish or esteem. We also, as John Stuart Mill saw at least in part, want the flaws, at least those we detect in others, to be recognized as flaws in them.[23]

Our mutual struggle for recognition takes place in all forms of action, but most obviously in speech. But as I have noted, action is both unpredictable in its outcome and transgressive. It is also both unpredictable in its occurrence and irreversible. What I do, I or another can counter but can never undo. Thus, the very action whereby we seek recognition at the same time threatens the mutuality required for recognition.

To preserve mutuality we must devise remedies for these "predicaments of action," as Arendt call them.[24] Our capacity for speech makes these remedies possible. To remedy the unpredictability of the occurrence of action, we can make and keep promises. We can both ask for and make commitments and pledges of allegiance. Through making and keeping promises and commitments we

> set up in the ocean of uncertainty, which the future is by definition, islands of security without which not even continuity, let alone durability of any kind, would be possible in the relationships between men.[25]

If we are sensible, we also recognize that the only worthwhile promises and commitments are those that people make freely and that do not fly in the face of their best considered convictions.

Making and keeping promises and commitments, by itself, however, is only a feeble remedy for the predicaments of action. Promises can neither cancel nor reverse a previous action. Nor can they keep any action from being transgressive. Effectively to remedy the predicaments and thus to preserve mutuality, promises must be complemented by forgiveness. We must forgive the impingements of others' actions on us and ask their forgiveness for our impingements on them. Without having and exercising the capacity to forgive one another we could not escape being trapped by the consequences of what we have previously done. We could never recover from them and the damage they do to mutuality.

To forgive a transgression is more than merely to react to it. It is to perform a new, unpredictable act. Thus,

> in contrast to revenge, which is the natural automatic reaction to transgression and which because of the irreversibility of the action process can be expected and even calculated, the act of forgiving can never be predicted. . . . Forgiving, in other words, is the only reaction which does

not merely re-act but also acts anew and unexpectedly, unconditioned by
the act which provoked it and therefore freeing from its consequences
both the one who forgives and the one who is forgiven.[26]

Taken together, our capacities to promise and forgive both display
our dependence upon one another and serve to preserve the mutuality
necessary for us to gain the recognition for which we strive. Both of
these capacities

> depend on plurality, on the presence and acting of others, for no one can
> forgive himself and no one can feel bound by a promise made only to
> himself; forgiving and promising enacted in solitude or isolation remain
> without reality and can signify no more than a role played before one's
> self.[27]

And yet each promise or commitment and each grant of forgiveness
is something that only an individual person can do. My promise is
mine to keep or break, not yours. And I receive your forgiveness only
from you. A group's promises and forgivings are nothing more than
the sum of its individual members' promises and forgivings. Plurality
is indeed a necessary condition for these sorts of performances but so
is the existence of fully individualized persons.

Hence part and parcel of my preserving the mutuality I need for
recognition is not only making promises and granting forgiveness. It is
also making and keeping myself ready to do so. By reason of my
thoughtly part I am capable of preparing myself for these performances. Through the exercise of this part I can take responsibility both
for what I have already done and for keeping myself prepared to act
anew. I thus take responsibility for myself.

At this point it is useful to recall the bodily dimension of our mutual
struggle for recognition. In all of our dealings with one another we rely
on and make use of the material world. Not only do we draw on its
resources to satisfy our natural needs. We also shape and reshape it.
Our power to shape nature lies at the root of both our social needs and
our ability to satisfy them.

What others have made and left behind when they died has arranged
the stage upon which we must live out our lives. The condition of the
material world and the set of cultural objects and institutions that they
leave to us is at one and the same time both the complex of things to
which we must respond in word, deed, and fabrication-consumption
and the complex of resources upon which we must draw to make our

response. We can gain recognition as unique individuals only because, by reason of our bodiliness, we are always geared into this complex and, by virtue of our thoughtliness, we either preserve its constituents or change them. Even the most thoughtless people among us cannot avoid rearranging the stage somehow. Their bodiliness makes the rearranging inevitable.

It is worth emphasizing here that it is a thoughtly task of the first order to give bodiliness its due. The thoughtless neglect of bodiliness, the reckless presumption that we can do just as we like with ourselves, each other, and our world has had, history shows, no less pernicious consequences than the neglect of thoughtliness. Pretending that we are gods is no less destructive than living as though we were beasts. In either case we abuse both ourselves and our fellows. Virtue lies in the Aristotelian mean that respects both bodiliness and thoughtliness. Fault lies in failure to locate the mean, and vice in refusing to concern oneself with the mean.

Integral to the task of concerning myself with the mean and taking responsibility for myself is reflection on who I have become and how I have done so. It consists in articulating a narrative of the life I have lived. This is a life of both doings and sufferings, a life that displays in all of its aspects both my bodiliness and my thoughtliness. Only through such narratives can we make sense either of ourselves or of others. Only through them can we know who and where we are.

So long as we live, our stories are of course incomplete. And they are always corrigible. No one's story makes sense apart from other stories. And neither alone nor together with others are our stories self-contained. They are always subject to verification by reference to the natural and cultural worlds that contextualize us.[28] And, of course, there is the constant danger that we will thoughtlessly or self-deceptively tell ourselves corrupt stories.

The responsibility for ourselves that we can take on by way of the stories we hold about who we are and how we have gotten to be so is temporally thick. It has a futural dimension inasmuch as we can recognize that we are responsible for even the long-term consequences of what we do regardless of whether we actually intend or foresee them. We know that the financial investments we make now will affect the estate we leave to our heirs. Or more to the present point, because our responsibility has a futural dimension, it can make sense for Jonas to argue that the way we use the technology now available to us makes us responsible for whether humanity can survive in the future.

My responsibility has a dimension of pastness as well. This dimension includes not just what I myself have already done or suffered. It includes as well the entire heritage I have received. Every heritage that we know about in any detail has brought its recipients burdens as well as benefits. Many parts of a heritage, legal codes for example, are simultaneously both burdensome and beneficial. Legal codes contain prohibitions. But they also make possible effective contracts and bequests.

Part of my heritage is the body I receive from my parents and their ancestors. And part of it is a distinctive cultural world into which I am inducted. Without this body and this world we could not exist, much less act. We exercise responsibility with regard to our heritage when we admit an indebtedness to it, an indebtedness we never finish with. To the extent that our heritage gives us unearned advantages over others, we owe them promises to help them relieve their disadvantages and we need their forgiveness. To the extent that our heritage leaves us undeservedly handicapped in some respects, it gives us claims against those who benefit from our disadvantages. It also prompts us to offer them our forgiveness.

And of course, responsibility has a present dimension. This present is distended, not punctiliar. It consists most radically in holding oneself durably constant. It demands that I am and should be "held to be the same today as the one who acted yesterday and who will act tomorrow."[29] In self-constancy I integrate what I now do and stand for with both the responsibility I have for the future consequences of all my own previous actions and the responsibility I have for the debts I owe and the claims I am entitled to advance by reason of my heritage.[30]

The capacity to act on the basis of an achievable self-constancy is the distinguishing mark of human persons. It entitles each of us to a respect from others that is inalienable.[31] We can exercise and increase our capacity for self-constancy by developing, through reflection, stable "considered convictions" that guide our conduct.[32] These convictions, though they are arrived at through serious reflection, always remain corrigible. In adopting them, we unavoidably take on what Rawls has called the "burdens of judgment."[33] There is thus always room for further reflection, and there is always reason to submit our convictions to the criticism of our fellows. When tested in these two ways, these convictions provide the surest ground for responsible action of which we are capable. To the extent that we act on them, we earn rights to recognition and respect over and above the entitlements we possess simply by virtue of being human.

At the beginning of this chapter I said that I proposed to construe human existence, in all its parts, as an interrogatory project. The description of our bodiliness and thoughtliness, on the one hand, and our ineliminable attachment to and relative independence from total absorption by the material and cultural world we inhabit, on the other hand, supports my proposal. We can make sense of everything that we do and undergo as so many parts of our life-long attempt both to fit into the world in which we find ourselves and to avoid being wholly absorbed by it.

The interrogatory project that is constitutive of each of our lives is radically dialectical and dialogical. My life is open-endedly intersubjective. There is no telling in advance which and how many other persons will be my interlocutors. It is ambivalent in the sense that in my dealings with my interlocutors I try to both join them and keep my independence from them. And it is finite and historical in the sense that my possibilities are circumscribed by the time in which I live, but in exercising them I contribute to a new determination of the circumstances of action, both my own and others'.

As an interrogatory project, I find that the several types of performances in which I can and do engage are both concordant and discordant with one another. My material and social needs and my desires both fit together and clash. Promises can both complete and clash with forgivings. And forgivings, while healing past transgressions, in effect open the doors for new ones. Convictions and commitments both shape and clash with desires. They also unite us with some people but divide us from others. And, as Plato suggests in the *Apology*, a person's sayings, doings, and makings regularly do not form a seamless whole.[34] What I do and what I say make at best a rough fit. My entire life is thus a process of trying to harmonize these disparate performances while at the same time giving each its own due attention.

Each of our lives, then, amounts to both a report of the responses we make to the issues or questions with which our world confronts us and our own rejoining interrogation that we address both to ourselves and to our interlocutors about the truth and worth of what we say and the goodness or beauty of what we do. Our report is never exhaustive and the answer to our question is never definitive.

Schematically, one can rightly say that a basic weakness in both the communitarian and the liberal conceptions of the human person is their failure to do full justice to its interrogatory character. Communitarians overstress the received answers that a culture passes on to its members. They underplay the questionableness of these answers and thereby tend to forget that each of us has his or her own new and individual question to ask. Liberals, on the other hand, tend to ignore the fact that each of us is reared in a particular tradition of inquiry that underpins our own interrogations. They instead implicitly or explicitly promote the notion that we can effectively bring our questioning to a conclusion by exercising individual choice. The answer that each of us chooses is regarded as no more questionable than we elect to make it.[35]

Even a liberal as sensitive as Yael Tamir is to the importance of the bonds that link us to our respective particular historical communities misconstrues our capacity to choose. She grants that communitarianism, or, in her frame of reference, nationalism, rightly teaches us the importance of belonging to a community. Liberalism complements this teaching by its insistence that persons are autonomous and possess rights as individuals. Taken together, these lessons lead to the conclusion that "no individual can be context-free, but that all can be free within a context."[36] We have learned, she says, both "the need to live one's life from the inside and the need to be rooted."[37]

She nonetheless argues that individuals are the best judges of the sort of cultural environment that fits their needs. Provided that they do not interfere with the choices of others, "there are no grounds for preventing them from pursuing their life-plans as they see fit."[38] Hence,

> not only should individuals have a right to choose the national group they wish to belong to, but *they should also have the right to define the meanings attached to this membership, that is, they should be the ones to decide on the cultural practices they wish to adopt, and on the ways of expressing them.*[39]

Granted, for the sake of argument, that we are free to specify the meaning some of our choices—for example, choices of diets, styles of clothing, and so on—just as we choose, we cannot do so in fundamental matters such as religion or citizenship. One who chooses to adhere to a religion does not genuinely do so unless he or she gives it its accepted meaning. One who chooses to give up the religion he or she previously practiced is a lapsed member, not merely a nonmember. Similarly, one is a good citizen of a state if he or she behaves in the prescribed way. And one who gives up his or her citizenship is an excitizen, not just a noncitizen. No chooser can negate these distinctions of meaning.

In any event, every choice, whether momentous or minor, is always an element in a history that is never merely the history of an individual. Like everything else that we do, it invites a response and thus is at bottom interrogatory. Conversely, as Tamir recognizes, one can acknowledge that each of us is inextricably tied to a particular community but that these ties are always open to our exploration and free response. They permit us—indeed, they invite us—to respond to them interrogatively.

However perspicuous the interpretation of human existence as an interrogatory project is, it still faces two straightforward challenges. One is posed by the fact that each of us is to die. The other is posed by the indifference of the cosmos to all human existence.

Consider first death and its counterpoint, birth. Each of us comes to be in our bodiliness and in our aptitudes for thought and action without asking to do so, and each of us lives with death as an unchosen ever-present possibility that is sure to be actualized some day. Even if the entire stretch of our lives between birth and death is construable as a complex interrogatory project, in what sense are the end points, birth and death, interrogatory? Briefly, they are interrogatory in the sense that they confront our relatives, friends, and acquaintances with new questions both about us and about themselves. Both our coming into their lives and our passing out of them call for their responses, which in turn invite interrogation.

More generally, we can grasp the interrogatory character of an entire human life, including its birth and death, if we follow a clue that Merleau-Ponty provides through his discussion of the history of painting. Each painting, he says, is linked to all others insofar as all of them are responses to the same problem or task. The problem is that which the world poses in presenting itself as paintable.[40] When a painter responds to this call to paint what appears to him or her, he or she "responds to an exigency like that which has called all other painters to their work."[41] The new painting enters into a history of creations, a history of attempts to bring to sight something worth seeing that has never been seen before.[42]

Analogously, each human life, with its birth and death, can properly be regarded as a distinctive interrogatory project that is a constituent of a history of such projects. It is the articulation of a line of inquiry that proposes either to preserve a previously established line or to inaugurate something new. It offers itself to those who survive it for their assessment, an assessment that itself is always open to question.

There is, however, a more radical challenge that my interpretation of human existence, like every other interpretation of it, must confront. A shadow thicker than death hangs over all human life. It covers all needs, desires, entitlements, choices, and convictions. It covers all thoughtliness. The shadow consists of the apparent indifference of the cosmic order to the existence of humanity. Like every other biological species, the human species came into existence at some moment of cosmic time and is destined to pass out of existence at some other moment. What does it matter in the long run that there have ever been human beings? Is not everything they have been and done ultimately insignificant? Is not meaning something that can occur only so long as there are people and, therefore, something that, like them, will one day be no more?

These questions confront us with a fundamental paradox. Ricoeur formulates it thus: "On the cosmic scale, our span of life [i.e., the span of the human species] is insignificant, and nevertheless, this brief lapse of time in which we appear on the scene of the world is the very place whence every question of significance arises."[43] Any attempt sensibly to deny that human existence matters founders, of course, on the fact that denials, no less than affirmations, presuppose sense and significance. But the shadow remains. Suppose that no saying, whatever its content or lack thereof, matters.

Believers in something divine and atemporal that can give a point and meaning to human life do not escape from the shadow. As Saint Paul said, those who see with the eyes of religious faith see only dimly and uncertainly. To see clearly in a pure light is reserved for the next life. But, of course, in this life we can have no more than faith that there is a next life. And it is the meaningfulness of belief, along with every other human performance, that is in question.

We come thus to a watershed. We must interpret the human condition either as a condition to be cherished and protected or as a fundamental absurdity, a condition that compels us senselessly to try to make sense. Philosophy gives us no ironclad answer. It is true that the question about what people can know and should aspire to is perennial. Every culture about which we have information displays beliefs about what makes human life worthwhile and struggles to live according to those beliefs. Each culture, in its own way, has held that "the good life for man is the life spent in seeking the good life for man."[44] The long history of this search does not, of course, settle matters, but it encourages one to hope that this search is not pointless.

And so, without ignoring the shadow of the apparently indifferent cosmos, I propose, in hope, an interpretation of the human condition that calls for us to live in the hope that speech and action are worthwhile. This hope, as Arendt saw, is made possible by our experience of the ability that people have to act.[45] In turn, this hope provides inspiration for us to preserve the capacity and conditions that make possible both our own action and that of others. In my interpretation, then, to live a fully human life is to act in such a way as to preserve the capacity for action.

My interpretation has several important consequences for political thought. Among the most basic of these is that it rules out what I have elsewhere called the politics of vision and the politics of might.[46]

Politics of vision, such as orthodox Marxism and the theocracies advocated by some Islamic and other religious fundamentalists, deny the paradoxical character of our search for meaning in an apparently indifferent cosmos. They claim to know eternal truths that remove the riskiness of action. For them, there are no ineradicable predicaments of action or burdens of judgment. But the certainty that they claim for the beliefs that they hold is indefensible. A politics that insists on the certainty of such beliefs is a tyrannical politics.

A politics of might, on the other hand, effectively sets at naught the political search for meaningful ways of living with one another. For such politics, the only thing of worth is the power to dominate others for no other purpose than the satisfaction of the will to do so. This sort of politics in effect dismisses the paradox involved in the search for meaning. For it, to take the paradox seriously is pointless. Domination justifies itself; or rather, justification is irrelevant to domination. Like a politics of vision, a politics of might is a tyrannical politics.

The resolution of the paradox of meaning that I adopt and the interpretation of human existence as an interrogatory project do not entail just one conception of the domain of politics or one constitutional form for it. But they do preclude the legitimacy of tyranny. They demand a politics that acknowledges the predicaments of action and the burdens of judgment. No tyrant can make such acknowledgment and remain tyrannical.

More positively, the account of human existence that I offer fits well with the Jonas imperative. If one hopes that interrogation is worthwhile and that we humans are interrogatory projects, then it makes sense to preserve the conditions that make interrogation possible.

In addition, though my interpretation does not strictly entail a democratic politics, it strongly supports it. Every human person is equally an interrogatory project and equally capable of agency. Whatever hierarchies people establish, including political ones, always remain open to their further questions and contestations. In the sameness of their interrogatory character, each person is in principle capable of political agency. Democracy is the historical form of politics that most explicitly acknowledges this sameness.

But even if every human person who has ever existed has been in principle capable of agency, there has not always been a distinct domain of politics. There have been societies in which no full-fledged distinctions were drawn between artistic, scientific, political, and religious activities. The existence of a distinct domain of politics is a historical achievement. Though its possibility is rooted in the very nature of the human condition, its actuality is contingent. It is the outcome of human performances that could have been otherwise. To complete the groundwork for the conception of citizenship that I argue for, I spell out in the next chapter the constitutive features of the domain of politics.

Chapter 4

The Domain of Politics

There is no generally agreed-upon definition of politics.[1] One can nonetheless identify within the tradition of Western political thought a collection of issues that have elicited perennial attention. Central among them are (a) the relationships between rulers and those whom they rule, (b) the nature and source of the rulers' authority, (c) the sources of conflict among people and its resolution, and (d) the very objective of political action itself. The thought and action devoted to addressing these issues and others closely related to them constitute a distinct domain of human endeavor.[2] How one conceives this domain and responds to its central issues will largely determine one's conception of the normative implications of citizenship.

In this chapter I argue that politics is an autonomous domain of thought and action, having its own distinctive norms and objectives. At bottom, everything political is either action or in the service of action; hence in some fashion or other everything political has the characteristics of action. But contrary to some claims, not all action is political. The political domain is not all encompassing. The political domain is the domain of speech, action, and production that has as its direct aim both the preservation and the well-being of a society. It is the domain of action that insists on the equiprimordality of these twin aims. But though the domain of politics is autonomous, it is inextricably linked to the domains of economics and ethics. Its autonomy is thus only relative.

My construal of the domain of politics is consistent with the interpretation of human existence that I presented in the previous chapter. No interpretation of what it is to be human gives one a set of premises from which to deduce straightforwardly a specific conception of politics, but every interpretation sets conditions that significantly affect how one construes politics. My construal is guided by a recognition of the human condition as one that is fundamentally an interrogative project.

This interpretation of the human condition, as I have said, has its origins in Aristotle's thought and draws heavily on the recent work of Arendt, Merleau-Ponty, and Ricoeur. So does my account of the domain of politics. It is also instructed by the liberal-communitarian debate.

The domain of politics is contingent. As long as there is action, it is possible. But it need not always be actualized and sometimes has not been. For example, there have been societies in which there was no significant distinction between the roles played by the one who was effectively both king and priest. Some early Celtic societies were apparently of this sort. And, as I point out in this chapter, temptations also remain today to reduce or subordinate the domain of politics to some other domain. Hence, the domain of politics is fragile as well as contingent. If it is to be durable, there must be citizens who exercise initiative and give it thoughtful care, but conversely, for citizenship to amount to more than an empty title, there must be an actual, relatively autonomous domain of politics.

One can identify in various historical eras inchoate forms of the mutual dependency between a relatively autonomous political domain and the existence of an institution of some type of citizenship, and one can distinguish them from mature forms. But there does not seem to be any way to determine just what brings an inchoate form to maturity. Both the beginnings and the flowerings of these forms are shrouded in darkness.

The account of politics that I offer deals with mature politics. It does not apply directly to warlords or despotic tribal chieftains and the people they control; nevertheless, in our internationalized world practitioners of mature politics must deal with such people in a way that is consistent with their own political maturity.

Before I begin to spell out my conception of politics, let me briefly respond to those who would claim that the term "politics" should cover not only what we do but what happens to us because we are affected by other people. For these thinkers, politics is all-pervasive. In this view, whether we wish it or not, we are enmeshed in struggles for power that have a life of their own. By virtue of their own dynamics, these struggles mold us, willy-nilly, to meet the requirements of their own "rules." All too often these views lead their holders to so naturalize both politics and human existence in general that they deny that there can be any genuine initiatives taken by individual persons.

But, as my interpretation of human existence shows, one need not deny that we are always contextualized in order to insist on our capacity for initiative. No human action would be intelligible unless it could be recognized as resembling the routine action associated with some institution. For example, an action is intelligible only if it can be recognized as being an action connected either with routine everyday practice or with some specialized institutional endeavor such as art or science or religion, and all routines and institutions have come into being in response to some widely recognized need or desire. Further, since all action is, in some respect or other, interaction, there is an irremovable political potential in every action.

Our contextualization does not, however, eliminate our capacity for initiative. Only if genuine initiative is possible can there be politics. Without it, there can only be a "human physics." In addition, the fact that there is an irremovable political potential in all action does not imply that all action and all institutions are reducible to the political domain. The direct object of the actions that the institutions of art, science, and religion make meaningful is not the same as that of political action. It is works of art, scientific discoveries, or religious worship. The direct object of political action is the perpetuation of a society and of its members' capacity for actions of all sorts, whatever their direct object. Part of the perpetuation of this capacity for various sorts of actions is the preservation of the conditions that allow the several institutions on which they depend for their meaningfulness to exist. Thus, for example, to the extent that Smith acts to produce a sculpture, he is doing something artistic. To the extent that this action and its product contribute to the preservation of the institution of art, they have political potential. When he or anyone uses either Smith's actions or its resultant sculpture to make arguments about the place of the domain of art or its activities and products in a society's overall life, to that extent he or she actualizes that political potential.

With these preliminaries in hand, I turn now to spell out in some detail my conception of the domain of politics. Let me begin by citing two partial characterizations of it. On the one hand John McDonald says: "Politics is the art of devising ways for men to live together in peace and relative comfort."[3] On the other hand, Ricoeur says that politics is the

> set of organized practices relating to the distribution of political power, better termed domination. These practices concern the vertical relation between the governing and the governed as well as the horizontal relation between rival groups in the distribution of political power.[4]

McDonald's remark, if read with Aristotelian eyes, shows an awareness that politics has to deal with both the bodily and the thoughtly dimensions of human existence. It draws attention to the good will or concord among a society's members that ought to be the ultimate objective of all of their political activity. This concord is not exclusively a communion of hearts or minds. It also requires a bodily ease or "relative comfort." I would add that not only is concord the goal of political activity but at least a modicum of it is a necessary condition for politics.[5] Those who truly despise one another can share only a perverted politics.

Ricoeur's comment, by contrast, reminds us not to romanticize politics. It reminds us that ruling and the threat of coercion are inseparable from politics. Politics always organizes coercive power and gives some people dominion over others. Politics takes its point of departure from a struggle for recognition and power, a struggle that is always already under way. It seeks to constrain the struggle in such a way that no actual distribution of power leaves any person or group wholly impotent. Were anyone deliberately made powerless, then those who made them so would have become tyrants.

To these two partial characterizations of the domain of politics, let me add that politics is the domain of thought and action that establishes and maintains a society of people for a dual purpose. On the one hand, it aims to inculcate in them a shared sense of identity, a political identity.[6] On the other hand, it aims to gather, protect, and distribute material and cultural goods as well as to fix and assign the burdens indissociable from the pursuit of these goods. The political society is meant to last indefinitely. It is, in Rawls's words, "conceived as existing in perpetuity . . . and there is no time at which it is expected to wind up its affairs."[7] Its own survival is one of its constitutive objectives. Political societies thus must always make provisions to incorporate new members to replace those who die, and they must be willing to impose on their members the burdens that are inseparable from the acquisition and distribution of goods.

Each of these three comments—McDonald's, Ricoeur's, and mine—thus refers to some important feature of the complex justice that it is the task of politics to pursue. It is a justice that has to do both with relations among people and with the acquisition and distribution of goods, it is a justice that refers to future generations as well as to the present one, and it is a justice that today has both local and global implications.

Taken together, these three remarks provide a framework for the conception of politics that I want to propose. They point to a domain of action whose objectives are multiple and in tension with one another. Many political regimes have claimed legitimacy on the grounds that they successfully promote one or another of these objectives. My contention is that a regime is legitimate and responsibly democratic just insofar as it both keeps in tension all of the objectives that make up the pursuit of justice and seeks to promote all of them optimally.

It is worth emphasizing at the outset that these three remarks about politics, each in its own way, take cognizance of both the bodily and the thoughtly dimensions of human beings. They all show recognition that both dimensions are to be respected and given their due. Because we are bodily, we are at home only some places with only some people. Those places are where we can best act and those people are the ones with whom we can most readily act in concert and find concord. But because we are also thoughtly, there is in principle no place where we could not act effectively at all, and there are no people with whom we could never act in concert at all.

Each of these remarks however, also admits, at least by implication, that giving both our bodiliness and our thoughtliness their due is a task that is endless, a problem that can have no definitive solution. Neither peace nor relative comfort can ever be definitively guaranteed, nor can any organization and distribution of power or resources be made permanent. This is so because, on the one hand, there are always deaths of members and their replacement by newcomers, either children or immigrants. Without the always pressing and never simple work of incorporating newcomers, no political society can survive. The task of giving due weight to both bodiliness and thoughtliness is interminable also because, on the other hand, there is constant change in the available material resources and in the technology with which to utilize them. Sometimes and for some people there is abundance. For others or at other times there is scarcity.

All three of these comments about the task of politics thus prompt us to recognize it as a domain of thought and action that is irreducible to other domains. It has its own distinctive issues and its own norms. Hence it is autonomous vis-à-vis other domains of thought and action.

Its autonomy, however, is only relative. On the one hand, political activity always involves judgments about the availability of resources and personnel and choices about their organization and utilization. It is, therefore, indissociable from economics. On the other hand, because politics always involves judgments about what is good for a society and its members, it is indissociable from the domain of ethics or morality.

Because politics is indissolubly tied to other domains, we find ourselves regularly tempted to subordinate political judgments to criteria drawn from them. Resisting these temptations is an essential part of practicing politics responsibly. Though our political judgments ought to take both economic and ethical considerations into account, they ought not to be wholly determined by them.

The twentieth century has seen more than one effort systematically to subjugate politics to economics. Orthodox Marxism regarded political alienation as a symptomatic manifestation of a more fundamental economic alienation. It took this economic alienation to be the product of the economic liberalism that is the true source of political liberalism. This reduction of politics to economics provided the orthodox Marxists with a justification for suppressing the benefits of genuinely democratic politics. For them, this suppression was simply the necessary price to be paid to eliminate the injustices that economic liberalism brought about. In fact, though, as we now know, this reductionism opened the way for justifying a murderous totalitarianism.[8]

Though orthodox Marxism appears now to be thoroughly discredited, other forms of the effort to subjugate politics to economics show, if anything, signs of waxing rather than waning. For example, organizational theorists such as Herbert Simon have long held that the primary rational objective of every organization is efficiency. An organization's fundamental task, therefore, is to adapt all of its resources—and the people involved in it count as resources—to the most efficient way to realize its objectives, whatever its objectives are. In this view, efficiency consists in having the organization's personnel act always for the best interests of the organization. People are rational just insofar as they promote the objectives of the organization of which they are members.[9]

Applied to economics, this notion of technical rationality would insist that the technical imperatives of a rationalized economy overrule any strictly political considerations that might challenge them. Proponents of some version of this position include rational choice theorists and cost-benefit analysts as well as organization theorists. In one fashion or another they all argue for making some version of technical rationality the ultimate basis for the disposition of legal and political matters.[10]

Whatever their motivation for subjugating politics to economics, for example, indignation at economic poverty or infatuation with economic wealth, those who would do so must deny the distinction between the rational and the reasonable. In this distinction, roughly, to be rational is correctly to derive conclusions from some set of premises. To be reasonable is to determine by appropriate reflection which set of premises to accept and what measure of credence to give it.

Proponents of the unequivocal primacy of the economic rationality thus cannot admit the appositeness of questions of the following sort. Are there not some noneconomic goods, for example, rich biological or cultural diversity, that a society should pursue even at the expense of some loss of economic efficiency? They too easily assume that the value of every human good can be exhaustively expressed in economic terms and that as a consequence economic efficiency is, in some long run, identical with what is good for people. To challenge their assumptions, as I do, is not to neglect the importance of economic efficiency. It is, rather, to ask about how a society does and should determine its objectives and about the relative worth of different degrees of efficiency in pursuing them.

Questions of this sort cannot, in principle, be answered in terms of any kind of technical rationality, economic or otherwise. They are questions about what "premises" to accept. That is, they are questions about which objectives are worthy of being pursued at all. They are not merely questions about the relative worth of one worthy objective when compared to another worthy one. Questions about the worthiness of objectives for what I, following Rawls and others, have called a political society are, in the strict sense, political. It is part of the practice of politics, understood as the exercise of a society's decision-making capabilities together with the implementation of these decisions by the use of its coercive authority, to determine to what extent the society will give sway to the norms of technicoeconomic organization and activity. It is for politics to preserve and make fruitful the tension between pursuits aimed at the society's survival and those aimed at its flourishing, its living well. It is politics' task to determine the reasonable response to claims advanced by technicoeconomic rationality.[11] Most fundamentally, it is politics' task to make sure that every response to these claims always remains open to reassessment.[12]

The capacity of politics, as an autonomous domain of discourse, decision, and action, to provide the continuous opportunity for people to raise and respond to questions about the weight that their society should give to technical demands of any sort is its glory. But the kind of response that politics permits also shows what Ricoeur has called its "fragility," its vulnerability to threats against its autonomy.[13] In the sphere of the production of economic goods, as in other technical fields—for example, medicine and weaponry—one finds a history of at least apparent progress. There is a progressive accumulation and sophistication of resources, tools, and techniques. This progress, or so it seems, is readily measurable and open to documentation. It is, in short, demonstrable.

There is no comparable record of progress in political matters. What a society learns in its political experience never becomes a settled acquisition that it can take for granted and straightforwardly build on. In many, perhaps most, cases there is no ready measure for determining unambiguously what counts as political progress. The political responses of yesterday are at best precedents, certainly not premises, for today. And none of the precedents is incontrovertible.[14]

The controvertability of all putative political progress extends even to the apparently secure claims advanced on behalf of the rightness of democracy and the propriety of universal freedom. These and similar ideas of supposedly progressive politics, for example, human equality, do not hold the status of transparent axioms. Rather, they mark the sites for investigation and argumentation. For political practice to have arrived at these sites is by no means trivial, but it has not thereby gained a settled acquisition to which it can give definitive expression in the norms it adopts. Who would deny that political programs whose designers aim for democracy or freedom or equality can reveal in implementation unexpected seeds of tyranny, anarchy, or totalitarianism? What Hans-Georg Gadamer says about freedom holds for other generally endorsed political ideals today such as democracy and equality. He says:

> The principle that all are free can never again be shaken. But does this mean that an account of this history has come to an end? Are all human beings actually free? Has not history since [Hegel] been a matter of just this, that the historical conduct of man has to translate the principle of freedom into reality? Obviously, this points to the unending march of world history into the openness of its future tasks and gives no becalming assurance that everything is already in order.[15]

Because it accumulates no unequivocal achievements, because the issues with which it deals are in principle beyond definitive resolution, politics requires indefatigable patience. Patience of this sort is hard to come by. One is persistently tempted to abandon the effort that political reasonableness demands in favor of the apparently more satisfying results that economic and other versions of technical rationality promise. This irremovable vulnerability of politics to impatience with the nondefinitiveness of its discourse and activity gives politics a fragility that no one concerned with protecting its relative autonomy can afford to ignore. Thus preserving the autonomy of his or her society's political practice is a responsibility that the good citizen never finishes with.

Besides being at risk from attempts to subjugate it to the requirements of economic or other forms of technical rationality, politics is also vulnerable to efforts to cancel its autonomy vis-à-vis the domain of ethics. There are at least two ways in which this second threat shows itself. Sometimes it shows itself as an attempt to subordinate politics to some ethical absolute, either religious or philosophical. Theocracies are obvious examples of this sort of attempt. Other times it appears as an effort to make politics into one of the constitutive parts of a comprehensive ethics. Ideal political theorists sometimes engage in an attempt of this sort. Ronald Dworkin has subscribed to such an effort in claiming that his version of democratic liberalism is part of a comprehensive moral doctrine.[16]

Just as there is no way to immunize politics completely against the threat from economics, so is there no way to do so against the threat from ethics. As with economics, the autonomy of politics from ethics is only relative. Since the ancient Greeks, Western thought has acknowledged a symbiosis between politics and ethics. "Although we can distinguish ethics and politics, they are inseparable. For we cannot understand ethics without thinking through our political commitments and responsibilities. And there is no understanding of politics that does not bring us back to ethics."[17]

The very effort to protect the domain of politics from domination by economic rationality itself reveals something of what Ricoeur calls an "ethical intention." To defend the autonomy of politics is a demand of politics itself. But it is not only that. It is also a demand of reason that appreciates the value of preserving politics' autonomy as one among several autonomous domains. The claim that it is important that there be a relatively autonomous domain of politics so that people can work out with one another appropriate relations among them implies in some fashion that the dignity that belongs to human beings by virtue of their humanity is no mere human fabrication. Neither is respect for this dignity to be treated as just one of several values of variables in some economic calculation. It is respect for this dignity, insisted on sometimes by religious doctrines and sometimes by philosophical ethics, that makes it important to preserve politics' autonomy vis-à-vis economics. Nonetheless these religious and philosophical considerations should not be stretched so far that they would deny the relative autonomy of politics vis-à-vis ethics as well.[18]

Some of the arguments that have been advanced against state citizenship in favor of some version of world citizenship deny at least implicitly the relative autonomy of politics. They claim that the characteristic values and norms of a state, in their particularity, always seek to favor their own members at the expense of foreigners. By insisting on the superior rationality of norms that fully satisfy the Kantian principle of universalizability or the Christian command of universal love, they in effect treat the political norms of particular states and the values to which they subscribe as, at best, deficiencies that can be temporarily tolerated pending their replacement as soon as possible by universal norms.

One can resist the penchant for universalizability and thereby defend the autonomy of politics by making use of Max Weber's famous distinction between an ethics of conviction or ultimate ends and an ethics of responsibility.[19] An ethics of ultimate ends is one that claims to articulate norms that are universally, though always abstractly, obligatory or commendable. An ethics of responsibility, by contrast, limits itself to claiming the obligatory character of norms that are concretely realizable with a reasonably limited use or threat of coercion or violence in some particular context. To maintain the autonomy of the domain of politics, its practitioners must hold fast to the spirit if not to the letter of this distinction.

An ethics of ultimate ends covers not only what is done but also what motivates doing it. It is concerned not merely with conduct and the set of values that this conduct displays but also with the motivations and justifications from which these values spring and which sustain them. This is the kind of ethics that confessional communities and some particular cultural and intellectual groups uphold as ideals for their members. One who accepts an ethics of ultimate ends thereby accepts a call to change his or her entire way of living.

By contrast, an ethics of responsibility is satisfied with a consensus only about the values to be acted on. In the interest in preserving this consensus, practitioners of an ethics of responsibility accept disagreement among themselves about the ultimate bases of the values they agree on. To avoid risking a destructive division in their society, they refuse to demand an unqualified commitment to a comprehensive way of life. They content themselves with mutual accommodation.[20]

A particular political society cannot demand that all of its members adopt some specific ethics of ultimate ends and still remain a genuine political society, a society that rejects any form of tyranny. But it can and should adopt and promote an ethics of responsibility. And it should leave as much room as it can without jeopardizing the consensus that sustains it for those of its citizens who wish to embrace an ethics of ultimate ends. Though a political society need not, and should not, make survival its sole ultimate objective, it must presume that there are discoverable reasonable norms that promote political goods such as justice and freedom that are compatible with its survival. In the absence of such a presumption, those who seek moral excellence would have to refrain from political life, and without such people, political practice will degenerate into a tyrannical politics of might.

For example, a political society should ask of its members no more than a consensus on common values. Consider the United States. Including as it does, tribes of native Americans as well as recent immigrants and descendants of earlier African, Asian, and European immigrants, it should promote a political identity and a consensus on values sufficient to make it durable. It should also, insofar as it is compatible with its own durability, permit particular groups of its members to promote and live according to their own conceptions of ultimate ends or the requirements of a comprehensive way of life. But in its properly political activity it should refrain from promoting any comprehensive way of life, whether it be a Dworkinian comprehensive liberalism or a Hasidic Judaism. To discharge this complex task successfully, a political society must provide its members with appropriate political education. I return to the issue of education in chapter 7.

To accept disagreements and different ways of arriving at the consensus on values that responsible politics requires is not to practice mere tolerance, it is to put into practice the mutual respect one owes to his or her fellow citizens. It is to join them in a common search for the politically reasonable. Technical rationality, for example, economic rationality, claims a capacity to mark off definitively the correct from the incorrect. Similarly, the theoretical rationality that purportedly underpins the demands of an ethics of ultimate ends claims to have established conclusively what is right and what is wrong. The politically reasonable, by contrast, claims only to arrive at better reasons for adopting *at this time for this society* one particular opinion or course of action instead of any of its presently available alternatives.

By its very nature, the claim to have found the reasonable is never definitively established. It is always open to reconsideration and reformation. Here again politics requires steadfast patience, and the fact that it requires patience makes politics fragile. It cannot be made entirely invulnerable to those who would obviate the need for patience by subjugating all action, political or otherwise, to the demands of some specific ethics of ultimate ends.

An ethics of responsibility gives full recognition to both the bodily and the thoughtly dimensions of human existence. On the one hand, it recognizes that our bodiliness always ties us to some locale with its particular population and historical moment. On the other, it recognizes that, because we are thoughtly, we can work out an accommodation, a modus vivendi, with those who are quite different from us. Many historical examples of ethics of ultimate ends, however, show strong tendencies to neglect one of these dimensions. Comprehensive liberalisms such as Dworkin's tend to neglect our bodiliness. They in effect regard people as equipped equally well to live anywhere, as native citizens of "nowhere." On the other hand, many nineteenth- and twentieth-century nationalisms tend to neglect our thoughtliness. They tend to treat natal religious, linguistic, or ethnic ties as a fate or destiny. Adherents of these nationalisms tend to stress these bodily bonds so strongly that they neglect to concern themselves sufficiently with the well-being of others.

Because it is sensitive to both our bodiliness and our thoughtliness, an ethics of responsibility will promote a specific sort of political identity. It is an identity that both accommodates diversity among its participants and admits the necessity and validity of the political identities of other societies. In this respect, it is a less strict identity than those that are so often promoted by nationalisms, but it is not as content-free as are the sorts of political identity that comprehensive liberalisms characteristically call for. It is sufficiently strict that it can underpin a strong distinction between those who participate in it and those who do not.

The autonomy of the domain of politics faces a second, perhaps more subtle, threat from the domain of ethics. Instead of subordinating politics to ethics, one might try to merge them. This latter threat, like the former, gains its initial plausibility from the ethical intention that prods politics to keep itself free from domination by economic or other forms of technical rationality.

Attempts to merge politics with ethics rest on a mistaken understanding of the essential contribution that the state makes to the society's historical survival. Though it cannot be a responsible state's sole objective, every responsible state must take as part of its fundamental task the preservation of the existence of its society. It must seek to maintain the society in spite of external or internal obstacles. If a state were to abandon this objective, it and the politics it makes possible would face extinction.

The state contributes to the society's survival both by reason of its form, especially its constitution and laws, and by reason of the force it amasses and is prepared to use.[21] Some people, though, exaggerate the role of form and slight the role of force in the state's activity. For them, the state's basic function is to harmonize technicoeconomic rationality with what the society's *mores* show to be reasonable for it. As Ricoeur puts it:

> The State would then be the synthesis of the rational and the historical, of the efficacious and the just. Its virtue would be prudence in the Greek and medieval sense of prudence. By this we mean that its virtue consists in holding together the criterion of efficacious calculation and the criterion of the living traditions which give the community the character of a particular organism striving for independence and longevity.[22]

This conception leads to the mistaken notion that the state is at bottom primarily the educator of its citizens, that its essential task is to bring its citizens to appreciate the synthesis it claims to have made between efficacy and justice. On this conception, the state's force can be completely harnessed so that it is never exercised except in service of the state's educative function.

If the state were able to confine itself exclusively to the role of educator, using force only in support of its educative function, and still survive, then perhaps one could collapse the distinction between politics and ethics. A state might then strive to be unequivocally a morally good state. But we have no good reasons for believing that a state can survive as a purely educational state. Even if force or power is not necessarily violence, no successful state about which we have historical records has wholly done away with the ruling of some people by others and the domination implicated in that ruling. "Political life," as Ricoeur points out, "remains ineluctably marked by the struggle for political domination."[23]

No constitutional or other formal features of a state can transform the struggle for power into nothing other than an exercise in education or a wholly subordinated aid to education. In the abstract, the struggle for domination could be a pure exercise of persuasion without any threats. But if this struggle is to lead to efficacious action, then, as history has constantly demonstrated, it is a practical impossibility to conduct it in the complete absence of coercion. The political struggle for domination must include in its aims some attempts to constrain what the thoughtless, the selfish, and the wicked would otherwise do. There is, however, no single best set of constraints and ways to implement it. Thoughtful, unselfish, and virtuous people can always have plausible reasons for disagreeing about who should be coerced and how it should be done, but if the coercion is to be effective, then those who hold dominating power must be prepared to coerce even the good and thoughtful fellow citizens who disagree with them. They must insist that the dissenters either lend support to or at least not impede the enforcement of the coercive measures they have decided on. This practical necessity for coercion holds true for international as well as domestic politics.

The practical ineliminability of coercion from effective politics clearly illustrates why political practice should adhere to an ethics of responsibility rather than an ethics of ultimate ends. There can be no definitive argument for any particular set of political institutions or practices, coercive or otherwise. Everything political can be contested without absurdity. An ethics of ultimate ends claims to have arrived at conclusions that there is no more reason to contest. An ethics of responsibility, with proper modesty, makes no such claims.

The dream of a pure educator state, history shows, has by no means been innocuous. Those who dream of the total merger of politics with ethics that the pure educator state implies, when faced with the messiness of the political life they are involved in, are tempted to become impatient with politics and to resort to calling not merely for the merger of politics with ethics, but indeed for the full subjugation of politics to ethics. They are tempted to embrace some theologicophilo-sophical rationality. To succumb to this temptation is to fall into pernicious ideology or utopianism.[24] Embracing a rationality of this sort has all too often led to "Thermidorian" dictatorships such as that into which the French Revolution degenerated or to theocracies. Though politics cannot be made invulnerable to the impatience that provokes such misadventures, it is crucial for its practitioners to resist these temptations.

To recognize that the domain of politics is both contingent and autonomous, but only relatively so, is to gain insight into some of the crucial features of any political thought or action that aspires to be responsible. As I pointed out in chapter 3, all thought and action is historical, ambivalent and ambiguous, and dialectical. Here it is important to spell out some of the capital implications of these features of action for political life. To ignore them is to be either reckless or ineffective or both.[25]

Consider first the thoroughly temporal, historical character of human life and the bearing it has on politics. Political sayings, doings, and makings, like all human actions, are never pure or perfect—that is, none of them is without unintended consequences—and none of them can claim to be the unqualifiedly best thing to do at the moment it is done.

To deny that there are pure and perfect actions is not tantamount to saying that there is something wrong with everything we do. It is, rather, to acknowledge the limitations that are ingredient in every political performance. This acknowledgment opens the way for us to appreciate that neither utopia nor dystopia are inevitable or achievable.

If the antecedents of our actions do not make them inevitable, neither can we wholly negate them. One cannot reasonably claim to start an action, political or otherwise, from whole cloth. We cannot recreate an archaic, prelapsarian moment. What Merleau-Ponty said about French colonial involvement in Madagascar holds good generally, as today's relationships between the French and their former African colonies testify. He said: "We are embarked and it is no small thing to have begun this game."[26] Kwame Anthony Appiah makes something of the same point from the standpoint of the colonized.[27] But just because we have started on some course of action does not condemn us to continue it.[28]

What politics calls for is timely action. Though there is no ideal action and no ideal moment for any particular action, some actions are both appropriate and timely and others are not. Time can run out for an action. It can also not yet be ripe.[29]

Because politics demands timeliness, it is unavoidably risky. It is characteristic of politics that it does not merely react to problems and situations but also seeks to transform them. Our view of the past, in light of which we plan these transformations, may provide us with probabilities or likelihoods. But it gives us no certitudes. We thus can do no more than hope that our political initiatives will later show themselves to have been well suited to their circumstances.[30] This is, however, a far from trivial or sterile hope.

Today, as I have noted earlier, politics must deal with the extensive internationalization of much of human life. This internationalization shows up in economic, cultural, and military matters as well as in political ones. State sovereignty has in recent years been attenuated and is likely to be further attenuated in the future; nonetheless, there is no single history or single politics that can synthesize human doings and sufferings into one all-encompassing whole. All political action bears the stamp of some particular locality. "There is," as Merleau-Ponty saw, "no universal clock, but local histories take form beneath our eyes, and begin to regulate themselves, and haltingly link themselves to one another and demand to live."[31]

It follows, therefore, that any attempt to base a politics on the assumption of a single ultimate direction and meaning of history—as orthodox Marxists on the one hand and some proponents of simplistic belief in an irresistible progress of democratic liberalism on the other have done—commits a fundamental error. This is the sort of error, as the historical record shows, that has all too frequently provided support for tyranny or destructive adventurism.

Even though human beings do make their own history, they nonetheless cannot fully know either the history they are making or that which they have already made. To pretend, as some Hegelians, Marxists, and others have, that there is some historical logic that in the last analysis is decisive and thus constitutes some ahistorical truth of history is indefensible. There is no "last analysis," and no logic can evade the contingency that is always ingredient in human affairs.[32] Because there is no historical totality and no sure line of march to historical progress, there are no political vanguards. No person or group of people can claim to be the vehicle or mouthpiece of a politics that will redeem humanity from the finitude and historicality that preclude it from producing perfect and definitive accomplishments. No politics can overcome the limitations that are constitutive of human life. There are thus no people who hold unqualified title to exercise political leadership, who hold title to political power by reason of some natural or apolitical right. This fact may well be a disappointment "for all who believed in salvation and in a single means of salvation in all realms."[33] A more fitting response to the limitations that are essential features of human existence is to accept the opportunities that the historical moment offers and handle them as adroitly as one can to improve the lot of all who are affected by this handling.

For an example of the sorts of claims that the denial of the possibility of pure or perfect speech or action rules out, consider the matter of interpreting written political constitutions. Some in the United States have argued that one can and should determine the original intent of the document's authors and make his or her interpretation or application of the Constitution conform to that intent, but if there are no pure or perfect moments of discourse or action, then such a proposal is thoroughly wrongheaded. Like everyone else, the authors, on the one hand, could do no more than respond to their own fallible grasp of historical antecedents and, on the other, could not reasonably claim to have spoken the last word on any matter. Even if one could do the impossible and discover their original intent, there is no good reason to believe that, all intervening contingencies notwithstanding, it could or should fully govern present applications. If one is to be faithful to a historical document, one must make a fresh response to it rather than simply to treat it as definitive.

Admittedly, even though there is no pure and perfect discourse, some discourse can rightfully be given a privileged status. The constitutions that democratic states adopt as their founding documents are obvious examples of such privileged documents.[34] It is appropriate that, when citizens deliberate about topics that their constitution addresses, they give special weight to what it says. Doing so contributes to the continuity of the process of political decision making and thus promotes the stability and order that a state needs to survive and flourish. A state can succeed, however, only if it also responds appropriately to the new exigencies that come to confront it periodically in the course of its existence. It cannot do so if its citizens insist on treating the constitution as a closed set of premises that are both necessary and sufficient for arriving at proper answers to all basic political questions or as an absolute standard against which all other political sayings and doings concerning constitutional issues must be tested.[35]

Just as politics is thoroughly historical, so too is it permeated by an ineliminable ambiguity and ambivalence. Three prominent aspects of this ambiguity and ambivalence deserve mention here.

First, attempts to divide the elements of any nontyrannical political situation into unqualified blessings and unmitigated curses are doomed to fail. No element is self-contained. It is always intertwined with other elements from which it gets part of its meaning and efficacy. Thus, for example, during the Cold War, American liberal capitalism and Soviet communism acted not only on the basis of their own inner principles but also in response to the other's doings. Given the internationalization of political and economic life today, the same holds true for any state in its dealings with other states. We can make

sense of a state's foreign policy only by taking note of its entangle-
ments with other states, and insofar as its domestic life is tied to its
international activity, it too is fully intelligible only by taking that
activity into account.

It follows that neither people as individuals nor states can be
neatly divided into what Merleau-Ponty calls cops and con men.[36] The
historical record shows us neither angels nor devils, only people.
And people both help and harm one another, both deliberately and
negligently and accidentally. Politics cannot redeem them from this
condition.

A second aspect of politics' ambiguity and ambivalence is displayed
in the phenomenon of political rule. If there is to be politics at all,
then, as Aristotle already saw, there must be a distinction between
those who are entitled to participate in ruling and those who are not.
Whatever rights may be accorded to all members of the body politic,
they do not all have equal title to rule. There must be a distinction
between those who hold office and those who do not. The latter may
be entitled to obey by way of critical response rather than by way of
mere acquiescence, but some must obey if others are meaningfully
to command. Nonetheless, all discourse, including that of political
command, is communal. Genuinely to speak, even to command, is
also to pay attention to, to listen to those one commands.[37] In politics,
if it is nontyrannical, rulers and ruled must interact in and through a
shared network of institutions that sustain them in their respective
roles. Strictly speaking, then, no one either commands or obeys absolutely.[38]

These political institutions display a third aspect of the ambiguity
and ambivalence that characterizes everything political. No institution,
political or otherwise, can be given a definitive form. They are all
perpetually open to improvement through new initiatives and to degradation by design or neglect. They always can and often do prevent us
from doing what we wish. They can and often do alienate us from one
another. But they do not merely constrict us. They also make it
possible for our actions to be durably efficacious. Institutions are thus
"the consequence and the guarantee of our belonging to a common
world."[39] They both allow us to contribute to a history larger than that
of our own lives and submit us to the constraints and results of
that history.

The ambiguity and ambivalence that pervades institutions is obvious
in a state's legal institution. Law both bears witness to the violence
that it aims to remedy and itself embodies a threat of further violence.

Like all political institutions, law makes and protects opportunities for exercises of freedom. But it also always exerts pressure on people. Even as an instrument of peace and order, law never surrenders its capacity for coercion, and, as I mentioned above, coercion is genuine only if it is prepared to turn into violence. The readiness for violence is inseparable from the unifying, peacemaking benefits that law makes available.[40]

For much the same reasons that it is completely historical and unavoidably ambiguous and ambivalent, politics is also inherently dialectical. In general terms, it takes place, on the one hand, at the intersection of what is already settled and what can now be initiated. On the other hand, it takes place in the interplay among members of a society and between a society and outsiders. This dialectic is multifaceted and gets played out in a struggle between pressures to adhere to a status quo and enticements to imagine and leap out to new possibilities. Roughly put, politics plays itself out between the poles of ideology and utopia. Responsible politics never eliminates the tension between these poles.

The dialectical character of politics shows up within individual political agents. Neither their aims nor their accomplishments are transparent to themselves. Their aims are never single-minded, nor are their accomplishments fully specifiable. Aims and accomplishments take their meaning, on the one hand, from the temporally extended interaction between an agent and his or her fellows and, on the other, from their joint encounter with their common world. No political agent, therefore, can come to the truth about himself or herself or the common world without help from others.[41]

Mutatis mutandis, the same lack of transparency characterizes group aims and actions. For one thing, the composition of a political society is always in flux. Births, deaths, and migrations constantly alter it. For another, politics always presses some people to expand the horizons of their individual interests by subordinating the differences among them to a more capacious unity. It never fails, however, to exclude some others. It always refers somehow to those it excludes in the course of defining itself. Nonetheless, because its own composition as well as that of the group it excludes are constantly in flux, its self-definition is never complete.

The dialectical character of politics calls for a constant critique of all of a state's institutions and practices. Its own members and those whom it excludes are all, in principle, appropriate participants in this critique. Criticism always involves opposition of some sort. The critical opposition that every state always needs, even an opposition that contains seeds of the state's overthrow, deserves welcome, for only a regularly criticized politics can remain a living politics.[42]

Perhaps nowhere does the dialectical character of living politics display itself more fully than in the discourse that seeks to legitimate either its system of rule or who should be the ruler or both. There is no set of arguments that can definitively answer either of these questions. Nonetheless, to have a durable political society, at least a sizable number of its members must regard the current answers as acceptable until they can find an at least equally acceptable alternative.

Failure to recognize the gap between these answers and the evidence that supports them would turn the answers into ideological pronouncements no longer in need of criticism. But to cite this gap, which is ineliminable, as a justification for rejecting the acceptability of any answers to these two questions is tantamount to embracing anarchy. Responsible critique searches for better answers, but it does not dream of definitive ones.

To dream of definitive answers is to dream of a utopia. Utopias, if embraced categorically rather than simply employed heuristically, have tended toward one or the other of two extremes. Some of them tend toward anarchy. These versions would claim that fully enlightened people, having realized that no sort of rulership can be fully justified, now find that they can dispense with ruling altogether. The other versions claim to have found a definitive justification for a specific sort of rule. These versions, denying that any dissent could be reasonable, are tyrannical. Their tyranny might present itself as benign, but it would be tyranny nonetheless. If implemented, utopian thought would undercut the political good by insisting on accepting nothing but the political best.

In the actual history of political thought and practice, at least in the West, there is compelling evidence of the importance of an ongoing critique that neither doggedly insists on the status quo, as unmitigated ideological discourse would do, nor blithely disregards the exigencies of reality in constructing and trying to implement an imaginary wonderland, as unrestrained utopianism would do. This evidence shows that, unless there is a healthy dialectic within a political society between ideological arguments that resist the wholesale dissolution of a status quo which has provided some substantial political and social coherence and utopian arguments that emphasize that the status quo is always in need of renovation, then that society's politics has ossified.

The preservation of a healthy dialectical tension is therefore an endless and crucial political task.[43]

Recognizing that the domain of politics enjoys a relative autonomy from those of economics and ethics and that all political action is historical, ambivalent and ambiguous, and dialectical has important consequences for how one should construe political identity on the one hand and political justice on the other. It helps us to see that in concrete practice, the effective meaning of political identity and that of political justice are tied to each other. As Hanna Pitkin has pointed out:

> Political life . . . is the activity through which relatively large and permanent groups of people determine what they will collectively do, settle how they will live together, and decide their future, to whatever extent that is within human power. . . . In deciding the perennial political question "What shall we do?" we are inevitably deciding at the same time both what each of us will get, and who we, as a community, will be.[44]

Attention to the features of political action that I emphasize here warns us away from two mistaken conceptions of political identity. It warns us away from the nearly context-free sorts of political identity that comprehensive liberalisms characteristically call for, but it also warns us away from conceiving of political identities as having nearly as strict a fixedness as material objects have. Some nationalists make one version of this mistake, and those who regard people as nothing but the products of their biological makeup or their cultural context make another version of it. Contrary to liberalism, a genuine political identity is always sufficiently strict that it can underpin a strong distinction between those who are entitled to participate in it and those who are not. On the other hand, though, to demand that people acknowledge a political identity so strict that they cannot rework it is historically unwarranted. To pretend that a permanently fixed political identity, even if not unavoidable, is nonetheless desirable is to be politically irresponsible.[45]

Much the same holds true for political justice. What Gadamer says about freedom holds for justice as well. All responsible politics aims to achieve justice among its members, but what this demands is always subject to local contingencies. To regard the content of justice as fixed once and for all and the task of politics as that of simply implementing this fixed content is to misconstrue both the domain of politics and one of its basic tasks. This misconstrual oversimplifies the complexities of political life. It is pernicious because it opens the way for an indiscriminate discrediting of much political practice.[46]

Consider for example the procedural safeguards that democratic states provide for those accused of crimes. No list of existing or proposed safeguards is perfect and deserving of universal adoption. There is no reason to believe that the set of safeguards presently in place in the United States is either irreformable or applicable elsewhere. Changes in kinds and frequency of crimes might make procedural reforms appropriate. Inhabitants of places where organized crime is deeply entrenched, as it is said to be in Sicily or Colombia or Bolivia, may reasonably argue that it is impracticable to grant the accused the same procedural safeguards as a more law-abiding society can.

Just as attention to the historicality, ambivalence and ambiguity, and dialecticality of everything political is instructive about the issues of political identity and political justice, so too is it instructive about the matter of political amelioration. The fact that all politics has these characteristics does not preclude the possibility of initiatives that ameliorate political life. What it does preclude is the claim that any action either has universal, ahistorical validity or is the unique and fully justified next step in a history of politics that is certainly progressive. Everything political has its costs. Nothing political is immune to interrogation.

The historical record provides compelling, though not definitive, evidence that some political practice has indeed been ameliorative of political life. Part of the evidence is negative. That is, it shows that political doctrines claiming to be definitively true or justified have regularly led to deeds that have wrought havoc not only on outsiders but also on a significant part of the society's own populace. Similarly destructive has been political practice that has adopted, explicitly or otherwise, the stance that might makes right. Given this history, a political practice that refuses to claim that it rests on apolitical, definitively true grounds or denies that might suffices to make right and admits instead its own finitude is already ameliorative. At the very least, it eschews tyrannizing or demonizing its opponents. Instead, it faces up to the predicaments of action and their consequences. It recognizes that they are ineliminable not only from their opponents' actions but also from their own.

The historical record does more, however, than supply us with negative evidence. It also gives us positive evidence of cases of political amelioration. These are cases of action that have proven to have been particularly well suited to their circumstances. Consider, for example, Abraham Lincoln's overall handling of the American

Civil War, Winston Churchill's leadership of Great Britain during World War II, and Willy Brandt's *Ostpolitik*. Even though one can raise reasonable objections about parts of these three examples, on balance one has good reason for admiring them. They provide warrant for saying that even though the historical record shows us no eternal truths, it does show us errors to avoid.[47] It also provides us, perhaps more hesitantly, with examples of political amelioration that encourage us to believe that we too can make improvements in our political life.

In today's world, however, those who would aspire to ameliorate political life in a democratic way have to face up to the widespread ignorance and thoughtlessness about many major political or politically relevant matters. Given the complexity and depth of the threats to the survival of the human species, a responsible politics must actively work against the adoption of policies or projects born out of incompetence. It can no longer assume that citizens have either the technical or the political competence to contribute to genuine political amelioration.

The historical record, though, gives one good grounds to be wary of tests for competence as conditions for admission to political participation. It prompts one to ask: Can a political society that refuses to presume that all of its normal adult members possess the competencies needed for responsible participation in politics really be democratic? One who would practice responsible politics today thus must ask: Can I work effectively to preserve the conditions necessary for the human species to continue to exist and do so in a way that remains democratic in more than mere name? The conception of citizenship that I present in the following chapters gives one reason to think that not only can one do so but that one is also obligated to do so. But, of course, no political solution to this or any other issue can be either definitive or guaranteed to succeed.

In sum, then, the domain of politics is relatively autonomous vis-à-vis the domains of economics and ethics. It is the domain of human action that holds as equiprimordial its twin objectives of human survival and flourishing. Everything belonging to this domain is inescapably historical, ambiguous and ambivalent, and dialectical. This conception of the domain of politics thus meshes neatly with my interpretation of human existence as fundamentally an interrogative project. It fully acknowledges the two orders of causality, the bodily and the thoughtly, that are operative in all human activity. It shows how both of them are in play in politics. And, because politics is not totally dissociable from either economics or ethics, this conception implies that, in the end, the concerns of economics cannot be exclusively for the bodily nor those of ethics exclusively for the thoughtly.

The sort of actual politics that best displays the features of such a domain now and for the foreseeable future is one that is democratic. It is one that gives all of its members an opportunity to exercise ruling as well as to submit to being ruled. In principle, a politics that is consistently democratic holds both (a) that to be human is enough to give one some claim to inclusion in some democratic political society and (b) that to be a normal adult is enough to give one some title to participate in the ruling functions of the democratic political society of which he or she is a member. Given the complexity of today's political issues, however, the title to participate in ruling can reasonably be no more than a title to the opportunity to gain the competencies needed to participate thoughtfully.

As I noted earlier, there are a number of plausible forms of democratic politics.[48] It is not part of my project to try to find the most plausible of them, for it is likely that because of the historicality, ambiguity and ambivalence, and dialecticality of politics, there is no single best form. Democracy is the name for a class of political forms that hold themselves open to contestation rather than a label for a fixed form of political organization.

There is, however, at least one trait that characterizes any politics worthy of being called democratic. Every democracy accepts a distinctive sense of power. For power to be democratic power, Claude Lefort points out, it must belong to no one and designate an empty place.

> To say that in a democracy power belongs to no one is to say that those who exercise power do not possess it; that they do not, indeed, embody it, that the exercise of power requires a periodic and repeated contest; that the authority of those vested with power is created and recreated as a result of the manifestation of the will of the people.[49]

To say, further, that power designates an empty place is to say that there is no unitary source whence the holders of power derive it. It does not come from God or nature or some putative unitary general will or will of the people. Power in a democracy involves the society's institutionalization of division, of conflict, as, for example, in campaigns for office and in voting. These activities always show division. Power, Lefort says, cannot be divorced from

> the work of division by which society is instituted; a society can therefore relate to itself only through the experience of internal division which

proves to be not a *de facto* division, but a division which generates its constitution.[50]

By institutionalizing division and renouncing all claims to a fixed identity, a democratic society eschews tyranny and totalitarianism. Democracy's power comes from no incontestable truth or law. It is sustained in and by the divisions that a society inscribes in itself in the course of "a debate which is necessarily without any guarantor and without any end."[51]

The repudiation of closure that characterizes the relationships among members of a democratic society likewise characterizes that society's relationships to other societies and their members, whether these other societies are democratic or not. A democratic society is always porous. It never seeks to isolate itself from foreign societies or insulate itself from foreign influences. This porosity makes democratic societies particularly well fit to function in a basically benign way in today's internationalized world. They are the societies that today are best equipped to give expression to the most fundamental but irreducibly complex of human desires, namely, "the desire to live well with and for others in just institutions."[52]

The porosity of democratic societies, however, makes them particularly fragile. They and their institutions are particularly vulnerable to corruption through either malice or thoughtlessness. More than ever before, they must make demands on their citizens if they are to survive, much less flourish. In the next two chapters I spell out the characteristics that one must possess today to be a good citizen in a democracy.

Because of the historical character of everything political, the conception of citizenship that I propose must take heed of its historical antecedents. In the next chapter I will therefore reflect on the features of democratic citizenship that have come to prominence during the past two and a quarter centuries. This reflection will help to ensure that the conception of citizenship that I propose is neither purely imaginary nor fundamentally nondemocratic. Then, in chapter 6, I propose transformations of the traditional conception of citizenship that will preserve its democratic character while still fitting it to meet the distinctive exigencies of our era. The conception that I arrive at respects not only the fundamentally interrogatory character of human existence. It also respects the present demands of internationalization and the conditions that give the Jonas imperative its pertinence.

Because my conception of citizenship is responsive both to the threats to the survival of humanity and to the aspirations of as widely shared freedom and well-being as is achievable, it belongs to the core of an appropriate conception of justice.

Chapter 5

Citizenship: Perennial Features

Every political society has the task of constantly concerning itself with its own perpetuation. It has to fend off enemies that would destroy it, and it has to ensure that there are replacements for its deceased members. The institution of citizenship has been developed in the West to fulfill this task.

Unsurprisingly, the conception of citizenship has evolved over time in response to changes in the material and cultural context in which political life takes place. Since the ancient Greeks, each successive age has found reason to rethink this conception. Our age is no different. Indeed, as Derek Heater has observed:

> Our own century presents us with a fascinating paradox. Never before has the idea of citizenship been so widely accepted and the need of education for status and function so widely appreciated. And yet, at the same time we may observe a greater diversity of interpretations than ever before of precisely what the role of citizens should entail.[1]

My proposal for how one should construe citizenship today makes no claim to have discovered the Platonic essence of a single true citizenship. Citizenship is a human artifact, always bound up with specific spatiotemporal conditions. My aim here is to present a normative conception of citizenship appropriate for our times.

The accounts of what it is to be human and of the constitutive characteristics of the domain of politics mark off the field within which any defensible interpretation of citizenship must fall. To interpret it in a way that is inconsistent with these accounts is to endorse normative standards that we have no good reason to believe that most, if any, people can meet. These accounts do not, however, entail just one and

93

only one conception of citizenship. To adjudicate between competing conceptions of citizenship that remain within the boundaries of this field, one must appeal to evidence drawn from the relevant historical circumstances. Ultimately, then, as I have mentioned above, the argument for any particular conception of citizenship is an exercise in what Aristotle would call deliberative rhetoric. My claim is that the interpretation of citizenship that I endorse, on the one hand, fully respects what human beings are and what politics is. On the other hand, it responds to the exigencies of political life today better than any available alternative. In brief, it respects both the relative autonomy of the domain of politics vis-à-vis the domains of economics and ethics. And it appreciates that politics is thoroughly historical, pervasively ambiguous and ambivalent, and fundamentally dialectical.

I develop my interpretation of citizenship in two parts. In this chapter, I reconsider the principal perennial features of democratic citizenship. For the most part, these features concern the proper relationship of the individual citizen to his or her fellow citizens on the one hand and to the institutions of the state on the other.

Even in this era of internationalism, as I have argued above, the particular state retains a political importance of the first order. People must still look to their state for military security and for the protection of their persons and property. People still, for the most part, work out basic elements of their political identity in conjunction with those who are fellow members of their state. They also find much of their political efficacy through interacting with their fellow citizens. By and large, it is the particular state that is the primary object of the individual's political loyalty. The state, rather than international political entities, remains that which people are prepared to die for.[2] The perennial features of democratic state citizenship thus continue to have great value and importance. A conception of citizenship that would either disregard or denigrate them would be foolishly ahistorical.

Neither the precise meaning nor the importance of these perennial features is, however, a settled matter. The no less perennial opposition of cosmopolitans to state citizenship regularly has had its roots in some objectionable conception of one or more of these features. To defend successfully my claim that state citizenship retains positive normative importance in our era, I must show that there are versions of these features whose normative implications are defensible. I do so in this chapter.

In the next chapter, I propose a way to construe these features so that the conception of citizenship and its normative requirements come to fit the two distinctive constituents of our era, namely, the internationalization of our lives and the threats to the human habitability of the earth. These two constituents give new urgency to two long-standing general questions about state citizenship. First, what does citizenship today call for from those who hold it concerning those who are not fellow citizens? Second, what does citizenship call for from its holders concerning international relations between their state and other states and the world community?

Taken together, these two chapters present a comprehensive conception of state citizenship that is appropriate for the present and the foreseeable future. This conception provides solid reasons for claiming that in our era the exercise of state citizenship is an integral part of the practice of justice. It is integral to the distribution and redistribution, either directly or through institutions, of the benefits and burdens of political life both within particular states and internationally.

I begin my reconsideration of the perennial features of citizenship by recalling that the history of the institution of citizenship shows that it has a two-fold purpose. On the one hand, the institution of citizenship has been designed to provide a political society with a self-replenishing supply of supporters, of people who pay taxes and take part in its defense against enemies. This institution thus promotes the stability and perpetuation of the society. On the other hand, the institution of citizenship gives a society's individual members a share in its political life. They receive, through rights, privileges, and immunities, both assurance that they and their property will be protected and a voice in their society's governance. The history of the development of democracy has given particular emphasis to this latter purpose. In this development, it has come to stress that individuals should have some entitlements not just because they happen to be members of a state that declares them but, more basically, because they are human beings. Although a society may, in order to respond to some particular circumstances, emphasize one of these two objectives of the institution of citizenship more than the other, in principle they are of equal weight. It is a fundamental task for any democracy to keep them in a balance appropriate to the times.

The dual purpose of the institution of citizenship gives rise to two basic questions that a normative conception of citizenship must address. Roughly, they are: To whom should a society's laws ascribe citizenship? And what obligations do citizens have to their political societies? Both of these questions pertain to justice. How one answers one of them has important consequences for how one should answer the other. They both bear on the difficult but crucial question of political identity and its perpetuation.

Historically, most people receive the ascriptions of citizenship that they hold through some circumstance of their birth. Some states recognize a blood right, a jus sanguinis, and ascribe citizenship to all the children of those who are already their citizens. Others recognize a right of the land, a jus soli, and ascribe citizenship to all those born with the appropriate link to the state's territory. Some states use both bases, with some restrictions, for ascribing citizenship. The differences in the ascriptive practices of states can make for awkward, sometimes painful, legal problems for some people. Thus far, these problems do not seem to be widespread, but should they become so, they will require prompt and equitable resolution.

More pertinent to this study is the fact that, besides "native born" citizens, most if not all democratic states provide legal procedures by which some people who have no birthright to citizenship in them can become naturalized citizens. Probably the most pressing question of justice pertaining to the ascription of citizenship today is that of the proper legal requirements for naturalization. Even if one rejects unmitigated cosmopolitanism, one would be hard pressed, especially in our era, to deny that at least some states have an obligation not merely to allow some immigrants to reside in them but also to provide opportunities for at least some of these immigrants to acquire citizenship in them. I deal with the issue of the naturalization of citizens in greater detail in the course of the next chapters, particularly in chapter 8.

The second basic question about citizenship concerns the obligations that citizens have to their respective political societies. It is generally agreed that normal adult citizens, at a minimum, are obligated to observe the laws that forbid crimes involving force or fraud, to pay the prescribed taxes, and to serve in time of need in their state's defense. People can, of course, free themselves from at least these two latter obligations by renouncing their citizenship. States should permit those who want to renounce their citizenship to do so, for an unrenounceable citizenship is a sentence, not a title. But states can reasonably specify the conditions that one must observe to make his or her renunciation effective.

According to some versions of the liberal tradition, to be a good citizen one need only keep the state's laws. In this view, citizenship is first and foremost a status that the state gives to individuals for their well-being. It amounts to an acknowledgment on the part of the state's authorities that they have a duty to protect the citizens' persons and property and not to interfere unnecessarily in their pursuit of their respective individual interests. Except for paying taxes, observing prohibitions against major crimes, and serving in their state's defense when needed, the citizen has no corresponding "active" obligations. Citizens may rightly, if they so choose, remain politically passive. Indeed, as Michael Walzer points out, "there are professional students of politics quick to tell them, what the early modern theorists also believed, that the security of the state is improved by their passivity."[3]

For example, in speaking about democracy in the United States, Thomas Dye and Harmon Ziegler argue:

> Democracy is government by the people, but the responsibility for the survival of democracy rests on the shoulders of elites. . . . [I]f the survival of the American system depended upon an active, informed and enlightened citizenry, then democracy in America would have disappeared long ago; for the masses of Americans are apathetic and ill-informed about politics and public policy, and they have a surprisingly weak commitment to democratic values. . . . [B]ut fortunately for these values and for American democracy, the American masses do not lead, they follow.[4]

But, as Walzer also sees, this minimalist view of the obligations attached to citizenship is inadequate. The institution of citizenship exists not merely to provide benefits to its individual holders. It has as no less important an objective the preservation and well-being of the political society of which it is a part. To achieve this objective, the state must ask more of its citizens than mere passive obedience. It must also ask them to concern themselves with maintaining the conditions that make its ascriptions of citizenship worthwhile. Of course, when it asks this of its citizens, then it has a duty to provide the institutional support that would enable them to participate actively and responsibly in its political life.

Justice, then, calls for citizens not merely to receive benefits but also to shoulder responsibility for their state's well-being. They must pay attention to the principal issues and problems that their society confronts. And they must engage somehow in the processes by which a society determines its response, by which it adopts and implements its policies and laws. To do so effectively will unavoidably cost citizens time and energy.

Obviously, though, the number and complexity of the large issues with which any but the smallest modern democratic state must deal and the size of the populations of these states make it difficult for the individual citizen to play a nontrivial role in his or her society's political life. If one considers only *direct* effective participation, one can expect to find opportunities for only a few citizens to be genuinely active.[5]

The bonds between the state and its individual citizens are not all direct, however. Some important bonds are mediated through the several groups that its citizens are members of. As Walzer has noted, "the citizen stands to the state not only as an individual, but also as the member of a variety of other organizations with which the state must relate in relating to him."[6] In participating in organizations of civil society such as cooperatives, professional organizations, environmental groups, neighborhood and charitable associations, and support groups, people can learn and exercise the civility, self-restraint, and sense of mutual obligation that are crucial to genuine democratic politics.[7] It is thus often, even usually, the case that a "citizen governs himself most actively in groups other than the state, groups that sometimes play an informal, sometimes an official, role in determining state policy."[8]

It is true that not every voluntary organization is an effective or appropriate mediator of the bonds between the individual citizen and the state,[9] but some of them are well constituted to play such a role. The state's authorities can rightly recognize this capacity and encourage its utilization. Leaders of such organizations should also recognize this capacity and encourage their members to exercise it. No voluntary organization, unless it is deliberately designed to be apolitical or to undercut fundamental democratic principles, is in principle an inappropriate mediator.

Citizens who are active in such groups have what can be called a pluralist citizenship. Through these groups they can make genuine positive contributions to the society's political life and thus come to a patriotism that is responsible, effective, and critical. For these citizens, the state is the most inclusive but not the sole group to which they belong. They have citizen responsibilities to all of these groups, "for there is no way to be a responsible citizen except to have more than one responsibility."[10] Thus, though it is not easy to be an active, effective citizen, it is by no means beyond the reach of many, if not most mentally normal adults. To be sure, it is a practical impossibility for most citizens to be responsibly active and effective in dealing with every important political issue, but citizens can deal with some of them.

No democratic state, therefore, can rightly neglect calling for its citizens to contribute actively to its activity or neglect providing institutional resources that enable them to do so responsibly. Issuing this call and providing these resources are distinguishing features of genuine democracies. If citizens are to be good citizens, they have an obligation to respond to their opportunities in some reasonable fashion. Only by so doing can they do their part to preserve democracy for others as well as for themselves.[11] To borrow an image from Hannah Arendt, every normal adult citizen has an obligation to contribute to the preservation and enhancement of the world, that is, of his or her society's democratic political life.[12]

Working within the liberal tradition, William Galston has developed a rich and subtle position concerning the importance of civic virtues for the well-being of any political society, particularly for liberal democratic ones. In the course of doing so, he takes heed of some standard communitarian criticisms of liberalism. The position that he arrives at is sufficiently close to the one I hold that it is worth considering here in some detail. By doing so I can clarify some of the distinguishing features of the conception I propose.

Galston recognizes that for any political society to survive, most, if not all, of its members must possess at least three virtues. First, they must have the courage to defend and, if necessary, be willing to die for their society. Second, they must be law abiding, that is, they must adopt a strong presumption that both they and their fellow members ought to obey the society's laws. Third, the members must have an active belief in the society's core principles.[13]

A liberal democratic society, Galston says, requires much more of its citizens than these three virtues if it is to be sustained. A democratic society is one that has

> a high degree of the following features: popular-constitutional government; a diverse society with a wide range of individual opportunities and choices; a predominantly market economy; and a substantial, strongly protected sphere of privacy and individual rights.[14]

It is a society characterized by individualism on the one hand and diversity on the other.

To sustain such a society, most, if not all, of its citizens must possess a distinctive set of traits or virtues. For, Galston argues, the operation of liberal institutions is affected in important ways by the character of citizens (and leaders), and . . . at some point, the attenuation of individual virtue will create pathologies with which liberal political contrivances, however technically perfect their design, simply cannot cope. To an extent difficult to measure but impossible to ignore, the viability of liberal society depends on its ability to engender a virtuous citizenry.[15]

Galston has proposed two sets of virtues that he regards as fundamental for citizens of a liberal democracy. First, in *Justice and the Common Good* he identified five traits that people should have to function well as citizens. None of them, he admitted, was wholly noncontroversial. First, citizens ought to be able to act independently and assume responsibility for their deeds. Second, citizens must be able to articulate their interests and to assess the effects of present or proposed public policies on them. Third, citizens ought to recognize the interests and claims of others and take them into account. Fourth, citizens ought to have a basic understanding of their society's language, beliefs, history, and institutions. Fifth, citizens owe loyalty to their society.[16] This loyalty, Galston says, has a two-fold object. Its object

consists in individuals, the fellow members of our community, and in the underlying ordering of individuals that determines our collective purposes and deliberative practices. We are asked to be loyal, then, to both the form and matter of our collective existence.[17]

More recently, in *Liberal Purposes*, Galston has presented a longer and more complex list of citizen virtues, one that implicitly includes some, but not clearly all, of the items on his earlier list. It is not necessary, Galston says, for the viability of a liberal democracy that all of its citizens possess these traits or virtues, but most of them must do so.

In addition to the general virtues of courage, law-abidingness, and active belief in their society's core principles that every political society must ask of its members, a liberal society needs at least most of its citizens to possess a distinctive set of liberal virtues. Galston distinguishes several sorts of liberal virtues. There are (a) virtues of the liberal society, (b) virtues of the liberal economy, and (c) virtues of liberal politics.

There are two principal virtues of liberal society. They correspond to the society's two key features, namely, individualism and diversity.

Thus, there is the virtue of independence. This is the disposition to take care of and accept responsibility for oneself, avoiding needless dependence on others. The second virtue of liberal society, corresponding to diversity, is the virtue of tolerance. Liberal tolerance need not be relativistic or radically skeptical. It is compatible with the claim that some way or ways of life can be known to be better than others, but it does call for one to hold that "the pursuit of the better course should be (and in many cases has to be) a consequence of education or persuasion rather than of coercion."[18]

The virtues of the liberal economy, Galston says, are of two different sorts. There are those that are proper to different economic roles and those required by liberal economic life as a whole. The virtues connected to economic roles are basically those that are appropriate to entrepreneurs on the one hand and organization employees on the other. The former include such qualities as initiative, imagination, determination, and willingness to take economic risks. The latter include such qualities as punctuality, reliability, and a capacity and willingness to perform assigned tasks within the frameworks that are established. Obviously, a society needs a variety of people with different combinations of these two sorts of role-specific qualities.

Besides these qualities, modern market economies call for three generic traits. First, these economies require a populace whose members have acquired a work ethic that includes both a determination to do their jobs well and the acceptance of the obligation to support themselves economically by their work. Second, they require a populace whose members observe a mean between self-denial and self-indulgence. These economies do rely on a multiplication and spread of consumer desires, but they also need investments and savings. Finally, modern market economies increasingly demand adaptability of those who live in them. This adaptability is "the disposition to accept new tasks as challenges rather than threats and the ability to avoid defining personal identity and worth in reference to specific, fixed occupations."[19]

In addition to societal and economic virtues, Galston identifies a set of virtues that are specifically political. Some of these are virtues proper to ordinary citizens, some to leaders and office holders, and some are common to both groups.

First, liberal citizens, Galston says, have no duty to participate actively in politics or systematically to subordinate their personal interests to the society's common good; neither are they called upon to commit themselves to accepting a collective determination of personal choices. But they must have the capacity to assess the qualifications of candidates for public office and the performance of those who have attained office. Second, they must possess both the disposition to keep their political and economic demands moderate and the self-discipline to accept necessary painful policies, laws, and regulations. Third, liberal citizens must acquire the capacity to discern and cultivate the will to respect the rights of others.[20]

Liberal political leaders ought to have several political virtues over and above those expected of them as citizens. They should have patience. Political patience is the ability and willingness to accept and work within the constraints imposed on their action by constitutional requirements on the one hand and the diversity of their society on the other. Political leaders also ought to have the ability and skill needed to forge a sense of common purpose acceptable to a diverse populace. Third, these leaders must persistently resist the temptation to seek popular support by pandering to immoderate public demands and acting as though all hard choices are avoidable. Finally, they should have the skill and will to persuade the citizenry to adopt sound views about what is politically feasible and worthy of their endorsement.[21]

Both ordinary citizens and leaders in a liberal polity ought also to have two general political virtues. The first is that they must acquire the capacity to engage in public discourse. This virtue demands a willingness to listen to others, even if they hold strange positions, as well as a willingness to present one's own view clearly and candidly. It serves as a basis for a politics of persuasion rather than one of coercion or manipulation. The second general virtue that ordinary citizens and leaders alike ought to cultivate in themselves and expect of one another is a commitment to admit and confront the flaws and inequities in their society and to work to overcome them. This virtue, like the other general political virtue, in effect requires both a disposition on the part of citizens to question authorities and hold them accountable and a disposition on the part of leaders to respond to this questioning and to give an accounting of their exercise of office.[22]

This complex set of virtues, Galston argues, is the set that is most conducive to the establishment and maintenance of a liberal social order. This order, in turn, is justified because, more than any alternative order, it contains the following elements:

1. social peace
2. the rule of law
3. a tendency toward inclusiveness

4. the decency to reduce the incidence of both desperate poverty and brutality as a tool for social control
5. a compatibility with economies that provide widespread affluence
6. institutions that provide extensive opportunities for the development of the individual's abilities and talents
7. a tendency to distribute benefits and burdens in a just manner, a manner that takes into account its individual members' claims springing from their needs, deserts, and choices
8. an openness to criticism and the truth-seeking that criticism implies
9. a respect for individual privacy that acknowledges the importance and legitimacy of spheres of human activity that are distinct, even if not wholly separable, from the political sphere.[23]

Galston rightly recognizes that his conception of liberalism and the sort of citizenship required to establish and maintain it do not provide detailed, conclusive answers to all political issues. He recognizes that his account of what human well-being consists of is relatively thin, is in large measure the outcome of reflection on "common bads," and leaves a number of questions open.[24] He correctly points out that

> the premise "B has a right to do X" does not warrant the conclusion "It would be right for B to do X." Between rights and rightness lies a vast terrain where moral argumentation and (in some cases) forms of public persuasion have a legitimate role.[25]

Galston further displays a sensitivity to the finitude and historicality that characterize liberalism no less than any other sort of politics. He acknowledges that even if a liberal political order minimizes moral coercion, it is nonetheless not neutral and neither does nor can wholly eliminate using "moral" coercion against its opponents and enemies.[26] He admits that liberalism is "a basket of ideals that inevitably come into conflict with one another if a serious effort is made to realize any one of them fully, let alone all of them simultaneously."[27] He recognizes that the task of determining the appropriate relations between the public and the private domains is "an endless task of imperfect adjustment."[28] And he agrees with Walzer that any concrete effort to specify just what equal access to political goods and the means to achieve them requires will inevitably reflect the local historical particularity of the society for which the specification is proposed.[29] In the end, however, for all of its many merits, the account that Galston gives of liberalism and the virtues that liberalism calls for in its citizens is insufficient for democratic practice today. In some respects, it claims too much; in others, too little.

The critique of Galston's position that I offer here is by no means comprehensive. It concentrates on three related parts of the account of citizenship virtues that he presents in *Liberal Purposes*. They are the parts that are particularly relevant to the conception of citizenship that I want to articulate. Galston's account, I contend, leaves the set of virtues he picks out underdetermined and is therefore vague. His account is inordinately dependent on political practice in the United States and thus lacks relevance to other democracies. And most fundamentally, his account is in several respects ahistorical and as a consequence it tends to claim more for the position he holds than is consistent with the contingency of everything political.

Consider at least three ways in which Galston's account is underdetermined. First, Galston gives insufficient weight to the distinction between needs and desires. His remarks about the tension among need, desert, and choice underemphasize the importance and difficulty particularly of the task of distinguishing between social needs and mere wants.[30] In actual practice this distinction gets drawn and implemented, well or badly, in the course of the complex interactions among a society's members. Their views find expression in what we call public opinion, in the use of their financial assets, and in lobbying, as well as in the formal political activities of voting and enacting and enforcing legislation. Being involved somehow in processes such as these is close to unavoidable. It is crucial, therefore for citizens to draw sensible distinctions between genuine needs and mere wants. Otherwise, they will tend all too often to subordinate their society's well-being to their own private interests.

Second, though Galston calls on the citizen to be self-disciplined and to restrain impulses to unmitigated self-aggrandizement, his claim that there is no duty either to participate actively in politics or to accept a societal determination of personal choices would leave the determination of what counts as restraint and self-discipline simply to the individual's private lights. I grant that a democratic society should seek to involve each individual member in the determination of the restraints it is to require. At the end of the day, though, the collective judgment it reaches must prevail, even though it is open to perpetual contestation and revision.

Third, and perhaps most important, Galston leaves his account underdetermined by failing to provide a ranking between the political and the economic virtues he identifies. This is a matter of no small importance for political practice. There is today a widespread tendency in both domestic and international activity to reduce or subordinate political values to economic ones. Democratic states are at least as prone to yield to this tendency as any other states.[31] It is clear that Galston would not countenance the unqualified subordination of political goods to economic ones, but in his account of citizen virtue he provides no systematic way for insisting on politics' relative autonomy vis-à-vis economics. For the reasons that I gave in chapter 4, this insistence is essential to politics. Part of the exercise of good citizenship is resisting tendencies to attenuate politics' autonomy.

The second basic weakness of Galston's position is its inordinate dependence on political life in the United States. This dependence substantially weakens the relevance of his position to other democracies. It also unwarrantly limits the sources for critical reflection on the United States' practice itself. Consider, for example, political practice in such democratic states as Germany, Finland, and Norway. Each of their constitutions differs in important respects. Finland and Norway each has an established church, and each of them makes special mention of the rights of one particular minority group of its citizens: the Sami in Norway, and the ethnic Swedes in Finland. The constitution of Germany displays, at least in part, a different approach to the issue of the relationship between constitutional provisions and legislation from that to be found in the United States' Constitution. In the latter, constitutional provisions basically serve as a test for the validity of legislation that deals with any subject matter that the constitution treats. In Germany, the constitution in several cases declares a right in general terms but explicitly leaves it to the legislature both to give the right further specification and to determine the appropriate conditions for its exercise.

Each of these documents obviously reflects the historical conditions that shaped the questions it is designed to answer. Galston holds that liberal societies "tend to be organized around abstract principles rather than shared ethnicity, nationality, or history."[32] But these abstract principles have their own history. They were forged out of reflection on some set of historical circumstances and there is a historical record of their implementation. The existence of democratic alternatives to Galston's liberalism and the virtues that support it give one reason to emphasize the contingent, political nature of every democratic regime, including the liberal regime of the United States. Like every political regime, this liberal regime can never be perfect or definitive. It is appropriate to assess its adequacy to the era at hand by considering not only the logical implications of the constitutional documents and the tradition of interpretation to which they have given rise. It is also worth drawing upon alternative democratic practices to do so. Each actual set of the practices provides food for reflection on the others. Mary Ann Glendon has indicated the importance of such wide-ranging reflection in legal matters.[33] I would hold that this is true of all political issues. Even if most citizens are unequipped themselves to introduce these alternatives, they ought to grant the appropriateness of doing so and give those who do so a hearing.

Both of the first two parts of my criticism of Galston's position turn out to be dimensions of the third, more fundamental criticism. At bottom, Galston's liberalism, with the virtues it calls for, is insufficiently historical. I grant that Galston does show some recognition of the historical character of everything political, but he fails to grasp all of its important implications.

Galston tends to treat the development of liberalism as a basically unidirectional progressive movement. He argues that, though liberal principles cannot be neutral, they allow traditional ways of life organized around other principles to survive and even flourish. When there is inevitable conflict with marginal groups, liberal societies can manage it "in a spirit of maximum feasible accommodation."[34] He cites in support of these claims the capacity of Orthodox and Hasidic Jewish groups to flourish in the United States and the exemption from some educational requirements that the United States Supreme Court has given some Amish children.

Galston then proposes a telling simile to describe the relationship between the liberal society and the traditional groups, religious and otherwise, that have basic principles that clash with liberalism's. He suggests:

> Think of a society based on liberal public principles as a rapidly flowing river. A few vessels may be strong enough to head upstream. Most, however, will be carried along by the current. But they can still choose where in the river to sail, and where along the shore to moor. The mistake is to think of the liberal polity either as a placid lake or as an irresistible undertow.[35]

The objection I have to the view that this simile expresses is not that, as Galston points out, the life of the marginal group will be pervasively modified by its determination to run counter to the liberal flow. It is, rather, that this view leaves the liberal, going with the flow, to take his or her liberalism as in need of no further questioning. Galston's liberal is too little pushed to reconsider whether liberalism, particularly in its present instantiation in the United States, is not too tolerant of a wasteful, self-indulgent consumerism, a political practice that countenances single-issue candidates and their supporters, and campaigns nearly wholly devoid of substantive debate. There are several religious traditions that provide bases for strong criticisms of such practices and, by implication, of the institutions that permit them. It is not evident that a liberalism that disregards these traditions has the strength to preserve a society that remains genuinely democratic.

The historicality of politics finds far better acknowledgment in Claude Lefort's conception of democracy as consisting fundamentally in the right of every member of the society to engage in a debate about political rights and duties. In this view, there are no settled positions, whether they are constitutionally inscribed or not. At bottom, everything about democratic politics is experimental and provisional. It is not, therefore, chaotic. History does show us such "common bads" as slavery, theocracy, and totalitarianism.[36] It also shows us the futility of attempts to achieve even small-scale utopias, but it yields no definitively beneficial practices or institutions. For all of its practitioners, then, democracy must remain a debate and a search for ways of living with one another that is necessarily without end.[37] It is part of good citizenship always to recognize the contingency, finitude, and historicality of all political thought and practice and to give them their due weight.

There is reason to suspect that the root of the flaws in Galston's account of liberalism and its virtues is his strong, near unquestioned, commitment individualism and diversity. He shows little recognition that the kinds and amount of diversity that a political society can accommodate are a perennial issue of great importance. And it is not evident that a thoroughgoing individualism, when put into practice, will yield a self-disciplined populace that is prepared to be moderate in its demands.

Whether because of his commitment to individualism and diversity or for some other reason, Galston's 1991 account of the virtues of the liberal citizen differs in one quite important respect from his 1980 account. His later account makes no explicit reference to the requirement that citizens ought to have a basic understanding of the society's language, history, and institutions. It refers only to an active belief in the society's "core principles." This change, wittingly or not, reduces the emphasis on political identity and subtly but importantly changes the object of loyalty. Such a change is a loss rather than a gain.

Consider first the matter of political identity, about which Galston has little to say in *Liberal Purposes*. All political identities, as cosmopolitans remind us, are troublesome. One comes to have a political identity by accepting as normatively binding a set of claims and practices that others, his or her predecessors, have devised. Among these claims are those that call for the division of humankind into an included "us" and an excluded "them." Every political identity, furthermore, is meant to be perpetuated through its inculcation in newcomers. The newcomers are primarily the children of its present holders but also, perhaps, some immigrants. Political identities thus seem to violate the autonomy that each person should exercise in determining both which associations he or she will enter and the terms for entering them. Political identities also seem to deny or at least to slight the common humanity that the "them" always share with the "us."

Nonetheless, for at least a large number of people, having a political identity is a sine qua non, or practically so, for enjoying a full human life. Being stateless is hardly a happy condition. Replacing political identities with a full-blown cosmopolitanism is not, for the foreseeable future, feasible. And apart from its feasibility, there are good reasons, as I mentioned in chapter 2, to deny even its desirability. The task is thus not to denounce all political identities. It is to determine ways of distinguishing responsible political identities, those that make only sensible demands on the society's members, from irresponsible ones.

Every political society, if it is to endure, must require its members to identify with its constitutive institutions and practices, even if doing so is costly to their individual preferences and aspirations. A society conveys this identity largely through a set of stories, stories of triumph over hardship or danger and stories of heroic dedication to the society's ideals or of betrayals of them. The objective of these stories is to shape how its members understand crucial parts of their lives. It is also to justify the society's political institutions and its ways of distributing political authority.

Unlike most stories, the ensemble of stories that convey a political identity do not tell of a definitive ending. They rather present a history that its recipients are to take up, continue, and add to. They exemplify United States Senator Eugene McCarthy's widely known remark that all politics is "second act."

The stories of political identity, however, as all stories inevitably are, are partial. They all exclude some relevant items, and they distribute emphasis among the items that they do include. There are thus always different plausible stories that one can tell about the same subject matter. Just as their subject matter includes contestations of various sorts, so too are the actual stories of political identity always open to contestation.

There are two other features of the stories of political identity that deserve explicit mention here. First, these stories embody claims to the exclusive right to some territory regarded as a homeland. Second, they embody the claim that their society has a uniquely strong title to continue in existence in perpetuity. Though the stories do not expressly deny that other societies also have territorial rights and claims to perpetuity, neither do they assert it.

Because these stories are inevitably partial, they always claim more than they can provide conclusive evidence for. No actual political society can provide incontestable evidence in favor of its political institutions and ways of distributing political authority. It cannot establish an impeccably "clear title" to its lands.[38] Nor can it give unimpeachable evidence that it has a uniquely strong title to be perpetuated. Hence these stories and the political identity they promote are always in some significant way ideological.

Though ideology is always dangerous because it claims more than it can prove, it is nonetheless indispensable for integrating people into a cooperative society. This is particularly true of societies in which unreflective moral and religious ways of patterning life have given way to the reflective distinction of different domains, each of which has its own distinctive norms and objectives. The political domain is, of course, one of these reflective domains. In such a society, Clifford Geertz argues, politics as we know it comes into being through the imaginative construction of a schematic ordering of its members, that is, through the construction of an ideology. In his words:

> The function of ideology is to make an autonomous politics possible by providing the authoritative concepts that render it meaningful, the suasive images by means of which it can be sensibly grasped. . . . It is when neither a society's most general cultural orientations nor its most down-to-earth, "pragmatic" ones suffice any longer to provide an adequate image of political process that ideologies begin to become crucial as sources of sociopolitical meanings and attitudes.[39]

Because political identities and the stories in which they are propagated are human constructs, they are always open to revision. No particular revision can eradicate their ideological character, hence it cannot remove their dangerousness. There is, nonetheless, a way to distinguish between responsible and irresponsible political identities. As far as I can tell, there is no set of principles whose application can be guaranteed in advance to yield a responsible political identity, but there is a set of questions that one should ask about a particular identity to determine its acceptability. Part of being a good citizen is to ask these questions about the identity his or her society is promoting.

To pass muster as a responsible political identity, one that respects those asked to embrace it, an identity and its constitutive stories should satisfy at least the following two related conditions. (a) Holders of the identity must admit that it is always both in need of improvement and in danger of being abusive. What the Lutheran dictum said of the church holds for the political society. It is always in need of reform. (b) Holders of a political identity must admit both (1) that there can be a multitude of responsible political societies each with its own distinctive political identity and (2) that there is no principle according to which these societies can be unequivocally ranked. There is no unequivocal paradigm case of a political society. Only a political identity that meets these two conditions encourages its holders (a) to acknowledge the historicality, finitude, and ambivalence of everything political, (b) to engage in critical reflection on their society's political practices, (c) to respect other states' politics, and (d) thereby to keep themselves ready to learn from the experiences of others.[40]

All political societies, particularly modern ones, are, of course, constantly undergoing changes; so are their respective political identities. Even if an identity passes the test that I propose at one moment, then, it remains subject to retesting because of changed circumstances. In practice, of course, no one can both have a genuine political identity and constantly put it in its entirety to the test, but there is no part of it that ever ceases to deserve testing. To accept a political identity is thus not necessarily to exempt any part of it from review nor to commit oneself irrevocably to any of its parts or moments. To commit oneself to a political identity is not to sell one's soul to it.

Let me briefly indicate some of the more important consequences of adopting the test of political identities that I propose. First, citizens of a society that passed this test would be led to admit the correctness of Arendt's claim that all action impinges on someone else. Whatever my society does has an impact on other societies, often in unanticipated ways. I therefore cannot claim that my society is ever wholly exempt from responsibility for having made the transgression. My society needs forgiveness. Conversely, I have to recognize that my own society cannot reasonably demand to be shielded from transgression from other societies. They cannot act without transgressing somehow. I and my society must stand ready to forgive a great number of transgressions. Never has this need for reciprocal forgiveness been more evident than it is now in the era of international commerce, communications, and travel.

A second major consequence of adopting my test of political identities is that citizens would have to admit that no society has an unqualified right to perdure. Though every society aims to endure in perpetuity, it may nonetheless become so dysfunctional that it can no longer sustain a politics that can make any reasonable claim to promoting human well-being. Citizens of such a society cannot rightfully work to perpetuate it regardless of the cost to themselves and others. For example, no citizens can defensibly adopt a position such as that which the Cold War slogan "better dead than red" encapsulated. They cannot rightfully say, "*Fiat civitas mea, pereat mundus*" ("Let my city remain, even though the world perish").

Finally, no citizen or group of citizens who adopt the test of political identity that I propose can rightfully claim to be the ultimate judges of the defensibility of their society and the identity it calls for its citizens to adopt. Each political society with its institutions and practices must face the judgment of others. These others include both its own members who will come to maturity in the future and foreigners. To paraphrase Merleau-Ponty, responsible citizens must work to ensure that the political identity to which they commit themselves today is one that later generations will judge to have been fitting for its times.[41]

Those who identify themselves with a political identity that meets my test will not give unqualified allegiance to their political society. They will always be open not only to its reformation but even to the possibility that it should cease to exist. Except in extreme circumstances, for example, devastation by protracted widespread war or persistent grave famine, these citizens are unlikely to entertain actively the radical dissolution of their society, but extreme circumstances are live possibilities. For example, a political society that can retain its identity only at the price of keeping its members woefully impoverished either economically or culturally should not continue to exist if it can merge with another viable society. Failed states, we must admit, are by no means impossible. Some present states, for example, Chad, may have already failed. Some secessionist movements, such as Welsh separatism, might well produce states destined to fail.

To admit that one's state may fail and thus lose its justification for existing does not preclude one from firmly committing himself or herself to it. But this commitment should be one that accepts the need to ask and give forgiveness for the transgressions that political societies inevitably inflict on one another. This commitment should not be made with blind faith. Rather, it should be made with a clear-headed hope that its results will prove to be on the whole good for one's fellow citizens and not bad for foreigners. Commitments to a state and to the political identity constitutive of it, made with forgiveness and hope, can be strong enough to lead citizens to die for them. But they do not warrant a fanaticism of any sort.

Reflection on the conditions for responsibly identifying oneself with one's political society is inseparable from reflection on political loyalty, for loyalty serves as a fundamental source for acting according to the political identity that one embraces. Loyalty, like its close kins patriotism and political identity, always divides humankind into two camps, a relatively small camp that is "us" and a much larger camp that is "not us." Political loyalty gives a special weight and priority to a set of ties to some particular past and assumes a set of obligations to work for a certain sort of future. One can acknowledge or repudiate these ties and obligations, but only infrequently, as, for example, in constitutional conventions, can one take part in establishing them.

Because loyalty so regularly consists in accepting bonds that one has not helped to forge, it has received strong philosophical criticism from the heirs of both Jeremy Bentham's utilitarianism and Kant's rational deontology. As these critics have seen, loyalty stands at best in tension, if not in downright conflict, with the principles of individualism, equality, and impartiality on which liberalism and many forms of democratic pluralism rest.[42]

Besides the philosophical considerations that raise doubts about the moral or political propriety of loyalty, there are all too many historical examples of loyalties that have led to disaster some or even all who have been touched by them, loyalties that are pernicious. There are loyalties that have arisen from a mental laziness that remains satisfied with received beliefs, relationships, and patterns of conduct without bothering to reflect on them. There are loyalties that have sprung from a jealous, self-interested, possessive attachment to institutions, persons, or places and that try to keep others from developing ties of their own to them. There are loyalties that have had their motivation in fear—a person may cling to the familiar sheerly out of fear of the strange or the unknown. There are loyalties that have been rooted in hypocrisy, cynically aiming to procure some personal gain or advantage. Then, of course, there have been blind loyalties. The blindly loyal are ripe for fanaticism. They are ready to sacrifice not only their possessions and themselves but even other people for a cause that they cherish as neither needing nor allowing for reflection or question. In effect, the fanatically loyal regard everything and everyone as a means to be used in the service of their cause.[43] For both philosophical and historical reasons, therefore, Alasdair MacIntyre rightly admits that loyalty and patriotism are constant sources of moral danger.[44] One can even see how Paul Gomberg has been led to claim that "patriotism is like racism."[45]

Despite its checkered history and the philosophical considerations that weigh against it, though, in the end there are no good reasons to believe that loyalty either can or should be eradicated from human relationships. We have no idea what a world in which there were no familial, religious, territorial, or ethnic loyalties would look like. Not only are loyalties not intrinsically perverse, there is good reason to hold that there is no genuine human well-being without loyalty.

What holds for loyalty in general holds for political loyalty as well. There is no evidence that without loyalty there could be any sustained and effective political action. A state without its citizens' loyalty, as a Hobbesion state would apparently be, is either unstable or prone to tyranny. It is not a state that is conducive to the well-being of its citizens. Loyalty, then, is something that a state must ask its citizens for if it is to perdure. But if the state is to be assuredly nontyrannical, and even more if it is to be democratic, it must also, through its institutions and the conduct of its authorities, work ceaselessly to earn their loyalty.

Under normal circumstances, citizens of democratic states are born and reared into multiple contexts of loyalty. There are loyalties to sets of values, religions or otherwise; there are loyalties based on ethnic, regional, and linguistic considerations, and there are political loyalties, distinct but not wholly separable from these other loyalties. Political loyalties need not all be loyalties to an established state. For example, one could be a loyal member of a pan-Islamist movement that does not accept state territorial lines as they are presently drawn. But if there are to be durable modern democratic states, then their institutions and their citizens must concern themselves with maintaining a common political loyalty. Such a loyalty provides the psychological underpinnings one needs to sustain a shared politics, particularly with fellow citizens who are in many other respects strangers to one another.

Times of widespread hardship tax this loyalty but also show its importance and not infrequently lead its holders to insist even more strongly on it.

Because we are bodily as well as thoughtly, the evidence that leads us both to give our own political loyalty and to recognize the others with whom we share it cannot be sheerly abstract. Similarly we cannot expect that those who share a different political loyalty will do so exclusively on the basis of abstract concepts and ideals. The sense and point of giving this sort of loyalty, a loyalty that may require sacrifice, even death, must have some basis in our daily experience of living with others. At least in its initial phases, loyalty thus arises among those who both are physically close to one another and are like one another. Family members and neighbors are the likely people among whom one would expect to find the first bonds of loyalty. Responsible politics will never condemn loyalty's first, bodily, upsurge. It needs this first experience of loyalty as a basis for promoting a thoughtly, specifically political loyalty that then unites people who are both strangers to one another and quite unlike one another.

Educators, Arendt points out, in teaching children, contribute to the preservation of their cultural world. They keep available to these newcomers the achievements of their predecessors.[46] Similarly, by their loyalty citizens contribute to the preservation of the political society. Their loyalty testifies to their conviction that it is a good society, one that deserves to endure because it has a record, its flaws notwithstanding, of promoting its members' well-being.

Considerations of this sort support Walzer's claim that politics presupposes a historical community whose members share a significant number of intuitions and sensibilities about important matters. Only rather rarely, for example, perhaps in Iceland, is there a one-to-one mapping of these communities into political societies. Political societies usually embrace more than one historical community. Conversely, many historical communities are spread into more than one political society. This fact presents political societies, particularly democratic ones, with a hard, urgent, and ongoing task. Through its practices, it has to forge the sort of bonds that hold promise of tying all of its members to it, regardless of the historical community to which they belong.[47]

A major task for a modern political society is thus to forge, promote, and defend its distinctive identity. To do so, it must overcome those deformations of loyalty that tend to pervert political loyalty by subsuming it under a religious or ethnic loyalty. The political society must call for its diverse members to acknowledge the common ties that they already share or that they can come to learn are worth cultivating. Nowhere is this call more urgent than in urbanized, pluralistic societies that receive immigrants.

On the other hand, the political society must defend its own distinctive way of life, its own identity, against those thoroughgoing cosmopolitans who would try to eliminate the efficacy of all historical community ties. The "thoughtly" ties, for example, the shared ideals, laws, and procedures, that responsible political practice promotes are not meant to break or set at naught all "bodily" ties. Rather, they are to complement them and, in doing so, change their weight and orientation.

From these considerations and from the test for defensible political identities that I proposed above, it is a short step to conclude that no political society can justifiably and responsibly promote loyalty to it by denigrating any historical community, whether presently represented in it or not. History shows the dreadful consequences of such denigration. Today, given the global interdependence of all peoples in commercial, environmental, and technological matters, the denigration of any historical community is politically irresponsible. It can only be destructive. In the final analysis a society shows itself to be worthy of loyalty from its citizens only insofar as the political identity that it promotes is consistent with respect for not only its own members but for other people and their reasonable aspirations as well. It must be a society that in its own distinctive way endorses and promotes in its members the desire to live well with and for others in and through political institutions that are just.[48] Conversely, it is the task of citizens to make and keep their political society one that observes this standard.

In modern societies, of course, the work of promoting a society that, through just institutions, promotes peace and well-being for its members is tremendously complex. It is a practical impossibility for the individual citizen to be knowledgeable about more than just a few of the important issues with which his or her society must cope. Even professional politicians and civil servants can be well informed about only a portion of these issues. All citizens nonetheless have a general responsibility to see that in their society there are appropriate conditions for dealing with all of them.

As I mentioned above, Walzer is right to point out the political importance of citizens' memberships in various voluntary associations. Through these associations—civic, religious, professional, and so on—

they can increase their civic competence and efficacy. It is their responsibility to see to it that when their associations promote some political project they do so in a responsible way.

Associations that are fit to play a constructive role in a society's political life all have at least two basic characteristics. These characteristics are analogous to those that any defensible political identity must possess. First, these associations must grant the legitimacy of other associations, even when they have competing political objectives. Second, these associations must admit the fallibility and reformability of their political objectives. They and their members must be prepared, should evidence warrant it, to modify or even abandon their political objectives in favor of some alternatives.

Associations that have these two legitimizing characteristics will eschew single-issue politics. Though an association may have a narrow purpose and hence address only a few political issues, it will not address them as though they were incontestably the most urgent and important ones. Nor will it pretend that any political issue is wholly isolable from all other ones. At the very least, most political issues have budgetary consequences that affect how other issues are dealt with. In short, whatever their internal organizations, these associations should interact democratically with other associations. The individual good citizen is one who belongs only to associations that do so.

I can now summarize my interpretation of the perennial characteristics of good citizenship. In general, I endorse the items that Galston places on his 1991 list. But I argue for a different conception of how these items are related to one another. First, though a democratic society must encourage the acquisition of the economic virtues, it can never rightly do so at the expense of the political virtues. Second, ordinary citizens are never wholly exempt from the responsibility to exercise some modicum of political leadership. They vote and they contribute to the formation of public opinion. A crucial part of public opinion is that which distinguishes social needs from mere interests and desires. To perform even these elementary functions well, citizens need traits that are not different in kind from those that Galston asks of leaders. Galston's 1991 list, furthermore is incomplete as it stands. Unlike his 1980 list, it does not explicitly include citizen loyalty. Loyalty based on a responsible political identity is crucial to a stable political life. It is that which sustains political practice in the face of hardships. It provides the motive for the courage and willingness to make sacrifices without which no political society can long survive. In short, without loyalty, the political domain, as a relatively autonomous domain, would collapse. This loyalty, in turn, must be based on a responsible political identity. Otherwise, it is prone to degenerate into a pernicious, destructive force.

Today, however, even more is required of one who seeks to be a thoroughly good citizen. The perennial traits of traditionally conceived good citizenship are no longer sufficient for taking part responsibly in political life. Given both the phenomenon of internationalization and the threat to the habitability of the earth, no political society can pretend to live in isolation. Its domestic political activity has unavoidable repercussions in other states. This activity is therefore subject to reasonable criticism by foreigners as well as by its own citizens.

This fact is perhaps most clear in ecological matters. Consider, for example, a state's legislation concerning the emission of fluorocarbons. The Mexican regulations obviously affect Brazilians and vice versa. But ecological issues are by no means the only relevant ones here. A state's trade regulations also affect foreigners. So too does its criminal law, as questions of international human rights make evident.

Today, the combination of the complexity of domestic political life, especially in large, stable, industrialized democracies, and its international ramifications requires a fresh conceptualization of good citizenship. A properly reconceptualized citizenship, I argue in the next chapter, is one that calls for the recognition of new issues, the need for new political institutions, and the adoption of new criteria for determining permissible political and economic initiatives. This reconceptualization will call for explicit attention to the question of citizen competence and a fresh consideration of what counts as responsible political loyalty. Citizens, I argue, now have global responsibilities. These global responsibilities do not threaten loyalty to a particular state. Now and for the foreseeable future, a necessary condition for effectively discharging these global responsibilities is that one be a loyal participant in the political life of a particular state.

Chapter 6

Complex Citizenship

Both the liberal and the communitarian traditions of thought about citizenship are surely worthy of respect. William Galston's conception of citizenship, which draws on both of them, displays something of the strength of both of them. But neither of these traditions provides grounds for hoping that it can yield a conception of citizenship that fits today's demands. The principal weakness of both traditions, and of Galston's own view, is that they are practically mute concerning the issue of the sustainability of democratic politics in an increasingly complex and fragile world. Though the traditional conceptions, including Galston's, presuppose both the indefinitely continued human habitability of the earth and the presence of the material and cultural conditions that democratic politics requires, they do not take into explicit account the possibility that citizens might have to work hard to ensure that these presuppositions remain well founded. Neither of these traditions, or so it appears, has sufficient conceptual resources to overcome this weakness.

Today, given the massive ecological problems that humankind both produces and confronts and given the sorts of internationalization of life that I have mentioned, the grounds for these presuppositions have become quite shaky. Today, therefore, Jonas's new categorical imperative takes on urgency. Good citizens must actively concern themselves in some nontrivial way with the task of protecting not only conditions for forms of political life that deserve to be called democratic but even the conditions for human life itself.

Of course, nothing that anyone can do can absolutely guarantee the continued existence of human beings. Natural forces are sure to eliminate the human species some day. More to the present point, however, no body of political thought or course of political action can

119

provide an ironclad guarantee against humanity's self-destruction. Not a few thoughtful people today find themselves deeply pessimistic about the efficacy of any program designed to avoid this self-destruction. I have no knockdown argument against this pessimism, but to act on it is likely to be self-fulfilling. My proposal for reconceptualizing citizenship is animated by the hope that what citizens do can make this self-destruction less likely. The heavier demands that I would place on citizens ultimately have no other justification than this hope. But all politics worthy of the name has always been risky and hence has had to rest on a hope of some sort.

Evidence that we can no longer take for granted the continued habitability of the earth is abundant. For example, the evidence that Paul Kennedy has marshaled in *Preparing for the Twenty-first Century* clearly shows that some threats to it are already quite well defined.[1] This evidence received corroboration in the 1995 State of the World report that the Worldwatch Institute issued. It says in part:

> In the mid-nineties evidence that the world is on an economic path that is environmentally unsustainable can be seen in shrinking fish catches, falling water tables, declining bird populations, record heat waves and dwindling grains stocks, to name just a few.[2]

How people should act to ward off or reduce these threats is both an immensely complex technical problem and a political problem that seriously challenges the adequacy of our present democratic institutions and practices.

Consider just one example, that of the emission of greenhouse gases. In 1992, participants in the Earth Summit in Rio de Janeiro agreed on a Framework Convention on Climate Change. A number of industrialized nations have since pledged to reduce their emissions so that by the year 2000 the annual amount of global emissions would not exceed that of 1990. Already, though, there is strong reason to doubt that the United States, one of the participating nations and the chief source by far of these emissions, will reach this goal. To do so would require nothing less than a very expensive, onerous transformation of its people's way of living. But there is little, if any, evidence that, given its present forms of political participation, the citizens of the United States would support the legal changes necessary to bring about so large a transformation. Neither the body of ordinary citizens nor their elected officials show signs of the political will to do so. Much the same can be said of the citizens both of other industrialized nations and of nations such as Mexico that are trying to become industrialized.

It is therefore far from implausible to conclude with Tim Beardsley that "the great experiment—how life will change in a high-carbon dioxide atmosphere—seems to be getting under way."[3] Of course, this is an experiment in only the crudest sense. Lacking any semblance of reasonable controls, it is a reckless gamble with the sustainability of significant portions of the biosphere and, hence, with the quality of human life. Indeed, it is by no means far-fetched to believe that this "experiment" threatens the sustainability of human life at any level above wretchedness. Nor is there any good reason to believe that democratic politics is a genuine possibility for wretched people.

There are two main obstacles to an effective response to the large-scale threats against the sustainability of both nonwretched human life and democratic politics. They are citizen ignorance and citizen thoughtlessness. Particularly harmful is the culpable ignorance that mental laziness leads to and the willful thoughtlessness that selfishness and small-mindedness generate. As presently institutionalized and practiced, democratic politics is insufficiently equipped to overcome these obstacles and thus to ensure its own continued existence. To overcome them will require both institutional reforms and significant changes in citizen conduct.

Good citizens today ought to adopt reforms and changes in their state's political practice that offer promise of satisfying the Jonas imperative in as democratic a fashion as possible. To adopt this objective, one need not unequivocally subordinate concern for democracy to concern for physical survival. Of course, without physical survival, there is no democratic living. But the historical record gives us no good grounds for believing that nondemocratic politics is more conducive to sheer human survival than democratic politics is. Nonetheless, given some particular set of circumstances, some versions of democratic thought and practice can conflict with some sensible programs that promise to promote survival effectively. Traditional conceptions of democratic citizenship can give rise to such conflicts. Some conceptions of constitutionally protected rights, for example, property rights, can do so. The conception of citizenship that I propose is designed to avoid these conflicts.

Put schematically, the fundamental task of citizens has always been that of preserving their political society, their political world. This task has always included that of making sure that the society had the material and economic resources it needed to survive. It has also always included making sure that, on the one hand, the institutions in which the society's cultural and political achievements are inscribed and kept efficacious are preserved. Particularly in the case of democratic citizenship, it has, on the other hand, likewise included making sure that citizens have opportunities to exercise political and cultural initiative, to bring about something new and different. The several parts of this task have never fitted together in an unproblematic way. Indeed, the fundamental task has always been to satisfy each part of the task in such a way that doing so does not undercut the capacity to discharge the other parts.[4]

Today, however, the world to be preserved is global. No society can ignore the rest of the globe and still preserve itself. The scarcity of resources that citizens must concern themselves with has, furthermore, taken on a different character. There are some resources, for example, water, for which there is no substitute. Some of these vital resources, if not judiciously protected, will be permanently lost. These differences make the citizen's task of contributing to his or her society's preservation more complex. They also demand a new understanding of political loyalty and identity as well as of several other traits or virtues traditionally expected of good citizens.

To deal effectively and democratically with the most crucial political issues of today, citizens need to reconceptualize the normative demands of citizenship. The appropriate reconceptualization, I propose, calls for (a) a new way of deliberating and reaching decisions about major political matters, (b) the recognition of new objects of citizens' concern, and (c) citizen support for new institutional arrangements that promote or facilitate (a) and (b). The new way of deliberating and reaching decisions amounts to a new way of assessing risks, a new casuistry. The new objects of citizen concern are (a) their own competence for sensible politics, (b) the well-being of foreign persons and states, and (c) the condition of the natural environment. A conception of citizenship that incorporates these new elements will require a fundamental recasting of the traditional traits of good citizenship. A conception of citizenship that gives preeminence to these new elements is the conception of what I call complex citizenship. Its principal demands are that individual self-interest must not control domestic politics, and the national self-interest should not control international relations.

Let me now offer a summary account of these new elements. Consider first the new way of deliberating about and reaching political decisions, the new approach to risk assessment or the new casuistry. This casuistry is by no means radically discontinuous with the sorts of argumentation long in use for dealing with practical issues. It, like they, has to deal with future contingencies, with matters about which there can be no certitude. It, like they, is a way of assessing risk that refuses to give the last word to economic criteria and, thus, contrary to approaches advocated by some people, properly acknowledges the relative autonomy of politics.[5] It, like they, is thus an exercise in what Aristotle called deliberative rhetoric. What distinguishes the new casuistry I propose is the recognition it gives to the distinctive exigencies of political life today and to the demands that these exigencies make on democratic politics.

Let me begin my argument for this set of claims by briefly describing the main features of classical casuistry. The new casuistry for which I call would have a structure that has much in common with classical casuistry. According to the *Oxford English Dictionary*, casuistry is "that part of ethics which resolves cases of conscience, applying the general rules of religion and morality to particular instances in which there appears to be a conflict of duties." The new casuistry that I propose would deal only with political issues and would not make use of principles or rules taken from religion, but like classical casuistry, it would resolve questions by paying attention to the particular circumstances that give specificity to these issues.

The classical discipline of casuistry rests on two basic assumptions.[6] First, it assumes that it is wrong for a person to perform an act while still in doubt about its moral probity. When doubts arise either because principles or duties are in conflict or because it is not clear whether a principle or obligation is applicable to the case at hand, one must resolve the doubt before acting. Second, casuistry assumes that no set of universal moral norms can be so self-interpreting that its applicability to particular cases in all their historical concreteness is always unambiguous. Given these two assumptions and given that sometimes abstaining from acting is tantamount to acting, then one should exercise an Aristotelianesque equity to tailor the principles to the case at hand. Casuistry is the discipline that aims to discern the equitable and thus to resolve doubts of conscience. It does so by showing how to give the concrete circumstances of the case the weight they deserve.

During its high period, 1550–1650, the discipline of casuistry employed a method that consisted of six parts. The method involved "the reliance on paradigms and analogies, the appeal to maxims, the analysis of circumstances, degrees of probability, the use of cumulative arguments, and the presentation of a final resolution."[7]

First, a paradigm case consists of a universal substantive rule and its obvious, unproblematic application to some particular instance.

Take, for example, the Fifth Commandment, "Thou shall not kill." Clearly, this rule covers every case of direct, deliberate, unprovoked killing of newborn babies. Arguing by analogy from this case, one can ask about other acts that lead to serious consequences. Is the attack direct, fully deliberate, or really unprovoked? Are its results sure to be death? Does this rule cover permanent maiming, temporary injury, psychological damage, and so on?

Second, casuists made use of conventionally accepted maxims used in moral argumentation. Some maxims originated in Roman law and became incorporated into canon law. Examples of maxims are "force may be repelled by force" and "one may tolerate a lesser evil to prevent a greater one." They also used more homespun maxims such as "one good turn deserves another."

Third, casuists considered the standard set of circumstances relevant to the case. They would ask: Who is to do what to whom for what reason and with what means? And when, where, and how is the deed to be done? Both the agent's condition—fearful, blood related, and so on—and the patient's condition—impoverished, aged, and so on—may turn out to be pertinent to determining the deed's rightness or wrongness. So too may the motive, means, and location.

Fourth, casuists qualified their conclusions in terms of likelihood or probability. Except for paradigm cases, they rarely claimed that the conclusions they reached about a particular case were apodictic or definitive. Rather, they claimed for their arguments only greater or lesser degrees of strength. An opinion acquired its strength, on the one hand, from the quality of the arguments that supported it and, on the other hand, from the agreement it gained from other casuists, other experts in the field.[8]

Fifth, casuists supported their opinions by amassing several supporting arguments of various sorts. They did not try to find a single deductive argument that would clinch matters. Rather, as in much everyday argumentation about all sorts of practical matters, they adduced a multiplicity of arguments and reasons that would lend credence to the conclusion they favored. "The 'weight' of casuistical opinion came from the accumulation of reasons rather than from the logical validity of the arguments or the coherence of any single 'proof.' "[9]

Finally, casuists always ended their analyses of cases with a resolution that would embody their advice about the moral permissibility of acting in one way or another. Without this advice, the use of the method would be fruitless, but, apart from paradigm cases, the casuists never forgot the moral ambiguity that pervaded so many practical and urgent questions. Hence,

> vividly aware that in morals, as in medicine, difficult cases can never be resolved by logical deductions leading to certain conclusions, they almost always presented their resolutions as "more or less probable." They would say, for example, "In these circumstances, given these conditions, you can with reasonable assurance act in such-and-such a way."[10]

Such resolutions were deemed strong enough to provide the moral certitude one needed to act with moral probity. Nothing more could reasonably be asked of the agent.

Though the history of casuistry shows that it was sometimes used to license outrageous conduct, its method embodies a profound respect for the ineradicable limits on the sorts of "certainty" that human beings can gain about any domain of practical life, whether the domain be moral, political, artistic, economic, or technological. In all of these domains,

> the most confident opinion about a particular case may subsequently be called in question in the light of fresh considerations. Even the most strongly supported (or "probable") of practical opinions can be presented only as the outcome of "presumptive," not "necessary" inferences; while the discovery of new facts about the circumstances of any particular case may always rebut, or force one to qualify, a former opinion about it.[11]

The whole point of casuistry was, of course, to provide guidance for action. It therefore had to find a practical way to resolve differences of opinion about whether, in the particular case at hand, a person was obligated to observe a general rule or was at liberty to act according to his or her own preference. In the course of casuistry's history, three principal ways of resolving differences of opinion were proposed. They were called probabilism, probabiliorism, and tutiorism.

According to probabilism, a person who is in doubt about the morality of a particular course of conduct may "lawfully follow the opinion for liberty, provided it is truly probable, even though the opinion for law is definitely more probable."[12] According to probabiliorism, a person in doubt must follow the opinion for law unless the opinion for liberty is clearly more probable. "If both opinions are about equally probable, the opinion for the law must be followed."[13] According to tutiorism, "one must follow the safer side (the opinion for the law) unless the likelihood that the law does not bind (the opinion for liberty) is most probable.''[14]

The discipline of casuistry thus never disregarded the importance and force of universal principles. But it also gave full weight to the particular circumstances and contingencies that affect the meaning and worth of each action. It recognized, furthermore, that assessments of the moral probity of a great deal of human conduct cannot achieve apodicticity. Many of these assessments always remain in the realm of reasonably contestable opinion. Thus, casuistry respects the finitude and historicality of human existence.

By reason of the assumptions on which it rests and its method, casuistry provides a fitting way for reflecting on the morality of our actions. It can also be, if properly reworked, a most appropriate guide for political deliberation, decision, and assessment dealing with some of the most difficult and risky political questions that our present complex world forces us to confront.

In the religious context in which it was developed, probabilism became the generally accepted standard to use to settle differences of opinion. It found favor because it gave liberty vis-à-vis law as much leeway as could plausibly be defended. In this context, one could presume that a good and merciful God would not condemn a person who adopted a course of action that was not lacking plausibility even if there were weighty reasons against it. Probabilism thus reflects a distinct optimism.

One finds a similar optimism in much Western thought concerning the exploitation of natural resources and the use of risky technological innovations. The basis of this optimism is, of course, not religious. Rather, it rests on a confidence that whatever damage people do, they can always find a way to repair it. This confidence also serves to support a probabilistic resolution of doubts about the propriety of such actions.

One thus often finds arguments supporting the use of risky technological innovations that amount to something like the following: First, if this innovation succeeds, it will make a notable contribution to human well-being. Second, if we who are careful and responsible do not proceed with it, others, who may not be as careful, will most likely do so. Finally, if by chance using the innovation does significant damage, there is a reasonable probability that it will be repaired either by time or by the discovery of some subsequent technological innovation. The conclusion to which this sort of argument leads is that, given all the relevant circumstances, there is sufficient probability that the use of the innovation would violate no rule and, hence, that one is free to use it if one wishes.

Structurally similar arguments are not uncommon concerning a number of other matters. They are used to justify commerce in armaments, trade policies, regulations or the lack thereof on currency movements and the activities of multinational corporations, and environmental policies. In all of these areas, we find optimistic arguments that in effect employ a probabilistic standard for resolving whatever doubts there are about the justifiability of the act in question.

Today, however, internationalization and the threats to the human habitability of the earth pose a host of problems to democratic political life that cannot be sensibly dealt with in a probabilistic manner. These problems are those for which we cannot reasonably expect second chances, for which we cannot reasonably hope that subsequent opportunities to rectify damage that we do will present themselves. For these political issues we need a new casuistry. Let me now sketch its principal features.

Every casuistry must have some substantive principles that, when applied, yield paradigm cases. It must have a domain of cases and a standard for resolving doubts about them. To function, it must have, on the one hand, a clientele that seeks advice and a cadre of experts who give it. On the other hand, there must be institutional arrangements that can bring clients and experts into contact with one another.

The new casuistry that I propose is designed first and foremost to prevent a "common bad." Even if there is no *determinate* common good that can serve as a goal for responsible political practice, there is a relatively determinate common bad that all responsible politics must seek to avoid. This common bad has two parts: first, the uninhabitability of the earth, and, second, the twin political calamities of anarchy and tyranny. This two-fold common bad gives rise to two principles, namely, the Jonas imperative and the democratic postulate.

The Jonas imperative, one will recall, reads:

Act so that the effects of your action are compatible with the permanence of genuine human life; or expressed negatively: Act so that the effects of your action are not destructive of the future possibility of such life; or simply: Do not compromise the conditions for an indefinite continuation of humanity on earth. . . .[15]

Unlike the Kantian imperative, which is addressed to the motives of individual conduct, the Jonas imperative is addressed to public policy

and its real, this-worldly consequences. This objective, Jonas emphasizes, adds

> a *time* horizon to the moral calculus which is entirely absent from the
> instantaneous logical operation of the Kantian imperative: whereas the
> latter extrapolates into an ever-present order of abstract [logical] compati-
> bility, our imperative extrapolates into a predictable real *future* as the
> open-ended dimension of our responsibility.[16]

The Jonas imperative presumes that it lies within our power to
devise and implement public policy that will substantially affect the
survival of the human race. Today, because of the scope and power of
the available technology, citizens have responsibility for preserving
not only their own political society but also the planet's habitability,
the fundamental condition for any politics at all.

Given human thoughtliness, however, a politics that would aim for
nothing beyond mere survival would be an unworthy politics. A
conception of politics that gave unqualified preeminence to mere
physical survival and comfort is compatible with the most thoroughgoing of tyrannies. Anarchy is not notably better. History has taught us
that to live in a fully human way people must be members of political
societies that give them opportunities to participate actively in the
political institutions that shape their lives. Today, the political societies
that best provide these opportunities are those that are in some
nontrivial sense democratic. The new casuistry should thus have as its
second principle the democratic postulate.

To count as a democratic society, as I said earlier, a political society
must have three characteristics. First, it must grant to all its qualified
members the right to participate, directly or through representatives
that they choose, in all of its political processes. Second, it must
provide all of its members sufficient opportunities to become qualified
for this participation. Third, it must both establish for all its members
a set of legal rights that restrict the scope of governmental power and
afford them protection against arbitrary uses of the power that the
government does have. These three characteristics are obviously in
tension with one another. Every democratic society has the ongoing
task of managing this tension, making sure that it adjusts the relationship among them to the exigencies of the times. Like everything
political, then, every democratic society has both a history-that-has-
been-made and a history-to-be-made. Nonetheless, for the most part,
it has not been difficult to distinguish genuine democratic societies
from pretenders.

Taken together, the Jonas imperative and the democratic postulate serve as the fundamental principles of the new casuistry. Responsible politics must acknowledge them and citizens ought to make certain that all political policies and practices to which they lend their support respect them.

The domain of cases to which the new casuistry applies includes, in principle, all political matters. But this does not mean that it wholly replaces more traditional forms of deliberation. Those forms, including the classical casuistry with its standard of probabilism, remain appropriate for a very large number of cases. For example, it has been suggested that the characteristic sort of reasoning used to decide complex legal cases in common law jurisprudence amounts to probabilistic casuistry.[17] The new casuistry would not require changes in most of these cases, nor would it require changes in the ways that democratic political societies deal with most tax questions, welfare issues, and crime, particularly unorganized crime. But if there is a doubt about whether a proposed course of action really does threaten to violate in a substantial way either of its two fundamental principles, then this doubt should be resolved according to the new casuistry. In short, in determining which issues are to be dealt with according to the new casuistry and which are to be left to more traditional forms of deliberation, one should employ the new casuistry. Then, of course, one should proceed to resolve these issues by again exercising the new casuistry.

Besides principles and a domain of cases, every casuistry must have a standard for resolving doubts about the propriety of courses of action. The probabilism of classical casuistry, as I have indicated, is not appropriate for the new casuistry's cases. The other two candidates that the history of casuistry provides are tutiorism and probabiliorism.

Tutiorism, or what has been called "the better-safe-than-sorry principle," however, both is simplistic and demands too much.[18] It would permit so little innovation that it itself could become dangerous either to the planet's habitability or to democracy. That is, it would so block innovation and experimentation that its practitioners would probably be overwhelmed by unavoidable changes in the circumstances that shape their political life. Tutiorism, furthermore, could all too easily lead to such unmitigated emphasis on survival that it would condone tyrannical practices. If democracy is inseparable from some risk to survival, it is a defensible risk. Its alternatives cannot guarantee survival, even if mere survival were worthwhile. It is thus only seemingly paradoxical that in a world such as ours a determination always to follow the safer course can itself turn out to be excessively risky.

Instead of either probabilism or tutiorism, the new casuistry should make use of the standard of probabiliorism to resolve doubts about the courses of action. Unless it is more probable that a particular course of action or set of institutional arrangements is consistent with both the Jonas imperative and the democratic postulate than is any available alternative, then citizens should not support it. And, to ward off conflicts between the demands of these two principles, probabiliorism requires that if one particular form of democracy is more probably consistent with the Jonas imperative than is any viable alternative, then that is the form that citizens should adopt and support. The viability of alternative forms of democracy will, of course, vary according to time and the particular society in question.

Political arguments calling for the adoption of the "safer course" are far from rare. For example, A. M. Rosenthal has argued that, in assessing the time that Iran would need to construct nuclear weapons, the United States should recognize that "it is *safer* to take the shorter estimate."[19] He has also argued that the United States should follow the safer course in matters concerning terrorists and the smuggling of weapons-grade nuclear materials.[20] My contention is that a mere ad hoc use of the "safer course" standard may be appropriate for some political issues, but today there is a large number of issues that are serious threats either to democracy or to the earth's habitability. Both to identify these issues and to respond to them, we need to adopt and institutionalize the use of a new casuistry that employs the probabilioristic standard to resolve doubts about the proper courses of action.

The new casuistry that I propose to guide political action can function successfully only if its practitioners have the competence to use it well. Accordingly, the second new element that distinguishes the conception of complex citizenship calls for citizens to extend their thoughtful concern to a new set of issues. The most fundamental of these issues is the competence that they and their fellow citizens have for participating well in politics. This thoughtful concern will show that the competence they need has two parts. There is technical competence, on the one hand, and political competence, on the other. Only those who possess both sorts of competence are fully entitled to take part in the deliberation and decisions about what I henceforth call the democratic survival issues. Those who possess this competence will understand that they must concern themselves both with the well-being of foreigners and their states and with the environment.

To raise questions about the competence of normal adult citizens to take part in any democratic process is controversial from the outset. Given democracy's history, one might well wonder whether there can be any democratic justification for making anything more than the competence to take care of one's ordinary personal affairs the condition for a citizen's active participation in political processes. Is it not actually undemocratic to propose making an explicit assessment of a person's fitness to exercise citizenship? Is it not indeed a defining characteristic of democratic states that they are expansive in their ascriptions of citizenship because they recognize that there is no more fundamental human right than the "right to have rights (and that means to live in a framework where one is judged by one's actions and opinions) and a right to belong to some organized community . . . ?"[21]

Questions of this sort reflect the undeniably preponderant view that one can and should presume without further ado that all mentally normal adults to whom a democratic state has ascribed citizenship are competent to exercise that citizenship in a way that is at least not harmful. One finds this presumption made explicit by Alexis de Tocqueville. He says:

> According to the notion of modern democratic and, I venture to say, the *correct* notion of freedom, everyman, being presumed to have received from nature the necessary intelligence to conduct his own affairs, acquires at birth an equal and imprescriptible right to live independently of his fellows in all respects that concern him alone, and to govern his destiny as he sees fit.[22]

Commenting on de Tocqueville's view of democracy, Claude Lefort points out that, for de Tocqueville,

> democracy's prime virtue is its characteristic agitation and not its political ability to facilitate the selection of the best and to improve the government's ability to conduct public affairs. While he agrees that the people often conduct their affairs very badly, he does not see that as something to be condemned, since it seems to him that the agitation which reigns in the political sphere spreads to the rest of society. It encourages initiative in every domain by promoting the circulation of ideas and by expanding everyone's field of curiosity.[23]

In support of his reading, Lefort quotes de Tocqueville's comment that

> [d]emocracy does not give the people the most skilled government, but it produces what the ablest governments are frequently unable to create: namely, an all-pervading and restless activity, a superabundant force, and an energy which is inseparable from it and which may, however unfavorable circumstances may be, produce wonders.[24]

De Tocqueville thus in effect dismisses the question of citizen competence. For him, in the long run it is better to encourage widespread citizen participation than to concern oneself with whether the citizens who do participate have the competence to participate well.

Even if, however, one does not share de Tocqueville's optimism about the consequences of presuming citizen competence, one might still resist opening the issue to public consideration. One might well hold that since we do not have the capability to make well-supported determinations of a citizen's competence, to open the question is very ill advised. Without hope of doing much good, one would just invite bad, even vicious, answers.

I have no definitive refutation for this objection. But because it concerns politics and its future contingencies, one cannot definitively establish its correctness, either. Everything in political life is not only contingent but also to some degree risky. This objection therefore does not lead to an absolute prohibition against raising the issue of citizen competence but rather leads to a strong caution about when, how, and about what specific matters one does so.

Let me emphasize again that the purpose of my proposal that a democratic society make citizen competence an explicit issue is not to search for some putatively "best" set of policies and practices that promote some determinate conception of the society's common good. Its purpose, rather, is to guard against the society's coming to suffer a grievous common bad.

If one could have reasonable assurance that one could avoid the common bads of disastrous environmental degradation, on the one hand, and the collapse of the political and social institutions on which democratic government is dependent, on the other hand, without raising the issue of citizen competence, the case against doing so would be compelling. Under such circumstances, raising it would be not only unnecessary but rash, perhaps even perverse.

The historical record and recent political discourse and policy formation, however, provide considerable empirical evidence against the easy assumption of widespread citizen competence. Too many citizens of democratic states all too often support policies that are ecologically destructive or xenophobic and candidates who advocate such policies. All too frequently they display the myopia of single-issue politics or give their backing to senseless or destructive economic proposals. And all too frequently they act on the erroneous belief that their own state can flourish regardless of what happens to people elsewhere. In short, all too often too many citizens, when they do participate in politics, do so ignorantly or thoughtlessly.

In practice, modern democratic states have gotten around the problem of widespread citizen incompetence in various relatively informal and often ad hoc ways. Their elected leaders get advice from lobbyists hired to promote special interests and from members of research institutes, or "think tanks." They also pay attention to "opinion makers." Some of these advisors are experts in some particular field, and some are paid advocates and supposedly are skilled at shaping and reflecting public opinion. As matters presently stand, it is hard to imagine how political leaders could avoid giving these advisors a role in formulating, implementing, and assessing major domestic and international political initiatives that is far greater than the sheer number of people they could plausibly be said to represent would warrant.[25] Indeed, all too frequently both the leaders and many of these advisors have worked not to involve ordinary citizens in political deliberations but either to manipulate them or to keep them uninformed. News media, rather than counteracting the forces that militate against well-informed citizen participation, have themselves often substantially abetted them.

Even if these informal arrangements for determining who become the advisors of political leaders do sometimes produce beneficial results, one would be hard pressed to argue that, in their present form, they promote genuine democratic political life. They do not constitute a satisfactory alternative to widespread citizen competency. For one thing, if these arrangements obscure the threats to democracy that citizen incompetence poses, then there is little incentive to provide institutional resources designed to promote competence. In the absence of such resources, it is likely that a significant number of capable citizens who would be willing to become competent will not have an opportunity to do so. There is, however, reason to expect that properly institutionalized support for promoting citizen competence would, at least in some modest measure, give greater voice to many who could come to deserve it. Without this institutional support, many citizens presently have practically no real opportunity or encouragement to gain this competence. A second weakness of the present arrangements that disregard the issue of citizen competence is that sound policies are in danger of being undercut or repudiated in elections and referenda by an electorate made up of large numbers of people who have no competence to deal with the issue at hand, or, conversely, they may well support folly. As history shows, incompetent citizens are ripe for demagoguery, and demagoguery is always antithetical to democracy.

My positive proposal concerning what citizen competence consists of and why it is proper, especially today, expressly to demand it of citizens rather than simply to assume it rests on two elementary, though admittedly contestable, considerations. First, democratic citizenship does not consist in possessing some static set of rights and obligations. More fundamentally, it consists in the right to take part in deliberations and decisions about which rights and obligations are to be ascribed to which inhabitants of the political society. It is a distinguishing characteristic of democratic states that they rest on *"the legacy of a debate as to what is legitimate and what is illegitimate*—a debate which is necessarily without any guarantor and without any end."[26] If citizens are sensibly and effectively to continue this debate, then they must have some grasp not only of the conclusions that their predecessors arrived at but also of the reasons that lead to these conclusions.

The second consideration that underpins my proposal is that citizenship should be regarded as the "first office, the crucial social and political 'place' and the precondition of all of the others."[27] As an office, citizenship has duties attached to it, basically the duty to help preserve the political society. In this view, the initial ascription of citizenship simply gives one an invitation and right to be a candidate for full citizenship. As such, mere ascription need impose no duties, but the recipient of the ascription is normally expected someday to assume the duties of the full-fledged citizen. By analogy with John Locke's distinction between birth to and birth in equality, one can say that by virtue of ascription one is born *to* citizenship but not born *in* it.[28] In my view, one attains full-fledged citizenship only when he or she acts on the ascription and thereby accepts the ascription and the duties normally associated with its acceptance. To accept the ascription properly, one should be competent to perform the duties.

As I have said, to participate responsibly and effectively in politics, citizens must acquire two distinguishable sorts of competence, namely, political competence and technical competence. Correspondingly, the state, if it is to be fully democratic, must provide both the resources necessary to achieve these two sorts of competence and the opportunity for all of its citizens to avail themselves of these resources.

Let me first briefly describe these two kinds of competence. Then I will indicate what sorts of institutional arrangements states should maintain to enable their citizens to become competent. Consider, first, political competence. Political competence consists largely of an understanding and appreciation of the constitutive characteristics of the domain of politics that I pointed out in chapter 4. It also includes, especially today, a grasp of the Jonas imperative, the democratic postulate, and the internationalization of both political and cultural life.

There are thus four basic constituents of political competence. First, the politically competent citizen will recognize that, though politics is inseparable from either economics or morality, it is not reducible to them. It has its own objectives, norms, and means. Political practice can and should acknowledge technical and scientific expertise and the universal normative force of moral ideals and principles. But it cannot rightfully allow itself to be wholly determined by extrapolitical considerations. Rather, it must both utilize technicoscientific expertise and be advised by moral principles. In the end, though, it must pursue its own purposes according to its own criteria.

The political utilization of both expertise and moral principles can and should be respectful and not co-optive. Co-optation would vitiate the instruction that politics would draw from these other sorts of reflection. To utilize rather than to co-opt them, the political practitioner should always admit that political proposals cannot rightly claim to be entailed by the results of these other forms of reflection. He or she can claim only to be informed by them. Consider the case of economic research. For sensible politics, the results of economic research do not dictate specific political policies or practices. Rather, they serve to mark off the field within which sensible political deliberation and decision will take place. Similarly, given the spatiotemporal specificity of everything political, no sensible political proposal can pretend to be fully warranted by some set of moral or religious ideals. Strictly speaking, there is no Jewish, Christian, Islamic, Hindu, Buddhist politics. As the discipline of casuistry illustrates, moral or religious norms and ideals are by no means irrelevant to human action of all sorts. But they are not self-interpreting in all circumstances. A politics that disregards all such norms and ideals is brutal. But one that aims to impose them on the unwilling is no less so.

Responsible political practice thus never claims that it can provide either redemption or salvation for its citizens. It can neither protect them from all the ills that befall people in the normal course of their lives nor can it redress all the harm they inflict on themselves and one another. Sensible political practice can aspire only to provide the structure and material and cultural resources for people to act and work together in a peaceful, orderly, and fair way. This aspiration is beyond definitive satisfaction. And its pursuit, as history shows, is never wholly free from strife.

The second basic constituent of political competence consists of the citizen's acceptance of the fact that all politics, like all action, is both risky and transgressive. It always impinges on some people in unforeseeable ways. There can be no certitude, furthermore, that a particular course of political action is unqualifiedly the best one. In politics one can work only with probabilities. Today, in some major matters, the politically competent citizen will submit his or her political deliberations and decisions to the standard of probabiliorism.

Third, the politically competent citizen recognizes the fragility of the domain of politics and of everything belonging to that domain. He or she recognizes that no politics can be made completely immune to the tendencies to tyranny, totalitarianism, or anarchy. Neither can it be made definitively secure against tendencies to subjugate it to either economic or moral imperatives. The politically competent citizen thus recognizes the need for vigilance against ignorant, thoughtless, or criminal people who threaten to undercut sound political practice. Such citizens recognize that they can never responsibly renounce all coercion and state-sanctioned violence. But at the same time they appreciate that the society's aspiration for peace requires it to seek ways to convert those who threaten it into its supporters. Even in their vigilance, then, politically competent citizens will always urge their political representatives to search for ways to reduce the frequency and intensity of exercises of state coercion.

Finally, the politically competent citizen never forgets that all human existence, and, hence, all politics, displays both bodily and thoughtly dimensions. The political participant cannot reasonably be asked to set his or her own blood ties, religious traditions, neighborhood associations, and long-standing customs absolutely at naught. But our bodiliness does not imprison us. Nor does it enjoy an unequivocal primacy in our reflections on how to conduct ourselves. For politics to recognize and sometimes call for a thoughtliness that overrides bodily considerations is not to demean bodiliness. Today, perhaps more than ever before, some features of our bodiliness can be preserved only by exercises of considerable thoughtliness. For example, to preserve the Welsh folkloric tradition may today require making it an object of international academic concern and commercial endeavor. Perhaps only in these thoughtly ways can the Welsh continue to find their bodily traditions worthy of their own esteem and their effort to preserve that esteem. In any event, the politically competent citizen will practice a politics that respects the dynamic, mobile interplay of the bodily and the thoughtly in all human affairs.

Besides political competence, citizens need a certain technical competence to participate sensibly in politics. They need some grasp of the relevant available factual information about the issues that they address politically. For example, to take part in deliberations or decisions about where to locate nuclear waste sites, they have to understand the health risks that these sites pose. To be technically competent, citizens do not, of course, have to have technical expertise. It would be fatuous to expect such expertise about every area of knowledge that bears on political life. Rather, citizens need the technical competence to make use of specialists' expertise.

More precisely, to be fully competent to take part in political life, citizens need to know which politically relevant beliefs have no plausibility for experts in the field in question and what sorts of policies or conduct experts in the field can show to be either almost certainly doomed to fail to achieve their objectives or most likely to be counterproductive. In short, citizens need sufficient technical competence to be able to dismiss "pipe dreams" from their political deliberations.

As I have intimated above, there are some matters about which there is comparatively little reason to make an issue of either the political or technical competence of citizens. Examples of such matters are elections of office holders for small towns or rural districts and referenda for financing local libraries and drainage projects. One can reasonably assume that citizens' ordinary experience will be enough to make them fully competent to discuss and vote sensibly. For other matters, however, such as managing large deposits of natural resources in an ecologically and economically responsible way or negotiating ocean fishing quotas, the ordinary experience of most citizens is too limited to sustain the presumption of competence. Similarly, the ordinary experience of citizens of relatively small, culturally and economically homogeneous states, for example, the citizens of Iceland, may suffice for sensible participation in deliberations about most domestic budgetary matters. But for citizens of large, culturally and economically diverse states, the sufficiency of ordinary experience in such matters is far more dubitable.

It is also true that people can gain both political competence and the relevant technical competence precisely in the course of political deliberations. Those who regularly attend school board meetings and zoning commission meetings quite often become fully competent to deal with those matters. But there is nothing competence forming about incompetent participation in large, complex matters. Bad habits of political participation are still bad even if those who have them exercise them with comfort.

Drawing the line between issues for which ordinary daily experience warrants the presumption of full citizen competence and those for which it does not is a practical matter. However one draws the line, it is always open to reconsideration. So too is the matter of how to deal with citizens whose competence is seriously in doubt. How long and at what cost does one continue to supply the resources and opportunities they could use to become competent? And of course, who is competent to deal with these matters?[29] In keeping with the new casuistry, I would argue that, at bottom, one should decide these matters of doubt about competence by adopting policies and courses of action that more probably than not will observe the demands of the Jonas imperative and the democratic postulate. That is, one should decide them by use of the standard of probabiliorism.

Whatever difficulties there are, however, in determining when one can safely presume citizen competence and how one should deal with incompetent citizens, it seems beyond reasonable doubt that the list of politically relevant fields of technical expertise is larger today than ever before. Today it includes economics, medicine, demography, and the applied physical and biological sciences. It also, of course, includes such matters as military capability and law enforcement capability. The state of knowledge in each of these fields is constantly changing. The task of keeping abreast of these changes and thereby being able to expose pipe dreams for what they are is obviously interminable, but it is a task that democratic societies must undertake if their citizens are to have a chance to take part in political activity that deals with some of today's most serious and urgent issues.

If a democratic society is to perform this task, it will have to maintain institutions that make available the instruction that citizens need to become and remain technically competent to take part in politics. It will also have to institutionalize restrictions on the political participation of those who fail to gain and maintain this competence.[30] Citizens, for their part, must support these institutions. This obligation is the third distinguishing feature of complex citizenship. Of course, citizens must themselves take advantage of the opportunities that these institutions provide for learning enough about the technical side of major political issues that they can avoid indulging in pipe dreams.

Citizens can avail themselves of these instructional opportunities in one of two ways. They can expend the time and effort they need to gain the necessary knowledge. Or, as is more probably feasible for most people, they can take part in voluntary organizations such as trade unions, civic organizations, business association, or religious organizations that have as one of their significant aims helping their members to achieve democratic competence. Such groups would perform a Walzerian mediating function in the instructional process. If citizens make use of the civic services that mediating groups provide, then they ought to contribute to their financial support.

Let me sketch out here a model of the institutional arrangements appropriate for supporting citizen competence.[31] First, let me reiterate that the purpose of the instruction that these institutions impart is to equip citizens to take part knowledgeably in political deliberations and decisions. It is not to give them answers or to persuade them to accept some particular, previously determined course of action. It is rather to equip them to reach sensible decisions of their own. The sole raison d'etre of these institutions is the preservation of democratic stability or environmental habitability or both. The instructors are thus not latter-day Platonic guardians. They should not claim to know precisely what to do. They can only claim to know what falls outside the range of plausible doings. And they must acknowledge that their knowledge is fallible. They are to be "guardians" only inasmuch as they provide defenses both against demagogues who would deceive citizens with pipe dreams and against citizens' own wishes for the unattainable.

The model of instructional institutions that I offer here applies only to institutions that are not part of the formal system of schooling. I deal with schooling in the next chapter. This model is a model for lifelong citizen education. To ensure the democratic character of this education, the model calls for the state to give official recognition to two different sorts of instructional institutions. Some of them should be explicitly established by law and supported by state funds. Others should be permitted by law and supported by private donations, perhaps encouraged by tax incentives.

Let me give examples of both of these sorts of institutions. Of course, these examples are meant only to be illustrative. There could be an excellent array of instructional institutions that do not include any that I mention.

Consider first those established by law and supported by state funds. A number of democratic states have official or quasi-official academies, standing commissions, or councils of science. In the United States, there is the National Academy of Science. It has on several occasions issued reports addressed to the public that have dealt with scientific or technological matters having important political implications. The members of this academy are selected by their peers for their scientific expertise. Though this academy has not wholly escaped political controversy, it has a solid record of independence from control by politicians. An agency such as this could be given legal standing without unduly jeopardizing its independence. I suggest that it, or an entity having much the same characteristics, could reasonably be charged by law with developing reports that are intelligible to the citizenry at large on important, politically relevant scientific matters. These reports should not advocate any specific political response, and they should acknowledge any significant scientific disagreements about their contents. The principal objective of these reports should be to make clear what the relevant scientific data is and what its implications are.

For today's complex world, states should establish and support several similar professional organizations with similar provisions to ensure their political independence. There might well be, in addition to an academy of science, academies of economics, ecology, medicine, demography, and military and police studies. Each would have a charge comparable to the one I suggest for the academy of science. Of course, these charges should not encompass all or most of an academy's work. Only if it remains first and foremost a prestigious organization that promotes first-quality scientific work in its own field can it gain the necessary respect to make an effective contribution to citizen competence.

It is worth noting that some legislative bodies have established nonpartisan agencies to provide technical information and advice to them. The United States Congress, for example, can call on its Congressional Budget Office, its Office of Technology Assessment, and so on. But these agencies presently can respond only to questions Congress asks. Under my proposal, the academies could determine at least part of their own agendas and should provide the electorate as a whole the sort of advice that I have sketched out above. That is, they should not endorse any particular proposal. Rather, they should confine themselves to demarcating the domain of defensible ones.

Besides the instructional organizations that they establish and support, democratic states should recognize other agencies that can make significant contributions to their citizens' technical competence. Some of these are international organizations and associations established and directly supported by treaties and agreements among states. The United Nations and its several agencies are prime examples. Other examples are NATO, the Organization of American States, the European Union, and the African Union. Reports on technical issues prepared by their staffs of experts are relevant to any democratic citizen who would be well informed. Unlike the reports of instructional agencies directly sponsored by single states, the reports of these international agencies should not be forbidden to advocate specific courses of action. One can safely assume that whatever they advocate would become no more than one opinion among many considered by informed citizens in their political deliberations and decisions.

Much the same holds true for another group of organizations that can play a vital instructional role and that a democratic state should permit and encourage. This is the group of nongovernmental organizations that deal with politically relevant issues either by aiding needy groups of people or by publicizing problems or both. Examples of such organizations are Doctors Without Borders, Amnesty International, Oxfam, and Catholic Relief Services. Precisely because they are not governmental, these organizations can provide a healthy critique of governmental policies and practices. Democratic politics should welcome their contribution to political debate and, where feasible, encourage it with tax exemptions or other incentives.[32]

Today, democratic states have a variety of means for making instructional material from these several sources available to their citizens. They can provide the organizations postal privileges, they can encourage or require either the electronic or the print media or both to give some exposure to these reports, and they can institutionalize ways of ensuring that at least the reports of the academies they directly support are made part of the discourse of those campaigning for major public office. Unquestionably, there will always be room for improvement in citizens' technical competence for political participation, but the means for substantially improving their technical competence are presently available. To make use of these means is neither prohibitively difficult nor antidemocratic. To the contrary, doing so holds promise of leading to an enhanced democratic political practice.

As I noted above, my conception of complex citizenship, by calling for a new form of political deliberation and decision making, by recognizing new objects of concern, and by demanding support for a new complex of political institutions, requires a fundamental recasting of the characteristics or traits traditionally deemed constitutive of good citizenship. In light of the foregoing account of citizen competence, briefly consider again a few of the items on Galston's list of citizen virtues. Today, citizens who avail themselves of opportunities to gain technical competence are far more able to distinguish well between the genuine social needs that they and their fellow citizens have and their plethora of mere desires. They are far more able to distinguish what is genuinely advantageous to them and those they hold dear from what deceptively appears to be so. For example, unless citizens today gain some understanding of economic realities, they are unlikely to be able to participate well in political discussions about their state's health care policies. Conversely, citizens are confronted with so many claims that economic considerations are the only reasonable bases for determining a state's policies that they also need the political competence to resist subjugating political issues to economic norms. Becoming aware that technical considerations are of different sorts and that they can clash with one another helps one to see just why it is important to insist on the relative autonomy of the political domain and its norms. One who comes to appreciate this autonomy is prepared to resist assigning excessive importance to the economic virtues and the commitment to affluence that Galston extols.

Even more important, citizens who achieve both political and technical competence improve their capacity to practice responsible political loyalty and increase the likelihood that the political identity they embrace will be reasonable. They will come to understand in some detail that their state is part of a world community. It cannot flourish in independence from the rest of the world. Accordingly, it has responsibilities that are global in scope. Good citizens will support political practice that accepts these responsibilities. They will define their loyalty so that it includes this support. And the political identity they cherish will be that of being a member of a political society that is drawing on its history of beneficent achievements for guidance and encouragement to shoulder the new global responsibilities it now has.

What I have said thus far about the conception of complex citizenship is enough to show that it makes significantly heavier demands on those who would be good citizens than the traditional conceptions do. The justification for making heavier demands lies in the distinctive exigencies and dangers with which political life must cope today and for the foreseeable future. To support further the claim that the heavier demands that my conception makes are the ones appropriate to today's political context, I want now to indicate the sort of guidance that it gives for dealing with some perennial political issues. The quality of this guidance strengthens the case for adopting this conception.

As always, citizenship today demands of those who would be good citizens that they address two basic sets of questions. Roughly, they are: (a) What policies and practices should citizens support and cooperate with to prepare their society's members to become competent citizens? (b) What policies and practices should citizens support and cooperate with to ensure that their society deals sensibly and justly with foreign individuals and societies? These two sets of issues pertain directly both to a political society's stability and to its justness. They also bear on the quality of the loyalty and the sense of political identity that individual citizens will embrace. Part of the merit of the conception of complex citizenship that I propose is that it provides solid guidance for responding to these two sets of questions. My conception of citizenship does not, of course, entail just one specific response. Rather, it provides recommendations and cautions that should be taken into account in the course of formulating and implementing appropriate policies for handling these matters.

The most effective way to show the kind of guidance that my conception of complex citizenship gives is to use it as a framework for concrete proposals for dealing with each of these two sets of issues. Chapters 7 and 8 contain my proposals. Though I believe that they do supply further reasons for adopting my conception of citizenship, not every argument against any part of them will also count as an argument against that conception. It is by no means implausible to believe that there are alternative and perhaps better ways to implement the requirements of complex citizenship concerning education and dealings with foreigners than those that I propose. Nonetheless my proposals do help to flesh out just what my conception of complex citizenship amounts to. I turn now to the matter of education.

Chapter 7

Education and Competent Citizenship

The most obvious way in which democratic societies have addressed the issue of citizen competence is through the educational programs that they either provide or encourage or allow. The constitutions of some democratic states, for example, Germany, Finland, and Spain, include explicit provisions for the education of their children. Other states, for example, the United States and Norway, deal with education through legislation that must satisfy the relevant constitutional criteria. For all democratic states, the overall objective of their concern for education is the social reproduction of their respective societies. As Amy Gutmann rightly says,

> "political education"—the cultivation of the virtues, knowledge, and skills necessary for political participation—has moral primacy over other purposes of public education in democratic society. Political education prepares citizens to participate in consciously reproducing their society, and conscious social reproduction is the ideal not only of democratic education but also of democratic politics.[1]

Few, if any, democratic constitutions, however, show any recognition that the human habitability of the earth may well be seriously at risk. They will need amendment if they are to provide the sort of education that will equip citizens to respond successfully to this threat. The proposal for citizen education that I make and defend implies that states should amend their constitutions to legitimate the provisions that my proposal calls for.[2]

I further take it that the legal support for an educational program strong enough to meet the demands of both the Jonas imperative and the democratic postulate will have to contain both carrots and sticks.

145

That is, because time for the political reforms necessary to meet these two criteria is short, the state's laws must not only reward citizens who take advantage of the educational program. They must also penalize somehow those who fail to do so, either deliberately or otherwise. Only citizens who have earned the right to participate in decision making should be allowed to do so. Nonetheless, no educational program can rightly pretend to be able to forestall the wickedness of those who know what should be done but refuse to do it. Only the state's legal deterrents can constrain them. Finally, like any sensible educational program, the program I recommend must recognize both the bodily and the thoughtly dimensions of its students.

My proposal for education to and for politics, like Gutmann's, calls for this education to continue in various ways throughout the citizen's life. In this respect, it clashes with Hannah Arendt's claim that education and politics are mutually exclusive activities. She says:

> Education can play no part in politics, because in politics we always have to deal with those who are already educated. Whoever wants to educate adults really wants to act as their guardian and prevent them from political activity.[3]

Perhaps in earlier times the education that one received as a youth would suffice for a lifetime of responsible political participation, but there is little reason to think that it could do so in the rapidly changing internationalized politics of today.

Let me begin my proposal with some remarks about what is required to make schooling genuinely democratic, to make it accord with the democratic postulate. Then I will outline a plan for political education that is appropriate both for the several different periods of a citizen's life and for meeting the demands of the Jonas imperative.

The constitutions of democratic states that do contain articles explicitly dealing with schooling show that their overriding objective is to preserve the state's unity while acknowledging and respecting the diversity to be found among its members. These articles, on the one hand, affirm the state's right to make some education both universal and compulsory as long as they also make it physically and financially available to everyone. They also affirm the state's right to supervise the curriculum and to determine and enforce the qualifications required of those who are to teach it. The state can and should possess and exercise these rights because it has the fundamental responsibility to preserve and promote its own democratic character. It can discharge this responsibility only if it has sufficiently competent citizens.

On the other hand, in at least some democratic constitutions, the articles dealing with education stand in opposition to a monolithic educational system organized and administered exclusively by the public authorities. They allow for, and sometimes encourage, the existence of private as well as public schools. They also recognize that parents have a right to exercise some control over both the curriculum and the management of preuniversity public schools. The Spanish constitution even grants pupils some say in these matters, though it is hard to see that it makes much sense to do so. In addition, these constitutions explicitly assign to parents the right to determine whether their children are to receive religious instruction in school or not.

When one considers the actual constitutionally supported educational practices of many democratic states, one finds, unsurprisingly, that they display a tension among competing pressures. There is pressure to provide an education that preserves the society's unity. And there is pressure to make available an education that respects and supports its diversity. There is, of course, ongoing debate about what would satisfy each of these pressures. I take it that the fundamental task of a democratic society's educational institutions is to preserve the tension between these two general pressures and thus to keep the competing pressures from either pulling the society apart or reducing it to homogeneity.

This tension is vividly expressed in the article on education in the German constitution. It is worth citing the article in full here not because I take it to be exemplary but because it so clearly both displays this tension and aims to preserve it.

Article 7 (Education) of the German constitution says:

(1) The entire educational system shall be under the supervision of the state.

(2) The persons entitled to bring up a child shall have the right to decide whether it shall receive religious instruction.

(3) Religious instruction shall form part of the ordinary curriculum in state and municipal schools, except in secular schools. Without prejudice to the state's right of supervision, religious instruction shall be given in accordance with the tenets of the religious communities. No teacher may be obliged against his will to give religious instruction.

(4) The right to establish private schools is guaranteed. Private schools, as a substitute for state or municipal schools, shall require the approval of the state and shall be subject to the laws

of the *Laender* [states]. Such approval must be given if private schools are not inferior to the state or municipal schools in their educational aims, their facilities and the professional training of their teaching staff, and if segregation of pupils according to the means of the parents is not promoted thereby. Approval must be withheld if the economic and legal position of the staff is not sufficiently assured.

(5) A private elementary school shall be permitted only if the educational authority finds that it serves a special pedagogic interest, or if, on the application of persons entitled to bring up children, it is to be established as an interdenominational or denominational or ideological school and a state or municipal elementary school or this type does not exist in the commune (*Gemeinde*).

(6) Preparatory schools (*Vorschulen*) shall remain abolished.[4]

Clearly, this article has been formulated against a particular historical background. It is designed to promote the political unity of a people who have strikingly different conceptions of the sort of education their children should receive. On the one hand, the article provides for a pluralistic system of schools. In so doing it in effect shows respect for the bodiliness of the citizens. It respects the fact that some of them have deep commitments to particular locales, religious groups, or ideologies but others of them have no such ties. At least some of those who have ties of these sorts will not unreasonably seek to reproduce them in their children. Those without such ties will probably either be indifferent or, more likely, opposed to efforts by schools to inculcate them in their children. This article attempts to respect both positions, giving no preference to either of them.

Even though this article shows respect for the citizens' bodiliness, it does not, however, neglect their thoughtliness. It calls on them to exercise it by refusing to let the society's educational activity be divided by wealth and poverty. It calls on all citizens to reproduce their democratic society by educational means that emphasize the historical and cultural heritage that unites them rather than the present financial conditions that separate them.

The article also gives weight to the thoughtliness of citizens by demanding that all of the children have teachers who have demonstrated their competence and facilities that meet reasonable standards. It enforces this demand by placing all schooling under state supervision. Having the constitutional right to ensure the quality of all schooling gives the state a capital resource for promoting citizen competence.

In general, the article on education in the German constitution is compatible with the core of Gutmann's theory of democratic education. Both of them recognize that neither states nor parents nor professional educators have either exclusive or unqualifiedly preeminent authority to determine the education that children are to receive. All three of these agents have important roles to play. For children to receive excellent education, the three agents must all cooperate and respect one another's reasonable concerns.

The goal of education implicit in this article, furthermore, fits neatly with the explicit educational goal that Gutmann endorses. For both of them, education's fundamental goal is to prepare the pupils to commit themselves to the collective task of reproducing the democratic society in which they live. In Gutmann's words:

> As citizens, we aspire to a set of educational practices and authorities of which the following can be said: these are the practices and authorities to which we, acting collectively as a society, have consciously agreed. It follows that a society that supports conscious social reproduction must educate all educable children to be capable of participating in collectively shaping their society.[5]

This ideal, Gutmann says, calls for the adoption of two principles, the principle of nonrepression and the principle of nondiscrimination. The principle of nonrepression forbids either the state or any group within it to use education to interfere with rational deliberation about any conception of the good life that has been or can be proposed, regardless of whether the state or any group within it finds this conception acceptable. The principle of nondiscrimination demands that every pupil receive adequate education to take part as a citizen in determining the society's future structure.[6]

This goal and these principles show that an appropriate democratic education neither can nor should be one that is wholly neutral concerning which sorts of lives are good lives to lead. Such an education neither can nor should be neutral concerning the value of democratic ways of living as opposed to nondemocratic ones. Even the most liberal states "will try, quite understandably, to teach children to appreciate the basic (but disputed) values and the dominant (but controversial) cultural prejudices that hold their society together."[7]

Gutmann, however, draws stronger conclusions from this goal and these principles than those that appear to be required by constitutional provisions concerning education like those contained in the German constitution. For her, not only must democratic education as a whole adopt this goal and these principles but so must each of its parts, namely, primary schooling, postprimary schooling, and adult education.

Consider her discussion of private religious primary schools. She denies that parents have a natural right to exclusive control of the education that their children receive in primary schools. Parents must share this control with the democratic polity. She grants that democratic states do not have to prohibit private schools. But they should do so if the private schools in fact either harm the public schools or insist on teaching moral or religious doctrines that are in conflict with the democratic purposes of primary education. These purposes

> include teaching children a common set of democratic values that are compatible with a diverse set of religious beliefs. A better alternative to prohibiting private schools would be to devise a system of primary schooling that accommodates private religious schools on the condition that they, like public schools, teach the common set of democratic values.[8]

In Gutmann's view, Catholic primary schools in the United States, as they presently function, are examples of schools that are democratically permissible. Their permissibility, though, hinges on empirical considerations. They in fact do not harm public schools, nor do they in fact fail to teach "the common set of democratic values."

Gutmann consequently concludes that, at least for the present in the United States, there are solid grounds for endorsing a mixed system of public and private schools. This system should try to achieve a delicate balance,

> permitting parents who are intensely dissatisfied with public schools to send their children to private school, but also trying to develop in all children—regardless of the religious commitments of their parents—a common democratic character. The balance is difficult because it constrains the moral doctrines that private schools may legitimately teach their students (the doctrines must be consistent with developing democratic character) at the same time as it limits the constraints that democratic states may place on private schools (the constraints must be necessary to developing democratic character).[9]

In this mixed system, there are limits to the permissible dissent from public schools. The limits are set by the curricular and noncurricular educational standards essential to democracy. These standards include teaching religious tolerance.[10]

There are, however, serious problems with Gutmann's position, problems that on the face of it, at least, are not necessarily generated by the provisions of the article on education in the German constitution. Consider just one of her basic contentions. For Gutmann, the education that public primary schools provide if they are functioning properly sets the standards against which private primary schooling, religious or otherwise, ought to be assessed. Only insofar as private schools sufficiently measure up to those standards are they permissible in a democratic state. These standards are not limited to those that deal with cognitive skills such as reading, writing, and mathematics. They also cover teaching religious tolerance. Private religious primary schools would thus be responsible for developing "democratic character" and "teaching their students a common democratic morality."[11]

One can make at least three objections to Gutmann's contention. First, it is far from obvious that one needs a democratic character that amounts to a complete way of life to participate well in reproducing a democratic society. As I indicated in my criticism of Rawls in chapter 2, one need not have ideal theoretic reasons for supporting democracy to engage sincerely and effectively in its reproduction. It would be enough for citizens to do so if they regarded democracy as now and for the foreseeable future the best available political modus vivendi. But even if Gutmann were right, however, that a democratic character is required, it still would not follow that one ought to begin its inculcation in the earliest years of a child's schooling.

Second, Gutmann's position appears to presuppose that the content of democratic character and democratic morality are now definitively fixed. If either of them is to undergo change, then apparently the change should result only from sources already internal to democracy. They should result only from the unfolding of its logic. Such a position, though, is tantamount to the denial of the historical character of democracy. Democracy has had no canonical form, nor is one to be expected. Rather, one should expect, and hope, that its form will be one that fits snugly with circumstances in which it must operate.

Third, and probably most concretely, it is highly likely that many people who establish private religious primary schools do so not primarily to express dissent from public schooling. Rather, they do so to provide a primary education that is pervaded by their religious convictions. Consider two lessons that are likely to be taught in primary religious schools established by Catholics, Orthodox Jews, and members of Islam as part of their central message. Each of them would teach (a) that the child who is a member of the religion in question is especially blessed in comparison with nonmembers and (b) that the member who abandons his or her religion is either an apostate and sins grievously or is seriously misguided. These are not messages that are designed to form democratic character. For the secular liberal democrat, giving up one's religion is always a permissible choice, one that deserves respect and no reproach. For the committed believers, the apostate deserves a communal rebuke and the misguided needs help to return to his or her religious belief and practice. To participate in reproducing democratic society, one need not interfere with schooling that teaches these messages. To take part in this work, one would need only to appreciate that democracy is worth reproducing because it has a particular, distinctive merit. Its merit is that it is the political system that now and for the foreseeable future best ensures that one can teach these religious messages to children without interference from political authorities.

Gutmann, then, is right to stress the importance of appropriate schooling for the successful reproduction of democratic society. But the standards she would set for what is to count as appropriate are excessively restrictive. They call for more uniformity than is necessary for social reproduction, and they take too little notice of differences between early primary education and later education.

My proposal for citizen education recognizes that Gutmann is right to emphasize the importance of schooling to democratic life. But schooling for children is no longer sufficient, if it ever was, to develop in citizens the democratic competence they need to take part well in political activity over the span of their whole lifetimes. To provide ways for citizens to gain this lifelong competence, democratic states ought to offer educational complements to schooling. It is not, however, necessary or even desirable to insist that every part of either schooling or its complements directly promote anything like a propositionally articulated "common democratic morality." My proposal provides for both schooling and its appropriate complementation. Furthermore, because it respects the democratic postulate, it is suitable for preparing citizens to discharge their democratic responsibilities. Because it is formulated in the light of the Jonas imperative, it responds to the distinctive exigencies of our times.

As I admitted above, no educational proposal can guarantee that, if implemented, it would yield thoroughly competent democratic political practice. No such proposal can guarantee that it would eliminate thoughtlessness or malice, nor can any proposal guarantee that those who would implement it cannot distort it into something antidemocratic. Like everything political, my proposal is unavoidably risky. The risk is worth taking because present democratic educational practice shows no sufficient evidence that it can effectively prepare people to deal well with today's political demands.

My proposal takes three points for granted. First, every citizen has an interminable right, in principle, to have access to opportunities to become competent to take part in all facets of political life. Even if a citizen has failed in the past to make use of these opportunities, he or she remains entitled to have access to them. Economic or other practical limitations might make it infeasible to give everyone interminable opportunities to become competent. But they are entitled, by reason of the democratic postulate, to have every feasible opportunity to do so. For example, if it makes sense to require some determinate level of functional literacy to participate in some parts of politics—for example, serving on a grand jury dealing with civil matters—then every citizen should have every feasible right to gain it. These opportunities should be available to everyone who can reasonably expect to be able to profit from them.

Second, democratic competence is a complex affair. One can be competent to participate sensibly in some political matters, for example, voting, but not others, for example, holding some political offices. It can also happen that, given the rapid changes in modern life, a person who has become competent in some matters has to work to maintain it on pain of losing it.

There are thus some political matters for which one's ordinary experience of life, perhaps supplemented by a rudimentary education early in life, is enough to equip a person for a lifetime of competent participation. Many local matters such as electing sheriffs or setting school tax rates are of this sort. But there are other matters for which this ordinary experience is not enough. It is, of course, hard to know exactly where to draw the line between these two sorts of matters. But one can say with confidence that all matters that have substantial international or ecological consequences are of this latter sort. It also makes sense to hold that, today, to resolve doubts about how to classify a particular case, one should use the principle of probabiliorism. That is, a state should permit citizens to participate in deliberations and decisions only about matters concerning which it is clearly more probable that they are competent than that they are not. The Jonas imperative demands this cautiousness. But the democratic postulate demands the exclusion from participation of as few citizens as is feasible. To satisfy both demands, a state must provide the opportunities for ongoing education that will give as many citizens as is feasible the opportunity to acquire the competence needed to take some part in all of their state's political activities.

Third, even though democratic citizens have a general obligation to take part competently in their society's political life, their participation is of value precisely to the extent that it is not coerced. The only legal penalty that those who fail to attain any particular level of democratic competence should suffer is, therefore, exclusion from participation in the corresponding political activities. Generally speaking, citizens who neglect or deliberately choose not to become competent to deal with as much of their society's politics as they reasonably can are failing to make the contribution to democratic practice that they are capable of. They are not pulling their weight and at least some of them are therefore blameworthy. But others may be excused for making such a choice. They may, for example, find that the very process of gaining democratic competence runs counter to their religious or moral convictions. Their choice, regardless of their own intentions, may in fact serve to help others understand more fully just how inclusive a democratic polity ought to be. For example, the refusal of the Amish in the United States to become democratically competent should not subject them to legal penalty. Nor for that matter should the lazy person's political indolence. Nothing about the Jonas imperative would demand that any of these incompetents suffer legal punishment. But nothing about the democratic postulate demands that people be allowed to participate in political activity for which they are incompetent. Indeed, the Jonas imperative requires that in some matters they be forbidden to participate.

With these three points in mind, consider now the role of primary education in preparing citizens to participate in politics. For present purposes, I take primary education to include all schooling that a child receives prior to specialized technical or vocational training or to college or university level education. I thus use the term "primary education" to refer to both elementary and high school in the United States and their rough counterparts in other democratic states. I distinguish further between early primary education, roughly for normal children up to thirteen or fourteen years of age, and late primary education, the last two to four years of schooling prior to advanced training or higher education.

Robert Fullinweider has articulated a sensible view about what primary education in a democracy can and should provide its pupils. He says:

> Moral learning for any child is learning by doing, under the supervision and correction of adults through imitation and practice with other children. Moral learning means becoming adept at the *forms* of perception, judgment, and criticism the moral practices of the community make available. What children will learn to do and be will reflect what the community's adults do and are; so different communities, if they are dissimilar, will turn out dissimilar children.[12]

Moral learning for children therefore amounts to their initiation into their community's moral and political practices. They learn through the example and tutoring they receive from their parents, their peers, and the contacts they have, for example, through television, with their wider society, and, of course, they learn from their school's curriculum and practices.

A good school provides its students with a context for learning that is free from intimidation and abuse. It adopts and fairly enforces a set of rules that teach, even if not in formal classes, the elementary moral concepts of fair play, individual dignity, and communal solidarity. By submitting to this discipline, pupils learn to see themselves as members of a community, to respect just authority, and to moderate their tendencies to selfishness.[13]

The sensible professional educator always keeps in mind that the school provides only part of what a child needs for good moral education, but it does play, for most children, a near indispensable part. It helps the child to learn the community's expectations concerning its members' conduct, it extends and enriches the range and complexity of the child's actual and vicarious experience and prompts him or her to reflect on and assess it, and it helps the child to find ways to explore and come to terms with his or her own talents and limitations.[14] In the final analysis, Fullinweider concludes,

> the school has only one thing it really needs to accomplish and that is to prepare young people to keep on learning the rest of their lives. . . . If students have learned, in a setting of mutual respect, the pleasures of discourse and the powers of imagination, they have gotten as good an education as we can give them.[15]

Using Fullinweider's view as a framework, I propose that, on the one hand, early primary education should reflect as well as it can the positive values of its pupils' parents, assuming of course that these values are neither criminal nor in violation of the requirement that all persons are entitled to equal respect. In practice, my proposal would lead to the acceptance of any primary schooling that would satisfy the provisions of Article 7 of the German constitution or other legal systems that were similarly permissive of all schools, public or private, that satisfy constitutionally authorized standards.

On the other hand, all primary schools should emphasize those disciplines that are crucial parts of a child's functional literacy for today's world. These are the disciplines that teach both spoken and written proficiency in the language in which the state's laws are articulated and its political discourse is most widely conducted. This functional literacy also requires the capacity to use mathematics and to understand the elementary formal notions that one needs to draw conclusions from evidence or to assess critically the conclusions that others draw. To whatever extent is feasible, furthermore, these pupils should have a chance to begin some second language. Though this latter subject matter is less urgent, it is a most appropriate way to help a child begin to understand foreigners. At any rate, imparting the functional literacy that this sort of curriculum provides and conveying something of its liberating potential is the fundamental instructional task for early primary education.

In the course of discharging this fundamental task, the teachers should use some literature that articulates, without making it a matter for controversy, historical or fictional narratives that express the society's moral and political traditions. These narratives help the pupils gain some initial sense of themselves, some initial sense of their moral and political identity. If judiciously selected, these narratives can also help the pupils to see new topics to explore and to find examples of ways of thinking and acting that are not to be found in their necessarily small world of daily experience. These examples can help them to take the first steps toward a critical reflection on their daily experience.

My proposal for early primary education is guided by two basic considerations. First, to participate well in politics of even the most local sort, a citizen must have functional literacy. Without functional literacy a citizen cannot make any nontrivial positive contribution to the discourse that shapes the political society and its projects, nor can such a citizen grasp and assess the contributions that his or her fellow citizens make. Second, early primary education should respect and offer responsible support for the bodily ties that children have both to their local communities and to their political society, ties established and promoted in large measure through living with their parents.[16] Through this respect and support the school provides a vital complement to the efforts of responsible parents. Together they give the child the wherewithal to make sense of his or her own experience and to begin to make those identifications with the political society that lie at the root of good citizenship and sound patriotism.

I admit, of course, that there are ignorant, thoughtless, and wicked parents. Schooling obviously should not support their values. But to the extent that it is reasonable to assume that parents are decent and sensible, schools should seek to work in tandem with them to initiate their children into the ethos of the community and society.

As I have argued above, the political ethos of every society is always in need of nontrivial reform. But young children are generally incapable of engaging in a fruitful critique of their local community's basic practices and values, nor are they well equipped to cope fruitfully with the strains of a sharp contest between school and parent over which examples and models for conduct are to be presented to them. Parents will rightly resist having their young children set at sea emotionally as well as intellectually by a forced and premature encounter with the limits to the evidence that underpins their values, limits from which no practical set of values is free. It is precisely to avoid wherever feasible such forced and premature encounters that I endorse the German constitution's expansive provisions that allow for a system of diverse private schools, as well as for public schools. The emphasis that I place on bodiliness in early primary education by no means precludes all attention to a thoughtliness that aims to expand the young child's horizons. Today, no sensible school curriculum can confine itself exclusively to local matters, nor can it ignore the fact that the political society has a diverse population and probably many schools do so as well. Even in early primary education children should be taught by both word and example to respect and appreciate this diversity. The schools should also encourage their pupils' parents to show this same respect. But the schools should do so by emphasizing as best they can the features of the community's values that are consonant with such respect and appreciation.

When children progress from early primary education to later primary education, their curriculum should be markedly different. The last two to four years of primary schooling should offer a curriculum that has three new components. At this age, students are capable of starting to relate their local experience and learning to a larger context.

These new components seek to utilize their newly developed capacity. They are all addressed to the students' thoughtliness. They call on students to counterbalance the attachments they have to their locales with recognition of and an appreciation for the unfamiliar with which they can now begin to gain some familiarity.

One new component of this curriculum should be civics. Civics should include the study not only of the state's actual constitutional structure but also of some of the reasons why the particular structure features were selected, rather than some other alternative that was proposed. Civics should also include a study of the usual practices, for example, campaigning and lobbying, that shape the way that the government actually works. It should also draw attention to the ways that one's state is tied to other states and the reasons for these ties. That is, it should show how and why there are treaties and international organizations such as the United Nations, the European Community, and the Organization of American States. The point of this curricular component is to introduce the students to their society's political life, giving them some taste of the debate that is always ingredient in all genuine democratic politics.

Second, the curriculum should include the study of the society's history. This study should help the child grasp both the society's uniqueness and the most substantial historical ties that it has to other societies. It should pay particular attention to the period of the state's founding or its adoption of democracy. Students should come to understand the ideals and aspirations that animated the inaugural period's principal political actors. This study should not, however, concentrate exclusively on political history. It should include the society's cultural history as well, taking care to draw attention to the diversity and variety of the contributions that particular groups of citizens have made to it. It should also acknowledge the social wrongs that the society has suffered from. Knowledge of this history provides the students with the historical background they will need to take part sensibly and effectively in political deliberations.

This study should also make clear that there are other societies that are democratic and good, though notably different from one's own. The point of this instruction is both to undercut tendencies to chauvinism and to give students an alternative with which to compare and assess their own society. Probably the most effective way to accomplish these objectives is to present students with a rather detailed picture of one other democratic society that has been historically important to their society. Optimally, this second society would be the one whose principal language the students were also studying. Instruction about these other democracies should also make clear that however superior democracy is to other forms of political life, every actual democratic state has nontrivial flaws and hence is open to reasonable criticism. Correlatively, not every nondemocratic state deserves unqualified censure.

Through these first two additions to the curriculum for later primary education, the schools help the students begin to develop a political identity that is reflective and critical. The aim of these studies is to help the students attain a political identity strong enough to commit them to their society's preservation in hard times as well as easy ones without falling into ignorant or thoughtless jingoism.

The third new feature of the later primary school curriculum should be an explicit introduction to the complexities, dangers, and opportunities that internationalization has brought into our lives. This introduction would aim to show students how vulnerable they and their society are to economic, cultural, political, and ecological conditions beyond their control. It would also aim to show how the practices and policies of their society affect people elsewhere. Through this instruction, pupils would learn both that their own well-being depends on foreigners and that they are likewise responsible for foreigners' well-being.

These three additions to later primary education complement advanced instruction in reading, writing, mathematics, and a foreign language. During these years of instruction, political competence becomes an explicit educational objective, but it does not do so at the expense of technical competence. Indeed, if properly taught, the subjects that deal with political competence will require the students to apply and expand their technical competence. For example, achieving even a rudimentary grasp of the many components of internationalization demands both rather sophisticated reading skills and the ability to comprehend and reflect on quantitative evidence.[17]

Because later primary education is the occasion for initiating students into a responsible political identity, the later primary curriculum of every school, private as well as public, should meet standards set by the state authorities. The standards should, of course, be sufficiently flexible that cultural, linguistic, or religious differences among groups of citizens can find reasonable expression. The standards should, nonetheless, be strong enough that every pupil is taught a curriculum that provides reasons for and encourages identification with the political society as a whole. To fulfill their purpose, the standards will have to undergo periodic revision lest they lose their relevance to the students' lives.

For example, Welsh and Scottish schools might well have parts of their later primary curricula that are different from their English counterparts, but all the curricula should share the same goal of preparing their students to commit themselves to British citizenship. No state should recognize the curriculum of a school that promotes the state's own dissolution. Where secession is a current societal issue, the curriculum may inform students about it. But it is not to advocate it. Further, it would not be surprising if some students or their parents objected on grounds of conscience to parts of the curriculum. This objection should be respected and the students excused. If the objection is to a part of the curriculum that the state authorities judge to be crucial for democratic competence, though, then those who receive the excuse should still be bound to gain by other means an appropriate competence.[18]

Of course, no matter how effective it is, primary education can be no more than an initial preparation for the democratic competence that one needs today to be a good citizen. To bring this preparation to fruition I propose that immediately after primary education, which should be compulsory, every pupil to whom the state has ascribed citizenship and who is not prohibitively handicapped should be required to perform a full year of national service. A program of universal national service can provide a uniquely favorable opportunity to promote political competence.

Fullinweider rightly says that political involvement is a function of what comes after schooling. It is a function of gaining concrete rather than merely abstract interests in the society's political affairs. "Adult projects, responsibilities, and institutions, not schools, make adults into good citizens, good neighbors, and good people."[19]

A program of national service is the best available bridge leading from primary education to adult life. Even if many youths return after their national service to advanced education or training, this service, if properly arranged, can serve well to link their advanced studies more to their future adult life than would be the case if such service did not intervene after their primary education.

The advantages of a program of universal national service for both the individual participants and the society as a whole are numerous and substantial. First, if properly organized, a program of national service can bring together participants from several locales. Through their ordinary daily associations with one another, they can have a chance to escape the provincialism that is typical of the milieu of most students in primary education, regardless of how urban or affluent or well traveled they or their parents may be. They can be helped to adjust to strikingly different living conditions from those to which they have been accustomed. And they can come to know young people whose experiences are quite unlike their own but who are nonetheless no less citizens than they are.

Second, a well-run program of national service can give its participants important, even if not prestigious, work to do. No modern society is free from the need for massive amounts of public work. There are always the elderly, the handicapped, and the ill who are in need of help, conservation projects always in need of manpower, public facilities always in need of maintenance and repair, and, at least in some democratic states, immigrants in need of help to become equipped to live in a new land. A program of national service can contribute substantially to filling these needs. In doing so, it could bring its participants to experience directly some pressing societal issues. And through their labor, the participants would find themselves investing in their society and thus able to see it as the society in whose well-being they have a lifelong stake.

Third, the new experiences that participants in national service have can provide a rich setting for explicit education for democratic competence. On the one hand, participants' concrete experience can show them the importance of technical competence for dealing with the needs they address. Not only must they possess or gain some skills but if they are to have success they must work in programs that have support and guidance from experts. Through this experience they can come to appreciate both the importance of expertise and its inescapable limits.

On the other hand, a sound program of national service should include provisions for education for politics. Part of the program should consist of instructional sessions for the participants themselves. This instructional component of national service should deal explicitly and thematically with the ethnic, religious, racial, and sexual differences among fellow citizens. Through this instruction these young people can learn that all of their fellow citizens deserve not merely toleration but respect.[20]

In addition, the instructional component of national service should aim to help participants to understand both the value and the limitations of politics. As I said in chapter 4, politics should be understood and respected as a relatively autonomous domain of action, one that is irreducible either to economics or to religion or ethics. Even at its best, however, politics has its limits, and its practitioners must always guard against the perversions that always threaten it.

Finally, the instructional program should make its participants vividly aware both of today's internationalism and of the dangerous factors that give the Jonas imperative its relevance. In this connection, it should provide an explanation of the principle of probabiliorism, and it should show which sorts of issues one should apply it to today.

These educational features of a good program of national service should serve as the inaugurating phase of a lifelong exercise in preserving and enhancing one's democratic competence. At its conclusion, the young citizens should have come to understand their citizenship as not only a status but also an office with obligations. They should see that to discharge these obligations, citizens need both political and technical competence. On the one hand, then, they should support institutions that provide opportunities for citizens to become knowledgeable about political issues and candidates subject to their vote. On the other hand, they themselves should take advantage of these opportunities.

For present purposes, I will pass over without much comment the institutions of higher education and advanced training to which many young citizens will no doubt return after their year of national service. This further schooling may very well increase not only their technical competence but also their political competence. For one thing, it will likely increase their sophistication about some forms of technical expertise and the limits thereof. For another, it will likely set some of them on the path to become themselves experts of one sort or another. But even though I would support some curricular proposals designed to improve democratic competence, my proposal does not envision any other tasks for higher education than those it has traditionally undertaken or provided an opportunity for. One can, nonetheless, reasonably expect that their year of national service would improve the students' capacity to profit from whatever opportunities to gain increased democratic competence that higher education and training make available.

If one agrees, though, that acquiring and maintaining democratic competence is a lifelong task, then one should support a number of institutional ways to promote citizens' doing so. Some of these ways should offer positive opportunities for citizens to enhance their competence. Others should consist of sanctions for having failed to attain or keep the minimally acceptable competence.

Let me indicate the sorts of institutional arrangements that I have in mind. Though I give relatively specific examples, any number of alternatives might well do a better job of promoting lifelong political and technical competence.

Consider first some ways to impart politically relevant instruction to adults other than through schooling. There are, of course, traditional institutions such as state-supported television, radio, and public libraries. There is also the information that trade and civic organizations disseminate either to their members or to the public at large. These sources of instruction are valuable and deserve continued support. But there is no good evidence to claim that they are sufficient for promoting adequate democratic competence in today's complex and fragile world. They need supplementation if they are to be sufficiently effective.

Here is one scheme for supplementing the traditional sources of instruction. On the one hand, it builds on the proposal that I made in chapter 6 for quasi-official academies, standing commissions, and councils of experts in some politically relevant scientific fields. On the other, it recognizes that citizens are likely to take advantage of this instruction only if they feel some pressure to do so.

The bodies of experts that I have proposed, one will recall, would be charged by law with preparing reports that citizens could understand concerning the scientific knowledge pertinent to major political issues facing the society. In fashioning their reports, these bodies of experts should cooperate with their counterparts in other states and in the relevant international organizations. The state should give these bodies nonpartisan staffs of civil servants to prepare and communicate their findings to the public. Through imaginative tax incentives and subsidies it should encourage educational and civic organizations and commercial news media to disseminate these bodies' findings and to discuss their political implications. Today, sufficient technology is available for most, if not all First World democracies to make this instruction readily available to large numbers of their citizens.[21]

Let me reiterate that these bodies are not to be authorized to make specific proposals. They are only to help indicate the parameters within which specific proposals should fall if they are to be well founded. Note further that these bodies are not charged to intervene directly in political debates or campaigns. They will, of course, select their topics because of the topics' practical relevance, but they need not and should not themselves explicitly endorse or oppose a particular candidate or proposal.[22]

The work of these bodies and their staffs would come to fruition in political campaigns. I propose that, on the one hand, nonpartisan boards, using previously published material and criteria, examine prospective candidates for national elective office and assess their qualifications according to previously established criteria. Boards should not be able to forbid a candidate from running for office. But they should be empowered to assess those who do run.[23] On the other hand, the state should require that news media that accept political advertising make these bodies' findings available to their audience. Candidates or advocates of proposals to be voted on would, of course, be free to make proposals that are incompatible with the expert findings. But doing so would subject them to criticism from their opponents and, one would hope, from the news media as well. The more hopeful outcome would be that candidates would make no proposals that were inconsistent with these findings unless they had reputable experts to support them.

Providing ongoing politically relevant instruction to citizens will be of no avail, however, unless citizens take the trouble to pay attention to it. Recent history in several democratic states does not encourage one to think that a large majority of citizens is eager to receive such instruction. If the Jonas imperative is relevant to today's political practice, though, and if probabiliorism is the appropriate principle to guide that practice, then it makes sense to permit only democratically competent citizens to participate in political decision making. Hence my adult political education scheme does not shy away from making demands on those citizens who want to participate actively in political processes. It demands evidence of their competence instead of simply presuming it.

To call for this evidence, one need not, and should not, suggest that any state change either the norms according to which it ascribes citizenship or most of the set of rights, privileges, and immunities consequent upon its ascriptions. But this call for evidence would make the right to vote contingent on some acquired competence rather than on mere ascription. To do so is consistent with treating citizenship not only as a status but also as an office. Ascription grants status. Evidence of appropriate competence entitles one to hold and exercise the office of citizenship.

To implement the demand for evidence, I propose that a citizen be required to obtain a license to vote. Gaining this license should take some effort and some accomplishment, And, because significant parts of the political agenda today change so repeatedly and so extensively, citizens who want to vote, as good citizens generally will, should periodically have to requalify for the license to vote on at least some issues.

A state should probably have two classes of licenses. Licenses of the first class would entitle its holders to vote in elections for local elected officials and in referenda that deal only with local matters having no substantial ecological implications. These licenses should be available to all citizens who have reached the legally specified age and can demonstrate that they possess a rudimentary functional literacy. Ordinarily, all those who have completed later primary education or its rough equivalent should be presumed to qualify for a license of this class. Once obtained, these licenses could be valid for life for votes of this sort.

Holders of licenses of the second class would be entitled to vote in all elections and referenda for which they were otherwise qualified. They would have to renew these licenses periodically, perhaps every seven to ten years. Citizens would first become eligible for these licenses when they have both reached the legally specified age and completed their year of national service or its instructional equivalent. Candidates for this license should have to pass a standardized test. Those who initially fail to pass it should be able to take it as many times as they wish until they succeed.

The periodic applications for renewing licenses of the second class should contain (a) evidence that the applicant has rather frequently exercised his or her right to vote and (b) evidence that he or she has taken advantage of some significant portion of the adult political instruction that the society provides. With the technology available today in economically advanced societies, it should be quite easy to gain access to this instruction. It should also be easy to devise and administer to those who want it a test that would elicit the relevant evidence.

The obviously relevant evidence is that which displays the applicant's sufficient acquaintance with the determinations made by the boards of experts that I described above. No greater acquaintance with these determinations should be required than is necessary to listen intelligently and with discrimination to arguments advanced by candidates for office or by those who publicly debate questions to be decided in referenda.

The most obvious objection against my proposal for licensing voters based on educational criteria is that it amounts to instituting a regime of experts who would resemble all too closely the ruling class in Plato's *Republic*. Such a regime would be incompatible with democracy.

This objection is not, however, well taken. First, it presumes that democracy is incompatible with any program promoting democratic competence that rewards those who attain it with rights that others do not receive. But current democratic practice includes renewable licensing for many activities that affect society's well-being. There are licenses to drive automobiles, practice law or medicine, teach school, and operate restaurants. There are or should be legal protections against either unreasonably high thresholds for granting licenses or irrelevant discriminations among applicants for them, and every citizen should be given ample help and opportunity to qualify for licenses. But there is nothing inherently undemocratic about licensing to vote only those citizens who have given evidence that they can do so thoughtfully. Today, given the complexity of the issues at stake, demanding licenses or their equivalents to vote is not merely permissible. Political prudence demands it.

There are two other respects in which this objection to my proposal is not well taken. First, in my proposal the function of experts, as I have said above, would not be to make specific political decisions. Their role would simply be to mark off the boundaries within which policies and practices must remain if they are to be responsible, if they are not to be fatuous or worse. It would be for political debate among all competent citizens to determine which of the available responsible actions to take. It would also be reasonable for political debate to contest the boundaries that the experts draw. But democratically competent citizens would demand that contestations of these boundaries be based on evidence. They would not allow them to be disregarded cavalierly. In my proposal, then, experts are not rulers—they remain advisors.

Finally, this objection to my proposal is not well taken because it would apparently canonize precedent. I admit that the history of democratic politics is one in which citizen competence has been presumed rather than established, but to canonize this history is to beg the question at hand. The question is: Given the radically new and dangerous context in which politics must today take place, what can be done to increase the likelihood that the decisions taken are the outcome of thoughtful deliberation? If one denies either that this context is as dangerous as I claim or that this danger is as proximate as I take it to be, then the case for retaining the precedent of presuming competence is strong. If, however, I am right to say that the dangers of today are unprecedented in their gravity, proximity, and complexity, then there are good reasons to doubt that precedents, no matter how well established, remain authoritative.[24]

Rather than being undemocratic, my proposal for licensing voters would work to preserve democratic states that adopt it. Let me recall crucial conditions that an implementation of my proposal ought to respect. First, there should be no legal penalties for those citizens who do not attain a license. Second, every citizen should always have an opportunity to earn the license. Finally, and more generally, my proposal is a political proposal. As I have argued throughout this work, everything political is always open to review, amendment, and supersession. So is my licensing proposal. Nonetheless, a fundamental task today is to block political practice that is either thoughtless or wicked. My proposal would not forestall wickedness. But it holds promise of blocking thoughtlessness. It is certainly possible that there are better proposals than mine for this purpose, but simply to insist on continuing to presume competence is not one of them.

Demanding democratic competence could contribute in important ways to harmonious political practice. It would do so by promoting mutual respect between voters on the one hand and candidates for office or protagonists in referenda proposals on the other. Voter competence would discourage demagogic and manipulative campaigning. It would instead prompt campaigners to make cases that serve actually to increase the electorate's competence.

Voter competence would also reduce the likelihood of misguided conflict between citizens and their officials. If out of ignorance or thoughtlessness an electorate confronts its officials with dangerous, even destructive demands, how should they respond? Should they risk either paternalistically overriding the demands or should they bow to them? Either choice comes at the expense of democratic ideals. The former does so by reducing the electorate's control over officials. The latter does so by threatening to bring damage and instability to the society. My proposal aims to avoid having the dilemma arise.

Even if my proposal concerning citizen competence is not contrary to the requirements of sound democratic practice, however, there are two other obvious questions that one can quite reasonably ask about it. First, if it were adopted and implemented, would my proposal be sufficient to meet the demands of the Jonas imperative and the democratic postulate? Second, is there any genuine possibility that a democratic society will, by democratic means, adopt and implement any proposal that calls for the sort of changes that mine does?

In response to the first question, I have to admit that I do not know.

Wickedness and thoughtlessness are always formidable threats, and under extreme pressure, it may be exceedingly difficult to satisfy both the Jonas imperative and the democratic postulate. But in politics there is no ironclad guarantee. Authors of alternative proposals would also have to admit that they could not be sure of their success. My proposal, though, precisely because it does demand democratic competence, holds promise.

In response to the second question, I admit that I have doubts about the likelihood of my proposal's adoption. Perhaps it can be adopted and implemented in stages. The first stage, I would think, would be to adopt and implement a universal national service program. It has precedents in industrialized democratic states, and it could readily be so planned that its young participants could come to see the need for the remainder of the reforms that my proposal would require. It is thus not baseless to hope that my proposal can win the support needed to adopt it. But the obvious obstacles, to say nothing of the unforeseeable ones that are likely to appear, allow for only a quite modest hope. That one can have only a modest hope for my proposal's practical utilization, though, does not count decisively against its worthiness of acceptance. To despair is no responsible alternative. Until a more promising response to today's dangers appears, my proposal deserves support.

In sum, then, my educational proposal would obviously bring about major revisions in democratic practice as we have known it. The motivation for accepting it is the unprecedented dangers to the human habitability of the earth. Its justification is the probabilioristic conclusion that making democratic competence an explicit, institutionally addressed issue, rather than continuing simply to presume competence, offers the best available protection against these dangers. Making these revisions, then, is the best available way to preserve both a politics worthy of being called democratic and the earth's habitability.

The education for democratic competence that I propose would have consequences that would extend well beyond those that affect a state's present citizens. It would significantly affect how a democratic state would deal with foreigners. In the next chapter I address some principal parts of this general issue. Doing so will furnish further evidence of the fruitfulness of the conception of complex citizenship that I articulated in chapter 6.

Chapter 8

Citizens and Foreigners

The conception of complex citizenship that I propose has substantial implications for the ways in which democratic states and their citizens should deal with foreigners. In this chapter I explore some of the most pertinent of these implications.

In very important respects, the internationalization of so many aspects of life today makes large numbers of foreigners potential or actual newcomers to one or another large industrialized democratic state. Even if there is no real prospect that all these people might physically migrate, they now have a discernible impact on the economic, cultural, and political well-being of every industrialized state. The well-being of the citizens of every democratic state is thus tied in important respects to other states and their peoples. Every state thus has good reason, and some obligation, to adopt policies and practices for dealing with other states and peoples that they can reasonably claim contribute to their common well-being. And individual people have reason to regard it as part of their duty as citizens to support policies and practices that are designed for this purpose.

Today, then, what is genuinely in any particular state's national interest is indissociable from the fundamental interests of the global community of people. Of course, it does not follow that the national interests of all states are in all respects identical. Finland, a small state, certainly has different national interests than do large states such as the United States or Mexico. Any state's genuine national interest, nonetheless, cannot be at the expense of that of another state. Rather it must be such that other states can acknowledge and accept it as compatible with their own.

If they are responsible, today's democratic states and their citizens will display by what they do and refrain from doing both a concern for

169

the political well-being of other states and a concern for the political well-being of individual foreigners. In expressing this two-fold concern, the democratic state, through its authorities, and its citizens should respect their own bodiliness and thoughtliness as well as that of the foreigners. They should not neglect the bodily task of nurturing their own distinctive political and cultural identities. But neither should they, through want of thoughtliness, disregard foreigners and try, vainly and destructively, to practice isolationism. An isolationist policy is vain because the forces of internationalism are too strong for it to be effective. It is destructive because it disregards opportunities to shape these forces so that their effect is beneficent.

For convenience of exposition, let me first point out some prominent ways in which citizens, through their political activity, express appropriate concern for the well-being of other states. Then, I will discuss some of the principal ways that they do so for the well-being of individual foreigners.

Citizens of democratic states today can and should give expression to concern for the well-being of other states principally by supporting their government's sensible foreign policies dealing with three overlapping sets of issues. First, they should support their own state's participation in international organizations such as the United Nations and the World Court. Second, they should participate thoughtfully in debates concerning which alliances and treaties their state enters into with other states. Third, they should participate critically in debates concerning their state's involvement in the internal affairs of other states.

Obviously, the more economic and military power a state has, the more substantial is the duty of its citizens to shape its use of them. But even small, weak states are not wholly impotent in these respects. Hence, their citizens too have some obligations in these matters.

No less obviously, most citizens will be unable to participate directly in the handling of these issues, but they can and should do so through their society's mediating institutions. At the very least, they can and should refuse to endorse or support policies whose fundamental justification is that they give their state's self-interest, construed as clear-cut competitive advantage, unqualified preeminence. Normally, however, the avenues for the expression of public opinion allow citizens nontrivial opportunities to make positive contributions to the formulation and implementation of their state's foreign policies. Good citizens take advantage of these opportunities, and they take steps to make themselves competent to do so well.

The general basis for these three responsibilities is the two-fold fact that (a) each person is part of a single human race and (b) that each state is part of a single global human habitat. The human race, as Kant says, shares in common the "right to the earth's surface." All human beings, he says, "are entitled to present themselves in the society of others by virtue of their right to communal possession of the earth's surface."[1] It follows, then, that, "no-one *originally* has any greater right than anyone else to occupy any particular portion of the earth."[2] All state borders are, at bottom, historically contingent and the artifacts of human devising.

Not only does no one have any unique original right to any particular territory, but neither can we trace back to an origin any factual distribution of property. That is, no actual state has, or has ever had, absolutely clear title to the territory it claims, and, therefore, it cannot provide an absolutely clear title to any individual citizen for the property he or she holds.

It does not, of course, follow that one person's or state's title to a piece of property is no better than any other person's or state's. But the significance of recognizing that no title is without color is by no means trivial. It affects the force of the normative claims that one can make on the basis of property rights and, in the case of states, the claim that can be made in the name of state sovereignty. All of these claims rest in some degree on convention. Thus, none of them can conclusively trump all other considerations.

That said, not all titles are equally colored nor are all colored titles arbitrary. Conventions, like any artifact, can have good reasons that support them, and, often, the longer they are in force, the stronger are the reasons that support them. But they and the reasons that support them remain always historical. Because circumstances are never fixed, conventions can lose their justification. They are always, in principle, contestable.

Let me now comment briefly on each of the three foreign policy responsibilities of today's democratic citizens. One of the principal reasons for organizations such as the United Nations and the World Court is that they provide a stable order for the relations among states. They provide support for the existing territorial divisions among states while at the same time furnishing mechanisms for adjudicating challenges to those divisions. They provide guidelines for appropriate intervention in a state's internal affairs. And the United Nations also sometimes supplies police enforcement for the provisions of this order.

Like all institutions, neither the United Nations nor the World Court is beyond reasonable criticism. The actions they take can be either ineffective or wrongheaded and their organizational structure can need reform. Indeed, their very usefulness can come to an end. Now and for the foreseeable future, however, the functions they perform are crucial to peace and justice. Either these institutions or more effective alternatives to them must continue to perform these functions.

Democratic good citizens will understand in general terms the need for these functions and will demand that their state participate constructively in the institutions that perform them. Obviously, the detailed workings of these institutions will have to be left to professionals. But if a state is to be thoroughly democratic, its authorities must encourage its citizens to exercise informed oversight over these institutions and their activities by providing them with appropriate information. Citizens, in turn, if they are responsible, will engage in this oversight. Given the conceptions of politics and citizenship that I have presented above, citizens cannot reasonably expect the activities of these institutions to be either risk-free or always conducive to their state's material prosperity. But neither can they reasonably neglect assessing both the efficacy of these institutions' activities and the bearing of their activities on their own state's economic, political, and cultural well-being.

A second area that demands the citizen's thoughtful participation is that of the debates concerning federation and secession. Today, debates of this sort are numerous, complicated, and fraught with dangers of several kinds. Consider first the matter of federation. As Allen Buchanan has pointed out, "we can imagine a continuum of degrees of closeness of political association, starting at one end with a unitary, centralized state, progressing to an extremely loose federalism, sometimes called *con*federation and ending in alliance (for example, a defense treaty) among sovereign states."[3] It is not part of my purpose here either to draw sharp distinctions among types of political association or to consider the relative merits of each type. Rather, I want to indicate some of the consequences of all types of political association among particular states.

Every association among states is meant to bring benefits to each member state. But every association that is not at least as inclusive as the United Nations divides the world into the included us and the excluded them. NATO includes some states and excludes others. So does the Organization of American States and the European Union. Sometimes the exclusions are trivial. Today, the existence of the Organization for African Unity that by its nature excludes, among others, Canada and South Korea, imposes no burden of consequence on either of those two countries. But it is far from obvious that the present European Union's exclusion of Romania and Latvia, for example, does not place them at a nontrivial disadvantage in several important respects.

Exclusions from some political associations can, of course, be defensible, even if the excluded were to seek inclusion. Unless there could be defensible exclusions, the only permissible associations would have to have no more stringent membership requirements than the United Nations does. Experience has shown, however, that some associations with restrictions on membership have been benign, not only for their own members but also for nonmember states. In some cases there are good reasons to fear that their ability to be benign or even to exist at all depends on the restrictions they place on membership. OPEC, for example, can bring and sometimes has brought stability to a commodity market of near universal interest. The Organization for African Unity holds some promise of improving its members without harming nonmembers.

Even if exclusions are sometimes defensible, though, today they all need defense. They need defense because, given the phenomenon of internationalization, the presumption must be that every exclusion places the excluded at some disadvantage. This presumption is, of course, rebuttable. Some exclusions can perhaps be shown to provide some compensatory advantage, for example, more focused material aid, for the excluded. Like everything political, though, every actual rebuttal is effective only for so long as the relevant circumstances remain unchanged. Hence, in these sorts of exclusions even successful rebuttals must be held open to subsequent contestation.[4]

Political associations also always cost the participants something. Today, so does refraining from joining associations. The costs can be economic, political, cultural, or all three. Political and economic costs, and, arguably, cultural costs as well, all affect a state's capacity to exercise its independence, its sovereignty.

Buchanan proposes that we understand sovereignty to consist in the power to make war and peace. Perhaps, he says, sovereignty also requires the power to control who enters and who exits the state's territory.[5] But even so spare a conception of sovereignty cannot pick out any particular power that a state can today exercise in radical independence from other states. The effective capacity to make war or to conclude peace today is inseparable from a state's economic strength, and its economy is in large measure indissociable from the global economy. So, even if a state can technically declare war independently of what other states do, it cannot sensibly do so without regard for its economy, an economy over which it is today vain to claim sovereignty. Analogous reasons hold for denying that a state can be radically independent in the way that it makes peace or in the way that it secures and polices its borders. However it performs any of these functions today, it does not thereby remain or become radically disentangled from other states.

One of the risks involved in joining some alliances and federations today is the incurring of what Stanley Hoffman and others have called a "democratic deficit."[6] That is, when a democratic state federates in some ways with others, it may be that efficiency will demand the creation of an administrative bureaucracy that is less answerable to the electorate than are their individual internal bureaucracies. The bureaucracy of the European Union is frequently cited as exemplifying this risk.

These bureaucratic elites or experts are not the same as the scientific experts, panels of whom I suggested in the last chapter should play a substantial role in the technical component of the ongoing education of a competent electorate. Rather, these are the civil servants or administrative technicians who manage the day by day functions of government. In any modern state, democratic or otherwise, they necessarily exercise considerable power. If a state is to preserve its democratic character, the electorate, through its representatives, must maintain supervisory control over the bureaucrats. In some modern confederations of states, it is quite difficult to maintain this control.

It does not, however, follow from anything I have said that political sovereignty has now become a bankrupt or obsolescent notion. Even if no state today is so radically independent that it can avoid with impunity all political associations with other states, states remain sufficiently independent that they can choose the associations in which they seek or maintain membership. These choices can be wise or foolish, but they are genuine choices. States thus retain a significant sovereignty and their authorities as well as their citizens have reason to concern themselves with its preservation by keeping democratic deficits in check.

The upshot of these remarks about federation and sovereignty is that all arguments concerning these matters are thoroughly contingent and historical. None of them has the form of a deduction from absolute, universally applicable principles. None of the claims made about these matters can be beyond contestation. The importance of this point is that it demands of all participants in concrete deliberations about any particular political association a clear-headed modesty. No one's case can ever be definitively established. It is always possible that an opponent can produce arguments against it that are worthy of acceptance.

The importance and complexity of present questions about which political associations a state should enter demand considerable technical expertise and political experience. They demand of those who would address them well a rather sophisticated, up-to-date competence. In a genuine democracy, every citizen who acquires this competence deserves a chance to be heard about these matters. Not only will they be affected by the outcome and hence are entitled to participate in these deliberations, but they also may contribute important questions and insights to them.

The issue of sovereignty is indissolubly tied to that of political identity. At the core of every well-established identity is a specific bodiliness made up of such elements as a common language, a common territory, and a relatively comprehensive set of political and cultural habits, ideals, and practices. As I have indicated above, these habits, ideals, and practices find expression in a set of narratives that claim to account for how this political identity came to be and how those who today share it come to do so. A shared bodiliness of this sort is constitutive of every viable state, at least of every state that seriously claims to give expression to its people's historical values and present aspirations. This bodiliness, as the capacity for forming political associations with states made up of people sharing a very different identity shows, is not an all-determining fate, but it is politically perilous to ignore it. Responsible citizens, in their deliberations about such associations, will take care to respect their society's distinctive bodiliness.

Attention to the reasonable claims of a society's political and cultural bodiliness leads to a consideration of the third foreign policy responsibility of today's democratic citizen. This third responsibility is more multifaceted than the other two and is often at least as demanding. In truth, this responsibility is not exclusively one concerning foreign policy. It is concerned with such matters as sovereignty, self-determination, and territorial integrity. Or, in other terms, it is concerned with such processes as secession, federation, and confederation. These are matters that may require addressing in the citizen's own state as well as elsewhere. Political and cultural bodiliness lie at the root of a number of today's political movements for which these issues are crucial.

Consider the numerous present day calls for political devolution. Buchanan's *Secession* provides good guidance concerning the sorts of questions that the thoughtful citizen should raise to determine which of these calls deserve support.

Political devolution can take several forms and have several different objectives. Groups of citizens who belong to a distinct cultural unit or who make up the population of a well-defined geographical district within a state may have or claim that they should have a constitutional right to declare items of national legislation null and void for the unit or territory in question. The Canadian constitution, Buchanan indicates, contains a provision that comes close to acknowledging such a right.[7] Or such a group may claim that, acting as a group, they have the right to block national legislative proposals. It claims a moral or a constitutional group veto right.[8] For example, the Swedish-speaking citizens of Finland, who in fact have the constitutional right to use Swedish for all legal matters, could be given group veto rights over all proposed amendments to the Finnish constitution that deal with the question of official languages.

Claims to a moral right to secede are more radical and usually more politically significant, for secession always consists in breaking an existing territorial state into two or more separate states. It thus always affects the people who remain in the former state as well as those who form the new state.

Buchanan's analysis of the most prominent moral reasons given for secession is quite helpful. Generally speaking, the strongest of these are (a) escaping discriminatory redistribution, (b) preserving a culture, and (c) rectifying past injustices.[9] For example, an American Indian tribe might claim that it has the right to secede from the United States or Canada because the state is unfairly taxing its territory or property or because it can preserve its cultural heritage only if it has its own independent state or because its territory had been forcibly and unjustly seized from it.

Though these and other reasons may count in favor of the moral propriety of particular secessionist movements, Buchanan and Thomas Christiano both rightly draw attention to the dangers and harms that today's welter of such movements threaten. Secessionist movements have already produced bloody civil wars, masses of impoverished refugees, and extensive violations of human rights. Hence, both Buchanan and Christiano rightly call for the concerted effort by international organizations such as the United Nations to seek ways to avoid secessions or at least to limit the damage they can produce. Christiano in fact argues that

> the integrity of any state that has a reasonably well functioning democratic order by which the main issues that confront its citizens are resolved ought to be protected by international law when there is a secession crisis within its borders. International law ought to state that secession under these circumstances is only legitimate when both parties agree (such as may happen in Quebec in the near future).[10]

Christiano does not, however, go far enough here. As recent history shows, it is quite likely that secession, no less than alliance and federations, will significantly affect third parties. Secessions are likely to lead to new associations with new economic, political, and military consequences for at least some states that were not parties to them. These consequences are often substantial and by no means always benign. The separation of Czechoslovakia into two states took place rather smoothly and peacefully, and the secessions of Estonia, Latvia, and Lithuania have been less smooth but not terribly bloody. But the secessions of Slovenia and Croatia have had catastrophic aftermaths for third parties in the former Yugoslavia as well as for Croatia itself. The numerous other bloody secessionist struggles in progress today give one no reason to think that what happened in Yugoslavia is atypical.[11]

In addition, Buchanan rightly points out that both secessionist conflicts and controversies over federalization regularly have at their heart disputes over the distribution of the property, resources, and opportunities for educational and cultural advantages. It is not rare that some secessionists and some federalists adopt their positions precisely to repudiate significant obligations to distribute these benefits fairly. That is, secessionist and federalist advocates not infrequently aim to perpetuate or perpetrate distributive injustices rather than to rectify already existing ones.[12]

Because of the dangers of secession, to which history testifies, good citizens will be cautious about the strains they place on their fellow citizens' commitment to their common citizenship and political identity. They will endorse and help implement practices that reduce the attractiveness of secession and promote the appreciation of the value of political union.

Similarly, good citizens will urge their government to be cautious about encouraging secessionist activity in other states, even if that activity were to bring their own states some material advantage. They will also urge their government to be slow to give diplomatic recognition to a state in the process of being formed through secession.

This conservatism about secession should not be dogmatic. But the presumption in all cases that do not involve secession from tyrannical rule should be in favor of stability, and there should be as impartial a forum as is possible to determine when the presumption in favor of the status quo ante has been successfully rebutted. As Christiano indicates, this is a task that an organization of states such as the United Nations should be charged to perform by interpreting and applying international law. Good citizens will demand that their governments acknowledge this international authority and obey it.

Activities promoting political alliances or federations can, of course, be just as disruptive of international peace and justice as activities promoting secessions often are. Recent disputes about the proposed admission of Eastern European states into the North Atlantic Treaty Organization illustrate this fact. It is probably true that, generally speaking, states in today's world exploring appropriate opportunities to form associations hold more promise for peace and justice than groups of people looking for opportunities to secede does. Nonetheless, an entity like the United Nations should have jurisdiction over cases of association, alliance, and federation. Without necessarily having the final word and the military power to enforce it, some such entity should have a recognized role in settling these issues. Its role should be to protect innocent third parties from harm and to give voice to the concern for global human well-being.

This general conservative concern to make present states genuinely habitable for all who live in them and hence to weaken or remove the reasons that people would have to secede is born out of reflection on and respect for the constitutive features of human existence. Advocates of secession, history shows, are frequently tempted to present a distorted account of them. On the one hand, they often exaggerate the importance of bodiliness. They claim that the bodily differences (language, ethnicity, religion, etc.) that distinguish them from those from whom they would secede are so great and so fixed that nothing positive can come from their continued political association. On the other hand, they often exaggerate a certain form of thoughtliness. They pretend that if they secede they will be at the dawn of a radically new day. By the power of imagination, they would wipe the slate of the past clean and be free to give pure expression to some supposed distinctive genius that vivifies their group.

If, however, my account of the constitutive features of human beings, the political agents, is correct, then there are no such radical distinctions among people. There are indeed important differences, both bodily and thoughtly ones, but none of them produce wholly unbridgeable gaps between people. We cannot wholly transcend our particular histories, nor is there good reason to want to do so, but these histories, no matter how different, always provide some points of support for finding common ground with others. The political task is always to look for this common ground and to explore it together.

Good citizens will therefore always support and, when appropriate, will help implement—in voting, business dealings, and so on—governmental policies that seek to convert enemies into opponents and opponents into collaborators. This objective, rooted in the appreciation of the common humanity that all people share, leads one to acknowledge and respect the bodily differences that distinguish us from one another. The good citizen will not pretend that these differences are either negligible or wholly abrogable. No one should be expected, for example, to willingly accept frequent and far-reaching changes in his or her habitual way of living. But neither will reflective citizens pretend that they are bound to be harmed if they make any accommodations to people with different heritages. The reflective person, the good citizen, knows that there are no fixed, definitive human enmities and acts accordingly. For example, a good citizen of the United States who is of Irish ancestry will not attempt to frustrate his or her government's efforts to help the Irish factions find a way to coexist in peace. Neither will the good Irish citizen.

Note that such a reflective person does not have to foreswear all resort to force or military might to protect either his or her state or the defensible associations to which it belongs. But any resort to force will be governed by norms that either have won widespread international acceptance or that one could propose for acceptance with a reasonable hope of success. An example of such a norm is the Geneva Conventions concerning the proper conduct of war. One crucial value of such a norm to regulate war is that it notifies enemies that they are still recognized as full fledged members of the human family and therefore are always welcome to return to peaceful coexistence. A second value of such a norm is that it gives at least oblique recognition to the fact that mere *raison d'Etat* is insufficient to warrant resorting to war.

Let me turn now to a consideration of the principal obligations that democratic citizens have for the well-being of individual foreigners. The guidelines that I propose for democratic governments to follow and for their people to support in dealing with matters of political association and dissociation among states have rough analogues for the appropriate handling of questions of the migration of individual people. Both immigration and emigration have nontrivial impacts on the well-being of a state. Today and for the foreseeable future, the issues they pose will be no less important than those posed by political association. Indeed, these two sets of issues are indissociable. The making or unmaking of associations is likely to prompt migrations, and migrations are likely to prompt associations and dissociations.

The pressures today that lead large numbers of people to seek to migrate are multiple and strong.[13] Some of these people seek only temporary relocation. Others seek a new permanent residence. Some seek a new citizenship. Among these migrants, some are political refugees with rights inscribed in international law, others, legally classified as economic migrants, do not enjoy these legal rights.[14] But even without legal rights, migrants raise important normative questions for citizens of democratic states.

Consider the size of the migrant population. In Europe, the number of illegal immigrants is in the millions and is increasing. So too is the number in North America. As a consequence, a number of states, including the United States, France, Germany, and the Netherlands, have either tightened restrictions on immigrants or propose to do so.

Roughly speaking, there have been three distinct sorts of proposals that have been advanced for how a democratic state should respond to this large influx of immigrants from poor states. First, some argue that immigrants strengthen a democratic state both economically and culturally. Furthermore, humanitarian concerns should lead to a willing acceptance of people in distress. Hence, a democratic state and its citizens should be as receptive as they can be to immigrant newcomers.

Second, some argue that whatever benefits immigrants once brought to European and North American states, today they are placing an inordinate burden on these states' resources. They are displacing citizens from jobs, overwhelming educational and medical facilities, and threatening the cultural heritages of these states. A state's immigration policy should, therefore, reflect the needs of those who already inhabit it, rather than those of immigrants.[15]

The third sort of proposal stands as something of a third way between the first two. Its proponents warn that failure to give proper attention to the ways in which immigrants are admitted and incorporated into a democratic state seriously endangers it. No responsible state or citizen thereof can ignore the task of preserving its political identity. This identity depends on shared ideals and a common dedication to the state's political structure and practices. Ordinarily, it also depends on the citizens' possession of a common language in which to conduct political affairs. They therefore argue that a state's immigration policies should be designed to ensure that newcomers assimilate into its political culture.[16]

Officials of the Catholic Church in twenty European states, meeting in Munich from September 29 to October 1, 1994 under the auspices of the Vatican Council for Migrants and Travelers adopted a statement that embodies features of both the first and third proposals. They emphasize the importance of the humanitarian considerations that animate the first sort of proposal, but they also recognize that states cannot reasonably permit unrestricted immigration.

These officials, calling the church a "fraternity without frontiers," demanded that states stop making immigrants, legal or otherwise, scapegoats for their domestic hardships and asked them to ease their restrictions on immigrants from poor states. The main cause of widespread migration, these churchmen said, is the huge economic imbalance among states. To reduce migration and the problems it brings, they called for large-scale reforms in the political and economic aid to poor states. Though these officials acknowledged that these reforms would not halt migrations in the short term, they argued that they hold promise for doing so in the long term. The success of these reforms would give inhabitants of these poor states solid incentives to remain in their homelands. In sum, these officials argued that "a balance must be found between people's freedom of movement and the right of countries to control immigration flows based on domestic situations."[17]

The proposal that I offer for dealing with the present problems that immigration poses for democratic states reaches a conclusion much like that of these Catholic officials. But my reasons, though not incompatible with theirs, are political rather than religious. They have as their backing the conceptions of (a) the human person, (b) the domain of politics, and (c) complex citizenship that I have articulated above.

My proposal has three parts. First, I argue that every well-ordered, sufficiently prosperous state has some obligation to help all desperately needy people wherever they are. But I recognize that no state can accept everyone who might want to immigrate to it.[18] Second, democratic states have a perpetual need for immigrants. They must therefore make institutional provisions for offering citizenship to at least some of them. Third, democratic states can and should establish requirements that immigrants who want to be citizens must satisfy. But there are some relatively clear-cut limits to what they can justly require.

Taken together, the three parts of my proposal yield a set of norms against which a democratic state's naturalization policies and practices should be tested. This set of norms by itself is insufficient to determine concrete policies. Each state will have to complement it with further considerations if it is to fashion policies and practices appropriate to its particular circumstances. But justice demands that these complementary considerations not negate my proposal's requirements.

Consider first the state's obligation to help all desperately needy people. Political refugees have the right, according to international law, to asylum. A state is obligated either to accept them or to help them reach another safe haven. States also have, however, some obligation to help foreigners in dire economic or medical distress. Sometimes and for some people the best help is to permit immigration. This obligation rests on several bases. For one, no state has such absolutely clear title to its own territory that it can rightly, under all circumstances, exclude all foreigners. For another, given the internationalization of today's economy, no society's prosperity is wholly independent of its dealings with foreigners. In fact, history shows that many presently prosperous societies have gained at least some of their wealth at the expense of other societies. Most, if not all, northern hemisphere well-established democratic societies have profited at the expense of the Third World. These societies have some obligation, when such profit results in destitution for others, to redistribute their wealth. Sometimes the most effective way to do so is to accept some impoverished immigrants.

No state, of course, can reasonably allow unrestricted immigration. There are territorial constraints, limits to available natural resources such as water, and limits to institutional resources such as schooling. Failure to heed these limits would jeopardize the society's durability.

On the other hand, migration to a prosperous democracy, even from an impoverished nondemocratic society, is never an unqualified boon for everyone who can do so. There is always loss for one who has to leave his or her natal society and land. Much of the pressure to emigrate is either unfortunate, because it springs from natural causes such as drought, or unjust, if it springs from willful oppression.

Immigration and naturalization very often have the character of a remedy for ills and not merely a promise of extra opportunities.

There are thus good reasons for prosperous democratic states to admit that an important way for them to discharge their obligations to desperately poor foreigners is to reduce the pressure to emigrate. They should give foreign aid not just to keep foreigners at bay but to preserve the habitability of foreign lands for their natal populations. Through this aid they not only alleviate the material needs of these impoverished people, they also help them to maintain their cultural and political identity, something that suffers severe strain should they have to migrate.

Not only do prosperous democratic states have an obligation to help desperately needy foreigners either by allowing immigration or redistributing wealth through foreign aid. All democratic states, whether particularly prosperous or not, also have an irremovable need for some immigrants. This need is, if anything, made more evident by the internationalization of political and cultural life. Because they have this need, these states have an obligation to make provisions for offering citizenship to at least some of their immigrants.

Historically, modern democracies developed as ways to achieve harmonious political unity among diverse groups of people. But we have learned that diversity is not at bottom a problem to be solved but rather is a positive good. Cultural and political homogeneity poses substantial problems for democracy. It tends to produce a conformism that is both narrow-minded and dysfunctional in an internationalized world.[19]

Hannah Arendt's reflections on speech and action, the central constituents of all genuine politics, help one to discern the grounds for holding that diversity in a political society is, or can be, of great positive worth. She has convincingly argued that speech and action, taken together, constitute necessary conditions for people to gain objectivity in their views not only about the material and cultural world they inhabit but also about one another and, indeed, about themselves. People achieve objectivity only through sharing with others their perspectives on what they encounter. "Only where things can be seen by many in a variety of aspects without changing their identity, so that those who are gathered around them know they see sameness in utter diversity, can worldly reality truly and reliably appear."[20]

A fundamental way for us to come to know ourselves is through the stories we tell, stories that include not only what we ourselves say and do but also the responses that others make to us.[21] Among these stories in a democracy are those that embody a multiplicity of perspectives about its political life and identity. These stories also embody views about the material conditions, for example, available economic resources, in which its members live out their personal and political lives. It follows, then, that only by not merely attending to the multiplicity of perspectives already at play in our state but also by seeking to make this multiplicity more inclusive do we obtain as much objectivity as we can about public matters and the material conditions in which they are situated.

Some important consequences for immigration policy can be drawn from this line of reflection. Citizens of a democratic state should want their political stories to be as objective as possible. However proud they are of these stories, they should never mistake them for fully finished stories, stories that need no modification or complement in order to deserve allegiance. Immigrants can make distinctive modifications and introduce complements that no natal citizens can.

No immigrant arrives empty-handed. Each brings to the host society a perspective and voice informed by a distinctive heritage. If, as Arendt holds, objectivity is the outcome of multiple perspectives on a thing or topic, then the distinctiveness of the perspectives that immigrants bring can provide indispensable aid to a host that wants to comprehend as well as it can both itself and the international context in which it is situated. The new perspectives and insights they bring can help the host society avoid a stultifying complacency about its political identity. Such a complacency, history shows, can all too easily turn into xenophobia. By welcoming the new voices that immigrants bring to their political discourse, natal citizens, citizens by birth, can overcome the ignorance that breeds prejudice and invidious discriminations.

It is true that foreign visitors and commentators can offer helpful perspectives on a society, but their offerings are no substitute for what immigrants can bring. However valuable the insights of visitors and foreign commentators, they are generally episodic and noncomprehensive. Immigrants, by contrast, are long-term residents who invest something of themselves in the host society. The new voices that they bring can be sustained and thoroughgoing in what they say, and, because they have a rather direct stake in the outcome of their contributions, they can claim a firmer title to be given a sympathetic hearing.

Because immigrants can contribute so importantly to a society's understanding of itself and its world, they have a claim to be offered naturalization. Only if they are naturalized can immigrants come to participate fully in the society's political life. There may well be circumstances in which a democratic state accepts more immigrants than it is prepared to offer citizenship to. But because citizenship in a democracy is so important a good, the ideal should be that every legal immigrant, on satisfying reasonable conditions, will be offered full citizenship.

Even if one grants, however, that a democratic state either is obligated to accept immigrants, to some of whom it ought to offer citizenship, or needs immigrants and so ought to offer it to some who allow it to satisfy that need or both, the question remains: Which and how many foreigners should it accept as immigrants? Since these are matters for perpetually revisable policies, one can do no more in a philosophical investigation than sketch out some relevant guidelines that answers to this question should observe as well as possible. Here I offer just two of them, one positive and one negative.

First and positively, a democratic society's need for diversity will be best addressed if, all other things being equal, it gives some priority to immigrants from lands that have strikingly different cultures. One can with good reason hold that immigrants from Third World areas will bring substantially more diverse perspectives to a northern hemisphere democracy than would immigrants from a less dissimilar society such as Croatia or Romania.

It is not inconceivable, of course, that members of some cultures are so different from any northern hemisphere democracy that they could not successfully adjust to it. If that is so and if they are destitute, then foreign aid is clearly better for them than immigration. With increasing internationalization, though, the distance between cultures is shrinking.

Part of the shock of dislocation for people from the Third World can and should be reduced by admitting enough of them that they can preserve some of their traditional practices and continue to find ways to give expression to their traditional beliefs and customs. Helping these people cope with the unavoidable shocks of relocation is part of being a respectful host.

The second guideline that I would propose for determining which and how many immigrants to admit is negative. Prospective host states should adopt immigration policies that work against "brain drain." Brain drain decreases the political and economic habitability of states that suffer it and hence increases the pressure to emigrate. It deprives a state of the technical and professional expertise its members need to engage in well-considered, independent political action. In the absence of this independence it is difficult, if not practically impossible, for them to achieve a defensible full-fledged political identity.

Justice therefore demands that prospective host states avoid promoting or even acquiescing in the flight of intellectual talent from states that are in dire need of such talent to ward off destitution. I grant that one should not apply this guideline simplistically. Immigration policies should be flexible enough to consider reasonably the specific features of each individual's case. But it is hard to see that Canada's new immigration policy, if it has been accurately reported, is just. Apparently, it calls for restricting immigration primarily to those who already have skills that will be of benefit to the Canadian economy.[22] Such a policy clearly countenances brain drain and minimizes, if it does not flatly deny, Canada's obligations to the world's destitute people.

In sum, then, the first two parts of my proposal lead to the conclusion that justice requires that the immigration and naturalization practices and policies of democratic states reflect all the implications of human plurality and diversity. Their policies and practices should both be consonant with a durable political identity and make available the infusion of fresh and diverse voices that every democratic state regularly needs to enhance the richness of its identity. Justice also requires that a state, in pursuit of these objectives, refrain from destabilizing or impoverishing other states by being the recipient of any substantial brain drain.

Michael Walzer has argued for a somewhat different view of the normative issues involved in immigration and naturalization than I have presented. He holds that what he calls the principle of political justice demands that

> the processes of self-determination through which a democratic state shapes its internal life must be open, and equally open, to all those men and women who live within its territory, work in the local economy, and are subject to local law.[23]

It follows, he says, that all immigrants who meet these three conditions have a right to naturalization "subject only to certain constraints of time and qualification, never to the ultimate constraint of closure."[24] Unless they are willing to forego the economic advantages of immigrant labor to their state, democratic citizens, Walzer concludes, must be ready to enlarge the ranks of those enjoying citizenship in their state to include all such immigrants.

Walzer's position, in my view, makes too much hinge on the immigrant's working in the local economy. By so doing, he fails to take note of the folly of citizens who would opt to close their state's borders to immigrants. Such a choice would be self-enervating not, primarily, because it would deprive them of the immigrant's labor but, rather, because it would deprive them of the immigrant's perspective and voice. They need the immigrant for their own self-comprehension. That need is unconditional and permanent.

Further, Walzer fails to recognize that, in the current internationalized world in which we live, a democratic state might have good reasons to accept more immigrants than it plans to naturalize. It might allow multinational corporations to operate in its territory with staffs selected according to their own criteria. These staffs might be made up largely of immigrants. It would not seem to follow that, even though these people "work in the local economy," they thereby gain a right to naturalization. Or, in an emergency, a state might accept refugees who have to stay for an extended period of time. There is no good reason for claiming that the state will incur an obligation to offer naturalization to all of them who happen to find work during this time in the local economy.

These two nontrivial differences notwithstanding, I concur with Walzer's concern that immigrants not be exploited. To accept immigrants either to satisfy the need for their perspectives and voices or to profit from their labor and at the same time to refuse to make provisions for naturalizing at least some of them violates the political justice that is constitutive of democracy.

Even granted, however, that a proper part of the activity of democratic states is making naturalization available to some immigrants, what defensible requirements can it impose on those who ask for it? The third part of my proposal is a response to this question. I claim that the democratic host state has not only the right but even the duty to make some demands on the immigrant before granting him or her naturalization. Principal among these demands are (a) that the immigrant learn the language or languages in which the host state conducts its public affairs and (b) that he or she not only learn but also agree to the fundamental norms and practices that constitute its distinctive political ethos. But, even though the host state can and should make some demands, there are substantial limitations on the sorts of demands it can justly make.

Two sets of considerations underpin these two demands. First, the cases of naturalization to which these demands are most relevant are those in which the candidates for naturalization migrate from some land that does not have democratic structures to a state that does. In such cases one can assume that the outcome of the migration is an improvement in the migrants' overall condition. That is, whatever losses they sustain by leaving their homeland, losses of familiarity, status, shared heritage, and so on, are more than compensated for by what they gain by moving to the new state. Hence, it is not unfair to impose some obligations on the recipients of these benefits.

If the populace of every land enjoyed genuinely democratic citizenship, or if there were no political refugees, then one major justification for emigration would disappear. There are good and often compelling economic, educational, cultural, or other reasons both for people from democratic states to want to migrate and for democratic states to receive them. But, given that two people have equally strong reasons of these sorts to migrate, if one already is a citizen of a democratic state and the other is not, then the latter has a stronger claim in justice to admission to a democratic state than the former does.

In a world in which democracy is not universal, states that are democratic not only provide a boon to their own citizens. They also provide a witness to people everywhere about what good politics can be. It is therefore a crucial part of the task of every democratic state to preserve its democratic character. Its authorities owe this preservation not only to its own members but also to people who do not enjoy democracy. In performing this task, the democratic state preserves a great good for its own citizens and their descendants. It also preserves its capacity to naturalize at least some foreigners into this good. It follows, then, that in its immigration and naturalization policies, a democratic state is obligated to ensure that the outcome of these policies does not undercut its democratic character.

Because there is no canonical form of democracy, these policies may permissibly introduce significant alteration into the state's way of being democratic. But they should not threaten the three fundaments of any democracy, namely, (a) that all qualified citizens should be equally entitled to participate in the state's political processes, (b) that all citizens be given every opportunity to become qualified for this participation, and (c) that citizens have rights that protect them against abusive or arbitrary exercises of governmental power.

The second set of considerations that underpins the demands that I would impose on immigrants who seek naturalization springs from the recognition that each human being is constituted as who and what he or she is by what Herbert Spiegelberg has called unavoidable "accidents of birth.''[25] Relevant accidents of birth in this context are those by virtue of which a person receives an allotment of material or cultural benefits or burdens that does not depend on what he or she has earned. The allotment depends solely on the characteristics that one has received by birth. Examples of accidents of birth that have historically been prominent in the allocation of benefits and burdens are parentage, sex, physical abilities and handicaps, and intellectual talent under some description.

Obviously, no candidate for naturalization can do anything about accidents of birth such as these. But there are other, less fixed accidents of birth that have a great political significance. Prominent among these are (a) the language one has been born and reared into, (b) the set of sympathies and antipathies, the set of prejudices, that one's rearing induces during his or her early years, and (c) the inevitable experiential and conceptual lacunae that one's formative influences leave one suffering from. Even if people cannot wholly eradicate these latter sorts of accidents of birth, they can compensate for them. Both the bearers of these accidents and others can contribute to this compensation.

One of the principal objectives of responsible democratic political practice is to help people alleviate the accidents of birth that are burdensome to them. Though it does not pretend that it can wholly eradicate their burdens, this practice works to keep them from having their own political opportunities unnecessarily constricted by them. In particular, responsible democratic practice aims to free its citizens, natal or naturalized, from complete domination by the sympathies and the antipathies that prevail in the particular locale and set of family ties in which they grow up. The genius of democracy has consisted in large part in recognizing that however important territorial and familial considerations may be for citizenship, they are insufficient for the fullness of political life of which people are capable. Fully democratic states therefore establish practices and institutions that link people of different locales and families. These states promote common political ties and activities that aim to prevail over the particularizing pressures exerted by ties to family and locale. They promote this unity both by the education they provide and by the laws they enact and enforce.

Immigrants, of course, unlike natal citizens, have no initial territorial title to citizenship, and many have no familial title either. The historical record gives us good reason to believe that the best way for the candidate for naturalization to compensate for these lacks is to learn the host society's official language. Except perhaps religion, there is nothing stronger than a common language to bind people of different locales and families to one another. Since the point of naturalization is to incorporate immigrant newcomers into a shared political life, they should learn the prevalent language. Religion, for generally recognized reasons, is a wholly inappropriate common bond for democratic states to promote. A democratic state should therefore require for naturalization a knowledge of its official language.[26] Without knowing the language one could participate in political life only through an intermediary who does know the language. These intermediaries will regularly function as filters, even if they try not to do so. Hence, they are obstacles to fully democratic practice. To preclude their need for such filters, candidates for naturalization should be obliged to learn the official language.

Linguistic bonds alone, though, are insufficient counterweights against the pull of family and locale. They are insufficient to ensure democratic political life. As history shows, the three-fold ties of family, locale, and language have seemed to underpin antidemocratic nationalisms. A linguistic assimilation of candidates for naturalization is therefore not enough to prepare them to contribute to, rather than to undercut, the host state's democratic political life. The state ought also to insist that they learn its democratic norms and practices, its democratic ethos, and give evidence that they are prepared to live accordingly. This ethos includes such things as an insistence on civilian rule over the military, a distinction between the police and the military, and free elections at fixed intervals. Constitutions give expression to principal parts of this ethos. But it is the ethos that informs, or should inform, the interpretation of the constitution.[27]

Like the linguistic requirement, this strictly political requirement need not prevent the naturalized persons from bringing important critical perspectives to bear on the state. As I have said, democracy has no canonical form. If a state is to be democratic, it must be open to alterations in the particular form of its democratic character. But it would be wrong for it to disregard its obligation to remain genuinely democratic. Accordingly, it is obligated to demand of its citizens, whether natal or naturalized, both an understanding of and an allegiance to its democratic character.

There may be good practical reasons for exempting some people from the requirement to learn the language and to subscribe to the ethos if they are to be granted full citizenship. Some of these reasons may be rooted in history. Finland, for example, has made special constitutional provisions for its Swedish-speaking citizens. And when

Italy was reunified, the Italian language that was made the official language was a language unknown to a number of the citizens of the new state. Thus some citizens, particularly elderly ones, could have full citizenship only if they were exempted from having to learn the official language.

Nonetheless, the state must take care lest these exceptions become so numerous and entrenched that they threaten to make a mockery of the democratic ideal of having all citizens be well equipped to participate in all facets of their state's political life. In a world in which antidemocratic politics is far from rare, citizens of a democratic state are obligated to preserve it as a potential political refuge. And those who seek refuge in it are obligated in justice to keep it available for future candidates for naturalization.

In sum, then, democratic states always need the cultural enrichment that immigrants can bring. In return for what they bring, at least some of these immigrants deserve to be offered naturalization, but neither the host state nor the immigrants can defensibly ignore the dangers of brain drain. Indeed, they are obligated to try to forestall it.

To preserve their democratic character, states ought to require those it would naturalize to meet two tests. First, they should either already know or commit themselves promptly to learning the official language of the host state, and second, they should learn and give allegiance to the political norms and practices constitutive of their host's political life. These principles and tests serve as the proper standards for assessing the justice of a democratic state's naturalization policies and practices.

Taken together, these reflections on how a democratic state should deal with questions concerning immigration and naturalization provide the framework for responsible dealings with foreigners. They do not yield specific prescriptions. Rather, they clarify the proper bases for these dealings and caution against pitfalls that threaten to vitiate them. This modest outcome is not a weakness. It is, in fact, a strength. It ensures against an ahistorical dogmatism and encourages instead the sort of historically instructed, cautious experimentalism that is so appropriate for the era of risky internationalism in which we live.

The proposals that I offer here and in chapter 7 flow from the recognition of the expanded scope of political responsibility that today's democratic citizens should acknowledge as their own. Today's citizens bear responsibilities that reach well beyond the territorial borders of their own society. Some of these responsibilities are global. They also extend to future generations not only of their own citizens but also to those of the peoples of other lands. To discharge these responsibilities, they must be willing to learn both from their own past and that of others. They must also find ways to incorporate into their political activity the best available technical knowledge. Whatever merit there may once have been to the distinction between the good and just person and the good and just citizen, the circumstances of political life today have surely weakened it.

Conclusion

As I indicated in chapter 1, the case that I have made for adopting the conception of complex citizenship is a piece of deliberative rhetoric. It is meant to be action guiding. The particular proposals for action that I have offered are, I believe, reasonable, but my case is not primarily designed to defend the details of any of them. It does not stand or fall with them. Rather, my case is designed to show how one should understand citizenship and its responsibilities today. Such an understanding ought to lead one to adopt the distinctive way of deliberating about and deciding on courses of political action.

Today, I have argued, political deliberation and the decisions to which it leads ought never to ignore three factors. The recognition of these factors has been the driving force for my case. They are (a) the internationalization of political life, (b) the soundness of the Jonas imperative, as well as the danger that it is subject to serious violation, and (c) the democratic postulate.

The set of conditions that constitute internationalization is constantly changing, and the relative importance of its several elements is never stable, nor are the relationships among them. None of us, therefore, has a firm grasp of either just what internationalization amounts to at any given moment or the sorts of changes that it is almost sure to undergo. The Jonas imperative is, I take it, fundamental, but taken alone, it is insufficient to guide action. It can only tell us what outcome we must always try to forestall. Nonetheless, we dare not disregard it. History, furthermore, gives us strong reasons for embracing a politics that is genuinely democratic, but there is no canonical form of democracy. It is always to be made and remade. And there is no ironclad guarantee that any genuine version of democracy is

strong enough either to give the Jonas imperative the practical weight
it deserves or to cope with the complexity of internationalization.

My case attempts to spell out what these three factors demand of
those who want to be good citizens today. No exercise of deliberative
rhetoric, as my case is, can plausibly claim to yield a Cartesianesque
certitude. It cannot even reasonably claim to give a definitive treatment
of any of the topics it does address. But a good case can and should
provide firm grounds for accepting it rather than any of its competitors.
My argument for the conception of complex citizenship does this. Let
me summarize it.

Good political practice today, as in the past, depends on good
citizens. But the received conceptions of good politics and good
citizenship are no longer sufficient. The new and different conditions
of political life today demand a reworking of the normative dimensions
of citizenship. To be a good citizen today one must learn the importance of the three factors that underpin the case I have made. They
must learn how to deliberate appropriately about them.

Both the liberal and the communitarian traditions of democratic
political thought embody normative conceptions of citizenship. Whatever merit these conceptions have hitherto had, they are not sufficient
for responsible political participation today. Both of them rest on
flawed views of the human person, the political agent. Under the
pressure of internationalization and the pertinence of the Jonas imperative, the seriousness of these flaws has become more evident and important.

At bottom, both of these traditions fail to give proper weight to the
person's fundamental historical character. This failure weakens their
conception not only of the political agent but of the domain of politics
itself. To remedy these flaws I have spelled out a conception of the
person as one who is in principle no less thoughtly than bodily and one
whose distinctive way of being is displayed in action. Action displays
human existence as finite, historical, and intersubjective, as fundamentally interrogative.

Because human beings are constituted as they are, the domain of
politics is always possible but is never necessary. When it is actualized,
it is fragile and needs active preservation to continue to exist. It is
always in danger of having its autonomy undercut by those who would
subordinate it to either the domain of economics or that of ethics. A
crucial part of the citizen's task is to resist these subordinations and
thereby to protect politics' relative autonomy. Good citizens therefore
must understand both their own makeup and the distinctive character-

istics of the political domain. They must understand both their need for politics and its unavoidable limitations.

In the past, the citizen's sphere of action and responsibility has been bounded by his or her state's borders and population. Today, however, internationalization forces one who wants to be a good citizen to acknowledge a far larger and more complex sphere of responsibility. Though one's own state and fellow citizens retain a certain priority in the good citizen's concerns, this priority is neither absolute nor exclusive. The citizen's responsibility regularly extends to many other people and many other places. Sometimes it is global. Whatever gap may once have existed between what makes one a good citizen and what makes one a good person has thus been substantially narrowed, if not completely closed.

Good citizenship today requires not only that citizens possess both technical and political competence but that they also demand them of their fellow citizens. To achieve and preserve this two-fold competence is a life-long task. To perform it well citizens need and must demand the institutional support that makes the attainment of citizen competence a feasible objective for all of their mentally normal fellow citizens. They must also support the institutional limitations placed on the political participation of those who are not competent.

As always, citizens have an obligation to concern themselves with the preservation and enhancement of their political society and its institutions. One part of this obligation calls for them to contribute to the induction of their young into their political life. Nothing is more important to their induction than proper schooling, but schooling is no longer enough. Because maintaining citizen competence is a life-long task, the good citizen ought, by word and example, support institutions that provide extraschooling citizen education and encourage his or her fellow citizens to take advantage of it.

Today, however, good citizens cannot effectively contribute to their political society's stability and well-being unless they extend their concern to foreigners. They must support their state's participation in the United Nations and other organizations that promote the mutual welfare of their member states without seeking to harm other states. They must support their state's giving economic and technical assistance to people and nonrepressive governments in impoverished lands. And they must support sensible and generous immigration programs, giving some preference to the politically and economically needy and avoiding policies that lead to brain drain.

Support for any particular organization of states or any particular set of foreign aid or immigration policies, of course, should be thoughtful. Like everything political, no organization or set of policies is ever perfect. They are always open to and in some respects in need of reform, but responsible reform today cannot move in the direction of disregarding the needs and aspirations of people anywhere. Today, no form of isolationism can make political sense.

The conception of complex citizenship that I propose is both rich and supple enough to lead those who adopt it to respond well to today's political exigencies. It demands of them a modesty and a diligence in their political participation that fits them well to work with diverse people with diverse interests for preserving the habitability of the earth and fostering the cause of democratic politics throughout the world. It calls for them to eschew both a disregard of and a despair about the conditions of political life. It calls, instead, for them to embrace a life of political participation marked by courage and patience, marked, that is, by a hope in and for politics.

The two most obvious objections to my proposal are (a) that it makes such heavy demands on citizens that only a few could satisfy them and (b) that its insistence on citizen competence is antidemocratic. These objections are two sides of the same issue, namely: Can one make such heavy demands without disqualifying so many members of a political society that it does not deserve to be called a democracy?

Let me briefly outline a reply. First, the complexity and urgency of internationalization and the threat to the human habitability of the earth cannot simply be willed away. They must be addressed. If they can be successfully addressed at all, which is far from sure, they can be so addressed only by those who possess considerable technical competence. The basic task, then, is to find a democratic way between a modern political Scylla and Charybdis. On the one hand, one has to avoid allowing a citizenry, through ignorance or thoughtlessness, to block the technically competent from addressing these dangers. On the other, one has to avoid making citizens so politically impotent that they exercise no control whatever over experts.

I grant that few citizens, acting as individuals, could gain the expertise to exercise sensible oversight and political control over technical specialists. But through participating in Walzerian civic organizations that mediate between ordinary citizens and the experts they can do so. The task of democratic citizens today is to provide to all of their fellows the opportunity to learn both the importance of these organizations and their obligation to make use of the mediations that they provide. No individual, of course, will make use of every mediational service of every organization. But one can hope that collectively they will make use of enough of them that they will exercise the oversight necessary to preserve the democratic character of their society.

I also recognize that my conception of complex citizenship almost certainly could not gain wide acceptance quickly. If it is ever to do so, there would have to be a long, patient educational effort mounted on its behalf. To be successful, this effort would have to convince its audience of two main points. First, this conception does not require that its holders jettison all of their traditional values. It does not demand their homogenization. To the contrary, this conception acknowledges the positive worth of their bodiliness, with all the differences that bodiliness causes. Second, the educational effort must convince the audience of the seriousness and proximity of the threats to the habitability of the earth and the practical implications of these threats for stable democratic political societies. My best guess is that the most effective way to begin this educational effort within a well-established democratic society is to construct a suitable program for a mandatory year of national service. Probably the best way to proceed internationally is to link this educational effort to the work of international agencies for economic and educational aid.

An educational effort of this sort is most unlikely to succeed unless it has some teeth. Those who support it ought to have their support officially acknowledged and rewarded by receiving increased political voice. Those who resist this effort need not be positively punished unless they actively seek to subvert it. But they should be left unrewarded.

In the end, I must admit that the prospects for widespread acceptance of this conception of citizenship are anything but bright. But even if they were, one might still reasonably fear that this conception, rather than demanding too much of citizens, demands too little to be successful against the present dangers. It nonetheless holds substantially more promise than do conceptions of citizenship derived from standard versions of either liberalism or communitarianism of guiding its holders past the modern political Scylla and Charybdis. If there were another alternative conception that held even more promise than mine does, I would gladly yield to it.

Endnotes

Chapter 1

1. Will Kymlicka and Wayne Norman, "Return of the Citizen: A Survey of Recent Work on Citizenship Theory," *Ethics* 104, (1994):352. Hereafter cited as *RC*.

2. *RC,* 352.

3. *RC,* 353.

4. Aristotle, *Rhetoric*, 1355a4–18 and 1356b35–1357a7. For helpful commentary on this point, see George A. Kennedy, *Aristotle on Rhetoric* (Oxford: Oxford University Press, 1991), esp. p. 33, fn. 23, and p. 45, fn. 68.

5. See Bernard Crick, *In Defense of Politics* (Chicago and London: University of Chicago Press, 1972), 145–50.

6. Herbert Spiegelberg, " 'Accident of Birth': A Non-Utilitarian Motif in Mill's Philosophy," in his *Steppingstones toward an Ethics for Fellow Existers* (Dordrecht: Martinus Nijhoff, 1986), 123.

7. John Rawls, *Political Liberalism* (New York: Columbia University Press, 1993), 18.

8. Michael Walzer, "Citizenship," in T. Ball, J. Farr, and R. L. Hanson, eds., *Political Innovation and Conceptual Change* (Cambridge: Cambridge University Press, 1989), 216.

9. See in this connection Hannah Arendt, *The Human Condition* (Chicago and London: University of Chicago Press, 1958), 175–88. Hereafter cited as *HC*.

10. For a good description of prominent forms of democracy, see David Held, *Models of Democracy* (Stanford: Stanford University Press, 1987).

11. J. E. S. Fawcett, "Security Council Resolutions on Rhodesia," *British Yearbook of International Law* 41 (1965–66): 112. Even though one might question whether these criteria have been faithfully applied, they do remain in place.

12. On democracy's indeterminacy, see Claude Lefort, *Democracy and*

Political Theory, David Macey, tr. (Minneapolis: University of Minnesota Press, 1988), 12–20.

13. David Held "Democracy: From City-states to a Cosmopolitan Order?" in *Prospects for Democracy*, David Held, ed. (Stanford: Stanford University Press, 1993), 37–44. For reasons I will give below, I do not agree with Held's cosmopolitanism.

14. Though I write as a native-born citizen of the United States, the conception of citizenship that I will present is appropriate for any democracy possessing a modicum of stability.

15. Robert A. Dahl, *Democracy and Its Critics* (New Haven: Yale University Press, 1989), 302. Hereafter cited as *DIC*. For an unsettling but well documented discussion of this list of problems, see Paul Kennedy, *Preparing for the Twenty-first Century* (New York: Random House, 1993).

16. For a good account from another perspective of the need to rethink the concept of citizenship, see Lolle Nauta, "Changing Conceptions of Citizenship," *Praxis International* 12, no. 1 (April 1992): 20–33.

17. *HC*, 250.

18. Among the important recent books about nationalism are Joseph Rothschild, *Ethnopolitics: A Conceptual Framework* (New York: Columbia University Press, 1981), E. J. Hobsbawm, *Nations and Nationalism Since 1780* (Cambridge: Cambridge University Press, 1990), James Kellas, *The Politics of Nationalism and Ethnicity* (New York: St. Martin's Press, 1991), *National Identities,* Bernard Crick, ed. (Oxford: Blackwell Publishers, 1991), Liah Greenfield, *Nationalism: Five Roads to Modernity* (Cambridge: Harvard University Press, 1992), William Pfaff, *The Wrath of Nations* (New York: Simon and Schuster, 1993), and Walker Connor: *Ethnonationalism: The Quest for Understanding* (Princeton: Princeton University Press, 1994).

19. Robert Heilbroner, "The Worst is Yet to Come," a review of Paul Kennedy, *Preparing for the Twenty-first Century, New York Times Book Review*, February 14, 1993, 25. Even if Amartya Sen is right that population problems can be solved without recourse to repression, the other items that Heilbroner points to are enough to produce severe political difficulties for democracies. For Sen's argument, see his "Population: Delusion and Reality," *New York Review of Books,* 41, no. 15, (22 September 1994): 62–71.

20. Hans Jonas, *The Imperative of Responsibility* (Chicago and London: University of Chicago Press, 1984), ix. Hereafter cited as *IR*. This book deserves much more attention than it has received.

21. "World Scientists' Warning to Humanity," a statement sponsored by the Union of Concerned Scientists and signed by more than 1,670 scientists including 104 Nobel laureates. The statement was issued in April 1993. Hereafter cited as *WSWH*.

22. *WSWH*.

23. *IR*, 11.

24. See in this connection William L. McBride, *Social and Political Philosophy* (New York: Paragon House, 1994), 136–48.

25. See *DIC*, 316–17.
26. See Yael Tamir, *Liberal Nationalism* (Princeton: Princeton University Press, 1993), 13–34.

Chapter 2

1. Yael Tamir proposes another alternative that deserves notice. I deal with it in chapter 3. See her *Liberal Nationalism* (Princeton: Princeton University Press, 1993). Hereafter cited as *LN*.
2. Derek Heater's *Citizenship: The Civic Ideal in World History, Politics, and Education* (London: Longmans, 1990) hereafter cited as *CCJ* is a helpful guide to the history of thought about citizenship. It also spells out provocative claims about how one ought to construe citizenship today, claims that I do not accept. Let me also note that, though I do not explicitly discuss anarchy as an alternative to state citizenship, at least some of my arguments against world citizenship count against it as well.
3. Reinhold Niebuhr, *Moral Man and Immoral Society* (New York: Charles Scribner's Sons, 1949), 91. Hereafter cited as *MMIS*.
4. Niebuhr develops his own critique of patriotism or state citizenship primarily in terms of the universalizability and the wisdom objections. See *MMIS*, 93–112.
5. Hannah Arendt, "Karl Jaspers: Citizen of the World?" in her *Men in Dark Times* (New York: Harcourt, Brace and World, 1968), 81. Hereafter cited as *MDT*.
6. *MDT*, 82.
7. See Paul Kennedy, *Preparing for the Twenty-first Century* (New York: Random House, 1993), 336.
8. See Allen Buchanan, "Federalism, Secession, and the Morality of Inclusion," *Arizona Law Review* 37, no. 1 (1995): 53–64.
9. Among influential present-day versions of democratic liberalism are those of Bruce Ackerman, Ronald Dworkin, George Kateb, and John Rawls. For statements of their respective positions, see Bruce Ackerman, *Social Justice in the Liberal State* (New Haven: Yale University Press, 1980); Ronald Dworkin, *Taking Rights Seriously* (Cambridge: Harvard University Press, 1977) and *A Matter of Principle* (Cambridge: Harvard University Press, 1985); George Kateb, *The Inner Ocean: Individualism and Democratic Culture* (Ithaca: Cornell University Press, 1992); and John Rawls, *A Theory of Justice* (Cambridge: Belknap Press, 1971) and *Political Liberalism* (New York: Columbia University Press, 1993). Hereafter I cite Rawls's books as *TJ* and *PL* respectively.
10. Allen Buchanan, "Assessing the Communitarian Critique of Liberalism," *Ethics* 99 (1989): 854.
11. *LN*, 20–25.

12. See in this connection Rawls's way of distinguishing his claims from those of Dworkin, *PL*, 211.

13. *PL,* xxv.

14. See in this connection Ronald Dworkin, "Foundations of Liberal Equality," in *The Tanner Lectures on Human Value* XI (Salt Lake City: University of Utah Press, 1990), 9–10.

15. *PL,* 368–69.

16. One holds a doctrine reasonably, in Rawls's sense, if one recognizes his or her fallibility and accepts the consequence that others can hold a competing doctrine without being less reasonable. See *PL*, 48–49, fn. 1.

17. *PL,* 10–11 and 226–27.

18. *PL,* 12. Rawls admits that the idea of a closed society is odd. He adds here: "At some point a political conception of justice must address the just relations between peoples, or the law of peoples, as I shall say." He proposes to do so by "starting from justice as fairness as applied first to closed societies." Just what this proposal amounts to will become clear below.

19. *PL,* 18.

20. *PL,* 18–19. See also 81, 103, 108.

21. *PL,* 280.

22. *PL,* 291. This formulation of the two principles, Rawls makes clear, nontrivially modifies the version of them that he gave in *TJ.*

23. *PL,* 197.

24. *PL,* 220–22. Rawls emphasizes that "the public vs. the nonpublic distinction is not the distinction between public and private. This latter I ignore; there is no such thing as a private reason." *PL,* 220, fn. 7.

25. *PL,* 228.

26. *PL,* 224–26, 241, 247.

27. *PL,* 251.

28. *PL,* 250, fn. 39.

29. *PL,* 251. My emphasis.

30. *PL,* 39, 147, 159.

31. John Rawls, "The Law of Peoples," in Stephen Shute and Susan Hurley, eds., *On Human Rights: The Oxford Amnesty Lectures* (New York: Basic Books, 1993), 42. Hereafter cited as *LP.*

32. *LP,* 50.

33. *LP,* 43.

34. *LP,* 62–63.

35. *LP,* 68.

36. *LP,* 44.

37. *LP,* 52.

38. *LP,* 62.

39. *LP,* 50.

40. *LP,* 71.

41. *LP,* 72.

42. *LP*, 73–75.

43. *LP*, 73–74.

44. *LP*, 55.

45. It is worth noting that Thomas Pogge has criticized what he takes to be the weakness of Rawls's understanding of cosmopolitan justice. Pogge argues that the logic of Rawls's project leads to a stronger version of cosmopolitanism. For my purposes I need not deal with Pogge's claims. See Pogge's *Realizing Rawls* (Ithaca and London: Cornell University Press, 1988). Hereafter cited as *RR*.

46. See Charles Taylor, *Multiculturalism and "The Politics of Recognition"* (Princeton: Princeton University Press, 1992), 25. He says there that the term 'identity' "designates something like a person's understanding of who they are, of their fundamental defining characteristics as a human being." Hereafter cited as *MPR*.

47. For an example of a stronger version, see Alasdair MacIntyre, *Three Rival Versions of Moral Inquiry* (Notre Dame: University of Notre Dame Press, 1990).

48. Charles Taylor, "Cross-Purposes: The Liberal-Communitarian Debate," in Nancy L. Rosenbaum, ed., *Liberalism and the Moral Life* (Cambridge: Harvard University Press, 1989), 159. Hereafter cited as *CPLC*.

49. There are important liberal views that argue for a substantive and not merely a procedural justice. See, for example, Martha Nussbaum, "Aristotelian Social Democracy," in R. Bruce Douglass, Gerald M. Mara, and Henry S. Richardson, eds., *Liberalism and the Good*, (New York and London, 1990), 203–52. I discuss her views later in this work.

50. Taylor explores the differences between strong and weak evaluation in several texts. See, for example, his *Human Agency and Language* (Cambridge: Harvard University Press, 1985), esp. 16–26 and 66–75 (hereafter cited as *HAL*); his *Sources of the Self* (Cambridge: Harvard University Press, 1989), *passim* (hereafter cited as *SS*); and his *The Ethics of Authenticity* (Cambridge: Harvard University Press, 1991), esp. 13–41, hereafter cited as *EA*.

51. *HAL*, 75. My insertion.

52. *SS*, 34.

53. *EA*, 32–33.

54. *SS*, 36. See also Charles Taylor, "Atomism," in his *Philosophy and the Human Sciences* (Cambridge: Harvard University Press, 1985), esp. 209. Hereafter cited as *AT*.

55. *SS*, 51. See also *EA*, 109–21.

56. Charles Taylor, "Hegel: History and Politics," in Michael Sandel, ed., *Liberalism and Its Critics* (New York: New York University Press, 1984), 192. Hereafter cited as *HHP*.

57. *HHP*, 193.

58. *HHP*, 195.

59. *MPR*, 37–44.

60. *HHP,* 197.

61. Charles Taylor, "The Diversity of Goods," in his *Philosophy and the Human Science* (Cambridge: Harvard University Press, 1985), 245. Hereafter cited as *DG*.

62. *AT,* 197–200. See also *DG,* 246–57.

63. *CPLC,* 166. My insertion.

64. *CPLC,* 179. Taylor's "rule and be ruled" obviously refers to Aristotle, *Politics,* 1332b25–26 and 1261a3–1261b6.

65. *MPR,* 61.

66. Jurgen Habermas, "Three Normative Models for Democracy," *Constellations* 1, no. 1 (1994): 6. Hereafter cited as *TNMD*.

67. *TNMD,* 7.

68. See Jurgen Habermas, "Discourse Ethics: Notes on a Program of Philosophical Justification," in Seyla Benhabib and Fred Dallmayr, eds., *The Communicative Ethics Controversy* (Cambridge and London: MIT Press, 1990), esp. 100–101, hereafter cited as *DEN,* and Jurgen Habermas, *Justification and Application,* tr. Ciaran Cronin (Cambridge and London: MIT Press, 1993), 163, hereafter cited as *JA*.

69. *JA,* 163.

70. *JA,* 164–65 and *DEN,* 105–6.

71. Jurgen Habermas, "Further Reflections on the Public Sphere," in Craig Calhoun, ed., *Habermas and the Public Sphere* (Cambridge and London: MIT Press, 1992), 446. Hereafter cited as *FRPS*.

72. *FRPS,* 448. See also *TNMD,* 10.

73. *FRPS,* 449.

74. Jurgen Habermas, *The New Conservatism,* tr. Shierry Weber Nicholsen (Cambridge: MIT Press, 1989), 256. Hereafter cited as *NC*.

75. *NC,* 262.

76. *NC,* 240.

77. *NC,* 249–51. See also Jurgen Habermas, "Citizenship and National Identity: Some Reflections on Europe," *Praxis International* 12, no. 1 (April 1992): 1–19. Hereafter cited as *CNI*.

78. *CNI,* 18.

79. It is by no means clear that either Rawls or Habermas could accept secessionist claims to a Wilsonian right of autonomous self-determination. See in this connection Daniel Patrick Moynihan, *Pandemonium: Ethnicity in International Affairs* (Oxford: Oxford University Press, 1993). I return to this general topic in chapter 8.

80. Aristotle, *Rhetoric,* 1358a36–b24.

81. *MPR,* 58–59. My emphasis.

82. *MPR,* 40–41.

83. For a good survey of standard criticisms of communitarianism, see Daniel Bell, *Communitarianism and Its Critics* (Oxford and New York: Oxford University Press, 1993).

84. *CPLC,* 180, and esp. *SS,* 532, fn. 60.

85. *CPLC,* 163, 182, and 281, fn. 21.

86. See Michael Walzer, "Philosophy and Democracy," *Political Theory* 29, no. 3 (August 1981): 393–94. Hereafter cited as *PD.* For a similar but not identical arqument against ideal theory, see Hannah Arendt, "Philosophy and Politics," *Social Research* 57, no. 1 (Spring 1990): 75–103. Hereafter cited as *PP.*

87. *PD,* 395.

88. *PD,* 386. For another sort of criticism of Rawls on this matter, see Joseph Raz, *The Morality of Freedom* (Oxford: Clarendon Press, 1986), 117–33.

89. See in this connection *PD,* 394 and 399, fn. 28, as well as Habermas, "Reconciliation through the Public Use of Reason: Remarks on John Rawls's Political Liberalism," *Journal of Philosophy* 92, no. 3 (March 1995): esp. 125, 128.

90. Michael J. Perry, *Morality, Politics, and Law: A Bicentennial Essay* (New York: Oxford University Press, 1988), 72–73.

91. See in this connection Stanley Hoffmann's critique of Rawls's "Law of the Peoples" in his "Dreams of a Just World," *New York Review of Books* 42, no. 17 (2 November 1995): 52–56.

92. See Hannah Arendt, *The Human Condition* (Chicago and London: University of Chicago Press, 1958), 236–43.

93. *PL,* 147.

94. As sympathetic as he is to Rawls's position, Thomas Pogge has also called attention to its ahistoricality. See *RR,* 105.

95. Indeed, Walzer makes his case in *PD* explicitly against Habermas as well as Rawls.

96. See in this connection David Ingram, *Habermas and the Dialectic of Reason* (New Haven: Yale University Press, 1987), 40 and 202, fn. 36; John B. Thompson, *Critical Hermeneutics: A Study in the Thought of Paul Ricoeur and Jurgen Habermas* (Cambridge: Cambridge University Press, 1981), 209 ff; and Shawn Gallagher, "Language and Imperfect Consensus: Merleau-Ponty's Contribution to the Habermas-Gadamer Debate," in Thomas Busch and Shawn Gallagher, eds., *Merleau-Ponty, Hermeneutics, and Postmodernism* (Albany: State University of New York Press, 1992), 77–79.

97. See Thomas McCarthy, "Kantian Construction and Reconstructivism: Rawls and Habermas in Dialogue," *Ethics* 105 (October 1994): esp. 50–53 and 61–63. McCarthy too finds Habermas's position superior to Rawls's in this respect.

98. See in this connection Thomas McCarthy, "Practical Discourse: On the Relation of Morality to Politics," in Craig Calhoun, ed., *Habermas and the Public Sphere* (Cambridge: MIT Press, 1992), 66–69. Seyla Benhabib proposes a weaker objective for a communicative ethics. Instead of consensus, it aims at "reading and understanding." See her *Situating the Self* (New York: Routledge, 1992), 75 and 88, fn. 18.

99. See in this connection *LN,* 112. What Tamir says there about the "morality of community" that always demands "untidy compromises" holds, in my view, for all responsible politics. In the domain of jurisprudence, Anthony Kronmann argues for the superiority of the approach that tests general theories by actual cases to that which deals with actual cases in accordance with the tenets of theories. See his *The Last Lawyer* (Cambridge: Belknap Press, 1993), 158–59.

Analogically, I argue that concrete political practice is not to be judged exclusively from the standpoint of some ideal theory. For an especially vigorous and cogent critique of ideal political theories, see Hannah Arendt, *PP,* 73–103.

100. Albrecht Wellmer has argued that Habermas's position "would make justified moral judgement a total chimera." See his "Ethics and Dialoque" in his *The Persistence of Modernity*, tr. David Midgly (Cambridge: Polity Press, 1991), 154–55.

101. William D. Ruckelshaus, "Toward a Sustainable World," *Scientific American* 261, no. 3 (September 1989): 166–74. Hereafter cited as *TSW.*

102. *TSW,* 169.

103. *TSW,* 174.

104. Isaiah Berlin, quoted in *LN,* 13.

Chapter 3

1. See, for example, Michael Walzer, "The Communitarian Critique of Liberalism," *Political Theory* 18, no. 1 (1990): 6–23, and Allen Buchanan, *Secession* (Boulder: Westview Press, 1991), 5. Charles Taylor, though, as I noted in chapter 2, has held out hope that the impasse might be broken, though he has not yet spelled out how he thinks it can be done. See his "Cross-Purposes: The Liberal-Communitarian Debate," in Nancy L. Rosenbaum, ed., *Liberalism and the Moral Life* (Cambridge: Harvard University Press, 1989), 163, 182. Hereafter cited as *CPLC.* For one recent proposal about how to resolve this debate, see Lawrence C. Becker, "Community, Dominion, and Membership," *The Southern Journal of Philosophy* 30, no. 2 (1992): 17–43. Becker makes his case by constructing a utopian communitarianism, but this utopian construct is a straw man. It is radically ahistorical. If anything characterizes communitarianism, it is its insistence on the importance of taking the community's concrete history into account in the formation of its political practices. For a more promising approach to resolving this debate, an approach that is generally consonant with the proposal I present, see Thomas A. Spragens, Jr., *Reason and Democracy* (Durham: Duke University Press, 1990), esp. 146–75 and 239–59. Hereafter cited as *RD.*

2. *RD,* 131, and Seyla Benhabib, *Situating the Self* (New York: Routledge, 1992), 77.

3. *CPLC,* esp. 159–64.

4. Alexander Murray, *Reason and Society in the Middle Ages* (Oxford: Clarendon Press, 1985), 3.

5. Martin Heidegger, *Being and Time,* tr. John Macquarrie and Edward Robinson (New York and Evanston: Harper and Row, 1962), 32.

6. Maurice Merleau-Ponty, *The Visible and the Invisible,* tr. Alphonso Lingis (Evanston: Northwestern University Press, 1968), 101–4.

7. Merleau-Ponty rarely, if ever, cites Aristotle. The similarities between his conception of the human condition and Aristotle's are nonetheless striking. Perhaps Hegel is the link between them.

8. Mary P. Nichols, *Citizens and Statesmen: A Study of Aristotle's Politics* (Savage, Md.: Rowman and Littlefield, 1992), 54.

9. Aristotle, *Politics,* 1275a20–30, 1277b7–33, and 1325b7–9.

10. Hannah Arendt, *The Human Condition* (Chicago and London: University of Chicago Press, 1958), 207–12 and 220–36. Hereafter cited as *HC.*

11. Michael Ignatieff, *The Needs of Strangers* (New York: Penguin Books, 1984), 27, hereafter cited as *NS.* This book has influenced everything I say in this chapter about needs and desires.

12. *NS,* 57.

13. *NS,* 28. Martha Nussbaum's defense of what she calls Aristotelian essentialism also relies in part on an identification of needs common to everyone. See her "Human Functioning and Social Justice," *Political Theory* 20, no. 2 (1992): esp. 214–18.

14. *NS,* 29.

15. *NS,* 29.

16. *NS,* 35–36, 44–45.

17. Paul Ricoeur, *Oneself as Another,* tr. Kathleen Blamely (Chicago and London: University of Chicago Press, 1992), 53–55. Hereafter cited as *OAA.*

18. Charles Taylor, *Sources of the Self* (Cambridge: Harvard University Press, 1989), 4, 14, and *passim.*

19. *OAA,* 86, and 292–93.

20. *HC,* 190. Recall that, unlike Arendt, I treat making as a form of action. What she says in the passage that I cite I regard as applicable to at least some work as well. I find some support for resisting Arendt's dichotomy between work and interaction in Mary G. Dietz, " 'The Slow Boring of Hard Boards': Methodical Thinking and the Work of Politics," *American Political Science Review* 88, no. 4 (1994): 873–86.

21. Maurice Merleau-Ponty, *Humanism and Terror,* tr. John O'Neill (Boston: Beacon Press, 1969), 166–67. Hereafter cited as *HT.*

22. G. F. W. Hegel, *The Philosophy of Right,* tr. T. M. Knox (Oxford: Clarendon Press, 1942), *passim.*

23. John Stuart Mill, *Utilitarianism,* ed. George Sher (Indianapolis: Hackett 1979), 49–52.

24. *HC,* 236.

25. *HC*, 237.

26. *HC*, 241. Arendt also points out here that punishment is an alternative to forgiveness but not its opposite, for "both have in common that they attempt to put an end to something that without interference could go on endlessly."

27. *HC*, 237.

28. Both Arendt and Ricoeur stress the narrative character of human existence. See *HC*, 182–88, and *OAA, passim*.

29. *OAA*, 295.

30. *OAA*, 294–96.

31. Handicaps may block a person's capacity to act, even permanently, but even if they are self-inflicted, the person continues to deserve respect because he or she is still a fellow participant in our common humanity.

32. *OAA*, 288.

33. John Rawls, *Political Liberalism* (New York: Columbia University Press, 1993), esp. 54–58.

34. Plato, *Apology*, 2lb–22e.

35. Among communitarians, see, for example, Michael Sandel, *Liberalism and the Limits of Justice* (Cambridge: Cambridge University Press, 1982), esp. 172–74, and Charles Sherover, *Time, Freedom, and the Common Good* (Albany: State University of New York Press, 1989), 16–26. Among liberals, see, for example, Ronald Dworkin, "Foundations of Liberal Equality," in *The Tanner Lectures on Human Values* 11, (Salt Lake City: University of Utah Press, 1990), esp. 57–71.

36. Yael Tamir, *Liberal Nationalism* (Princeton: Princeton University Press, 1993), 13. Hereafter cited as *LN*.

37. *LN*, 30.

38. *LN*, 31.

39. *LN*, 37. My emphasis.

40. Maurice Merleau-Ponty, *Signs*, tr. Richard C. McCleary (Evanston: Northwestern University Press, 1964), 56–60.

41. Vincent Peillon, *La tradition de l'esprit: Itineraire de Maurice Merleau-Ponty* (Paris: Editions Grasset and Fasquelle, 1994), 108. Hereafter cited as *TE*.

42. *TE*, 109.

43. Paul Ricoeur, "Le temps raconté," *Révue de métaphysique et de morale* 89 (1984): 440. My insertion.

44. Alasdair MacIntyre, *After Virtue* (Notre Dame: Notre Dame University Press, 1981), 204.

45. *HC*, 247.

46. Bernard P. Dauenhauer, *The Politics of Hope* (London: Routledge and Kegan Paul, 1986), esp. 2–3 and 100–101.

Chapter 4

1. Steffen Schmitt, Mark Shelly II, and Barbara Bardes, *American Government and Politics Today* (New York: West, 1985), 13.

2. See in this connection Sheldon Wolin, *Politics and Vision* (Boston: Little Brown and Co., 1960), 1–68. Hereafter cited *as PV.*

3. John D. McDonald, *One More Sunday* (New York: Alfred A. Knopf, 1984), 105. This book is a piece of light fiction, but the comment I cite is not trivial.

4. Paul Ricoeur, *Oneself as Another,* tr. Kathleen Blamey (Chicago and London: University of Chicago Press, 1992), 257. Hereafter cited as *OAA.* As I will make clear, this remark by no means does full justice to Ricoeur's political thought. Here I use it only as a stepping stone.

5. For a good discussion of concord in Aristotle's thought, see Judith A. Swanson, *The Public and the Private in Aristotle's Political Philosophy* (Ithaca and London: Cornell University Press, 1992), esp. 140–42.

6. Lawrence Biskowski has reminded me of this constitutive political objective.

7. John Rawls, *Political Liberalism* (New York: Columbia University Press, 1993), 18.

8. See Paul Ricoeur, "Ethique et politique," *Esprit* 101 (May 1985): 3–4. Hereafter cited as *EP.* Ricoeur's contributions to contemporary political thought have received far less attention than they deserve. For one indication of his contributions, see my "Ricoeur's Contribution to Contemporary Political Thought," in David Klemm and William Schweiker, eds., *Meaning in Texts and Action* (Charlottesville: University Press of Virginia, 1993), 157–75.

9. Herbert Simon, *Administrative Behavior* (New York: Macmillan, 1947), esp. 38–39 and 101–10. For Wolin's critique of Simon's views, see *PV,* 380–414.

10. See in this connection Anthony Kronmann, *The Lost Lawyer* (Cambridge: Belknap Press, 1993), esp. 225–40.

11. *EP,* 5.

12. For another argument in support of the distinction between the political and the economic realms, see Robert A. Dahl, *Democracy and Its Critics* (New Haven and London: Yale University Press, 1989), 324–26. Hereafter cited as *DIC.*

13. Paul Ricoeur, "The Fragility of Political Language," *Philosophy Today* 31, no. 1 (1987): 35–44. Hereafter cited as *FPL.*

14. Paul Ricoeur, "The Task of the Political Educator," *Philosophy Today* 17, no. 2 (1973): 145. Hereafter cited as *TPE.* Whether a form of putative technical progress is genuine or spurious is not at issue here. Even if much of this progress is illusory, history shows that many people have regarded it as so certain that it is beyond challenge. This widespread confidence is what makes politics, in its ineliminable ambiguity, so vulnerable.

15. Hans-Georg Gadamer, *Reason in the Age of Science,* tr. Frederick G. Lawrence (Cambridge: MIT Press, 1981), 37.

16. Ronald Dworkin, "Foundations of Liberal Equality," *Tanner Lectures on Human Values* 11 (Salt Lake City: University of Utah Press, 1990), esp. 20–22 and 36–42.

17. Richard J. Bernstein, *The New Constellation* (Cambridge: MIT Press, 1992), 9. Hereafter cited as *TNC*.

18. Claude Lefort, *Democracy and Political Theory,* tr. David Macey (Minneapolis: University of Minnesota Press, 1988), 216–25. Hereafter cited as *DPT*. For complementary reflection on the relationships between politics, economics, and ethics, see Maurice Merleau-Ponty, *Signs,* tr. Richard C. McCleary (Evanston: Northwestern University Press, 1964), 324–29. Hereafter cited as *S*. See also Vaclav Havel, *Summer Meditations,* tr. Paul Wilson (New York: Alfred A. Knopf, 1992), 63–71, 100–101. George Kennan finds merit in Havel's views about this matter. See his review of Havel's book in *New York Review of Books* 39, no. 15 (24 September 1992): 3–4.

19. Max Weber, "Politics as a Vocation," in his *Essays in Sociology,* tr. H. H. Gerth and C. Wright Mills (New York: Oxford University Press, 1958), esp. 120–26. It is important to notice that the category of ethics of ultimate ends includes, but is not limited to, ethics taught as part of a religious doctrine. Weber's thought is complex and often opaque. In using this distinction I do not mean to suggest that I endorse other parts of his work, but, of course, I do recognize the importance of all of his thought. See also in this connection *TNC*, 35–40.

20. *EP,* 10–11, and *TPE,* 149–50.

21. *EP,* 5–6.

22. *EP,* 6–7.

23. *EP,* 6.

24. Paul Ricoeur, *Lectures on Ideology and Utopia,* ed. George H. Taylor (New York: Columbia University Press, 1986), esp. 252–53 and 311–12. Hereafter cited as *LIU*. See also my comments on this book in my *"Ideology, Utopia, and Responsible Politics,"* *Man and World* 22 (1989): 25–41.

25. I have learned much from Merleau-Ponty about responsible politics. For a fuller documentation of my debt to him, see my *The Politics of Hope* (London: Routledge and Kegan Paul, 1986), 23–42 and *passim,* and my *Elements of Responsible Politics* (Dordrecht: Kluwer Academic Publishers, 1991), esp. 7–10 and 19–62.

26. *S,* 336.

27. Kwame Anthony Appiah, in *My Father's House: Africa in the Philosophy of Culture* (New York and Oxford: Oxford University Press, 1992), 72.

28. *S,* 323–24.

29. *S,* 328, 334.

30. Maurice Merleau-Ponty, *Adventures of the Dialectic,* tr. Joseph Bien (Evanston: Northwestern University Press, 1973), 225. Hereafter cited as *AD*.

31. *S,* 35.

32. *S,* 274–76. See also Maurice Merleau-Ponty, *Humanism and Terror,* tr. John O'Neill (Boston: Beacon Press, 1969), xxxii–xxxiii. Hereafter cited as *HT*.

33. *S,* 35. See also *DPS,* 13, 226–28.

34. I assume here that, even if a nondemocratic state has something called a constitution, its normative force is different in kind from that of constitutions of democratic states. This assumption's warrant is my claim that now and for the foreseeable future, democracy is the best available form of government.

35. On the historicality of the democratic process, see *DIC*, 312, 317–21.

36. *S*, 302–3. See also Maurice Merleau-Ponty, *Sense and Non-Sense*, tr. Hubert Dreyfus and Patricia Allen Dreyfus (Evanston: Northwestern University Press, 1964), 143. Hereafter cited as *SNS*.

37. Maurice Merleau-Ponty, *Phenomenology of Perception*, tr. Colin Smith (London: Routledge and Kegan Paul, 1962), 183–84 and Maurice Merleau-Ponty, *The Primacy of Perception*, ed. and tr. James Edie (Evanston: Northwestern University Press, 1964), 134.

38. *SNS*, 143, and *AD*, 120, 150–51.

39. Maurice Merleau-Ponty, *Themes from the Lectures at College de France, 1952–60*, tr. John O'Neill (Evanston: Northwestern University Press, 1970), 40.

40. *HT*, xxxvi–xxxix, and *AD*, 26, 205. See also Anthony Giddens, *Central Problems in Social Theory* (Berkeley: University of California Press, 1979), 63–69.

41. *AD*, 198–200.

42. *AD*, 56–57, 204–33. See also John Stuart Mill, *On Liberty*, ed. David Spitz (New York: W. W. Norton, 1975), esp. 18–22.

43. *LIU*, esp. 252–53 and 312–14.

44. Hanna F. Pitkin, "Justice: On Relating Public and Private," *Political Theory* 9 (1981): 343–46, as quoted in Lawrence J. Biskowski, "Practical Foundations for Political Judgment: Arendt on Action and World," *Journal of Politics* 55, no. 4 (1993): 877. Biskowski's entire essay deserves attention.

45. I discuss political identity in more detail in the following chapters.

46. For a criticism of one form of pernicious oversimplification, see my "Deconstructive Politics: A Critique," *Human Studies* 14 (1991): 311–30.

47. *AD*, 28.

48. For a good description of prominent plausible forms of democracy, see David Held, *Models of Democracy* (Stanford: Stanford University Press, 1987).

49. *DPT*, 225.

50. *DPT*, 226. See also 227–28.

51. *DPT*, 39.

52. *OAA*, 239.

Chapter 5

1. Derek Heater, *Citizenship: The Civic Ideal in World History, Politics, and Education* (London and New York: Longman, 1990), 94. Hereafter cited as *CCI*.

2. See in this connection Nicholas Colchester, "Goodbye, Nation-State. Hello . . . What?" *New York Times* (17 July 1994): E17. This essay summarizes a report of a recent conference at the Ditchley Foundations, Oxfordshire, England. I leave aside until chapter 8 the question of political loyalties to nationalities within multinational states.

3. Michael Walzer, *Obligations* (Cambridge and London: Harvard University Press, 1970), 210. Hereafter cited as *Oblig.*

4. Thomas R. Dye and Harmon Ziegler, *The Irony of Democracy,* quoted in Benjamin R. Barber, *Strong Democracy* (Berkeley and Los Angeles: University of California Press, 1984), 8. Barber disagrees with Dye and Ziegler.

5. *Oblig.,* 214–17.

6. *Oblig.,* 218.

7. Michael Walzer, "The Civil Society Argument," in Chantal Mouffe, ed., *Dimensions of Radical Democracy* (London: Routledge, 1992), 104–7.

8. *Oblig.,* 218–9.

9. Will Kymlicka and Wayne Norman, "Return of the Citizen: A Survey of Recent Work on Citizenship Theory," *Ethics* 104 (1994): 364. Hereafter cited as *RC.*

10. *Oblig.,* 221.

11. See in this connection Hanna Fenichel Pitkin and Sara M. Schumer, "On Participation," *Kettering Review* (Summer 1994): 17–26.

12. Hannah Arendt, "The Crisis in Education," in her *Between Past and Future* (New York: Penguin Books, 1983), esp. 186. Hereafter cited as *CE.* I return to this essay in chapter 7.

13. William A. Galston, *Liberal Purposes* (Cambridge: Cambridge University Press, 1991), 221. Hereafter cited as *LP.*

14. *LP,* 220.

15. *LP,* 217.

16. William A. Galston, *Justice and the Common Good* (Chicago and London: University of Chicago Press, 1980), 266. Hereafter cited as *JCG.*

17. *JCG,* 269.

18. *LP,* 222.

19. *LP,* 224.

20. *LP,* 224–25.

21. *LP,* 225–26.

22. *LP,* 226–27.

23. *LP,* 301–4.

24. *LP,* 168, 177.

25. *LP,* 281.

26. *LP,* 297–98.

27. *LP,* 195.

28. *LP,* 304.

29. *LP,* 184.

30. *LP,* 184–90.

31. See, for example, David E. Sanger, "Foreign Relations: Money Talks, Policy Walks," *New York Times* (15 January 1995): sect. 4, pp. 1, 4. According to Sanger, the United States Department of Commerce is regularly superseding the State Department in determining govermental policy.

32. *LP,* 221.

33. Mary Ann Glendon, *Rights Talk* (Toronto: Free Press, 1991), esp. 32–40 and 146–51.

34. *LP,* 295.

35. *LP,* 296.

36. I return to the topic of theocracy in the next chapter. It remains relevant today because of movements to govern states by Koranic law.

37. Claude Lefort, *Democracy and Political Theory,* tr. David Macey (Minneapolis: University of Minnesota Press, 1988), 39.

38. One might argue that at least some states, for example, Iceland, are counterexamples to my claim, but, as I show in chapters 7 and 8, today there are no counterexamples.

39. Clifford Geertz, *The Interpretation of Cultures* (New York: Basic Books, 1973) 218–19. See also Paul Ricoeur, in George H. Taylor, ed., *Lectures on Ideology and Utopia* (New York: Columbia University Press, 1986), 10–13.

40. I grant that my test may be incomplete, but at this time I do not know of any additions that should be made to it.

41. Maurice Merleau-Ponty, *Adventures of the Dialectic,* tr. Joseph Bien (Evanston: Northwestern University Press, 1973), 29.

42. George P. Fletcher, *Loyalty: An Essay on the Morality of Relationships* (New York and Oxford: Oxford University Press, 1993), 11–15, 166–70. Hereafter cited as *LEMR.*

43. On the perversions of loyalty, see Maurice Nédoncelle, *De la Fidelité* (Éditions Montaigne: Paris, 1953), 137–51. One can readily translate what he says about fidelity to fit loyalty.

44. Alasdair MacIntyre, *Is Patriotism a Virtue?* (a pamphlet published by the University of Kansas, n.d.), 15.

45. Paul Gomberg, "Patriotism Is Like Racism," *Ethics* 101, (1990): 144.

46. *CE,* 185–89.

47. Michael Walzer, *Spheres of Justice* (New York: Basic Books, 1983), esp. 28–29. See also *LEMR,* 33–36, 155–56, 164–65.

48. I paraphrase here Paul Ricoeur, *Oneself as Another,* tr. Kathleen Blamey (Chicago and London: University of Chicago Press, 1992), 239.

Chapter 6

1. Paul Kennedy, *Preparing for the Twenty-first Century* (New York: Random House, 1993), esp. 95–121.

2. 1995 State of the World report, quoted in *New York Times* (12 February

1995): Y12. According to the *Times* report, the World Bank concurs with this view.

3. Tim Beardsley, "Hot Air," *Scientific American* 271, no. 3 (September 1994): 22.

4. I borrow the notion of preserving a world from Hannah Arendt. See "The Crises in Education" in her *Between Past and Future* (New York: Penguin Books, 1983), esp. 186–93. I do not, however, accept the strong distinction she makes between education and politics. She is wrong to deny that there can be defensible political education of adult citizens.

5. For an example of a proposal to assess environmental risks primarily according to economic criteria, see Keith Schneider, "As Earth Day Turns 25, Life Gets Complicated," *New York Times* (16 April 1995): E6. Hereafter cited as *AED*.

6. My description of the classical casuistry depends heavily on Albert R. Jonsen and Stephen Toulmin, *The Abuse of Casuistry* (Berkeley, Los Angeles, and London: University of California Press, 1988). Hereafter cited as *AC*.

7. *AC*, 251.

8. *AC*, 252.

9. *AC*, 256.

10. *AC*, 256.

11. *AC*, 257.

12. F. J. Connell, "Probabilism," *New Catholic Encyclopedia* 11 (New York: McGraw-Hill Book Company, 1967), 814. Hereafter cited as *NEC*.

13. F. J. Connell, "Probabiliorism," *NEC* 11, 814.

14. F. J. Connell, "Tutiorism," *NEC* 14, 348. A fourth position, called equiprobabilism, came to occupy the ground between probabilism and probabiliorism. For my purposes, I need not consider it.

15. Hans Jonas, *The Imperative of Responsibility* (Chicago and London: University of Chicago Press, 1984), 11. Hereafter cited as *IR*.

16. *IR*, 12. My insertion.

17. *AC*, esp. 48–74.

18. *AED*, E6.

19. A. M. Rosenthal, "Here We Go Again," *New York Times* (13 January 1995): A15. My emphasis.

20. A. M. Rosenthal, "The Nuclear Smugglers," *New York Times* (20 January 1995): A15.

21. Hannah Arendt, *The Origins of Totalitarianism* (Cleveland and New York: Meridian Books, 1962), 296–97.

22. Alexis de Tocqueville, *L'Ancien Régime et la Révolution Française* 1, 62, quoted in Claude Lefort, *Democracy and Political Theory*, tr. David Macey (Minneapolis: University of Minnesota Press, 1988), 169. The latter is hereafter cited as *DPT*.

23. *DPT*, 168.

24. Alexis de Tocqueville, *Democracy in America* 1, 252, quoted in *DPT*, 169.

25. See Robert A. Dahl, *Democracy and Its Critics* (New Haven and London: Yale University Press, 1989), 332–35.

26. *DPT*, 39.

27. Michael Walzer, *Spheres of Justice* (New York: Basic Books, 1983), 144. Elsewhere, Walzer seems to treat citizenship as only a precondition for political office. He says, for example, "that all citizens, or *all citizens with some minimal* training or *skill*, have a right to be considered when offices are given out" (136; my emphasis). My contention is that today, when one considers citizenship's normative requirements, one should construe it as an office that one holds, the qualifications for which are less "minimal" than they once were.

28. John Locke, *Two Treatises of Government 2*, ed. Peter Laslett (Cambridge: Cambridge University Press, 1988) no. 55.

29. These questions are structurally similar to those that John Stuart Mill seeks to answer with his doctrine of qualified judges in *Utilitarianism*.

30. I deal with the matter of restrictions on political participation in chapters 7 and 8.

31. Ambassador George F. Kennan has also recognized the need for some institutional innovation to improve the quality of public discourse about major political issues. He has proposed what he calls a "council of state." My basic objection to his proposal is that he would give this council too much power. See his *Around the Cragged Hill* (New York and London: W. W. Norton, 1993), 236–49.

32. Present United States law—wrongfully, in my view—denies tax exemptions for dues or gifts to nongovernmental organizations that lobby the Congress. Bread for the World is one of the affected organizations.

Chapter 7

1. Amy Gutmann, *Democratic Education* (Princeton: Princeton University Press, 1987), 287. Hereafter cited as *DE*. In this work, Gutmann both presents a theory of democratic education and articulates its implications for educational practice. She claims no more for this work than that it holds good for the United States in its present form (p. 17, fn. 34 and 40). For my present purpose, I treat her theory as though it were applicable to any modern democratic society. So doing lets me use it as a background against which my own proposal can stand out with clarity.

2. One might object that constitutional reform and educational reform apparently presuppose each other and hence, neither can occur. I can only hope that this apparent dilemma is, in practice, no more than merely apparent.

3. Hannah Arendt, "The Crisis in Education," in her *Between Past and Future* (New York: The Viking Press, 1988), 177.

4. *The Basic Law of the Federal Republic of Germany*, ed. Ulrich Karpen (Baden-Baden: Nomos Verlagsgesellschaft, 1988), 228–29.

5. *DE*, 39.

6. *DE*, 44–46.

7. *DE*, 34.

8. *DE*, 117.

9. *DE*, 117–18.

10. *DE*, 118.

11. *DE*, 118.

12. Robert K. Fullinweider, "The Ends of Political and Moral Education," in *Moral Education I*, 1990, a publication of the Carnegie Council on Ethics and International Affairs, 2. Hereafter cited as *EPME*.

13. *EPME*, 5.

14. *EPME*, 12.

15. *EPME*, 13.

16. Schooling that respects and properly supports these bodily ties is not necessarily at odds with liberalism's universalism. See Allen Buchanan, "Self-Determination and the Right to Secede," *Journal of International Affairs* 45, no. 2 (1992): 350–51.

17. Students in the later years of primary education should also receive instruction in the natural sciences. I have no competence, though, to make a sensible proposal about what this instruction should include.

18. To establish and enforce curricular standards for later primary education, I propose that all democratic states should have nonpartisan institutions such as the British or the German ministries of education, whose jurisdiction is statewide.

19. *EPME*, 13.

20. For the difference between the outlook that leads to respect and that which leads to mere tolerance, see Amy Gutmann and Dennis Thompson, "Moral Conflict and Political Consensus," *Ethics* 101 (1990): esp. 76–88.

21. My proposal is on the whole consistent with the sort of relation between citizen and expert that Robert Dahl suggests is both possible and desirable. See his *Democracy and Its Critics* (New Haven and London: Yale University Press, 1989), 338–41.

22. For an example of the sort of activity that I would have institutionalized in political practice, see the article "House and Science Panels Clash on Wetlands' Fate," *New York Times* (7 April 1995): A10. It reports the criticism that a committee of the National Academy of Science makes of legislation proposed in the United States House of Representatives. My proposal would institutionalize the role of such a committee and provide for widespread dissemination of its findings.

23. In the United States, the American Bar Association makes assessments of the sort I have in mind of nominees for appointment to federal judgeships.

24. For a study that recognizes the dangers of today but draws far more

severe conclusions for them than I do, see Eric Hobsbawm, *The Age of Extremes* (New York: Pantheon Books, 1995).

Chapter 8

1. Immanuel Kant, "Perpetual Peace," in his *Political Writings,* ed. Hans Reiss, tr. H. B. Nisbet (Cambridge: Cambridge University Press, 1991), 106. Hereafter cited as *PP.* Though I admit that I have taken this passage somewhat out of context, the position I argue for is in no small measure compatible with the overall doctrine of "Perpetual Peace."

2. *PP,* 106. My emphasis.

3. Allen Buchanan, *Secession* (Boulder: Westview Press, 1991), 18. Hereafter cited as *Sec.* All of my remarks about federation and secession have been influenced by Buchanan's work.

4. My remarks here about exclusions spell out some of the implications of the transgressive character of all human action that Hannah Arendt emphasized. I discussed action's transgressiveness in chapter 3.

5. *Sec.,* 19.

6. Stanley, Hoffmann, "Goodbye to a United Europe?" *New York Review of Books* 41, no. 10 (27 May 1993): 27–31.

7. *Sec.,* 38 and 83, fn. 18.

8. *Sec.,* 38.

9. *Sec.,* 38–74.

10. Thomas Christiano, "Secession, Democracy and Distributive Justice," *Arizona Law Review* 37, no. 1 (1995): 70. See also Allen Buchanan, "Federalism, Secession, and the Morality of Inclusion," *Arizona Law Review* 37, no. 1 (1995): 62–63. The latter article is hereafter cited as *FSMI.*

11. See Misha Glenny, "The Great Fall," *New York Review of Books* 42, no. 5 (1995): 56–65.

12. *FSMI,* 58–61.

13. See Paul Kennedy, *Preparing for the Twenty-first Century* (New York: Random House, 1993), 41–46 and *passim.*

14. United Nations High Commissioner for Refugees, *Handbook on Procedures and Criteria for Determining Refugee Status* (New York: United Nations, 1992), 10–25.

15. Garrett Hardin has argued for a position like this one. See his *Living within Limits* (New York: Oxford University Press, 1993), 276–93.

16. These three sorts of proposals are sketched out in Keith Melville et al., *Admission Decisions: Should Immigration Be Restricted?* (Dayton: National Issues Forums Institute, 1994). Though these proposals were prepared with the United States in view, they are, mutatis mutandis, applicable to most, if not all, democratic states.

17. *Georgia Bulletin,* 20 October 1994, 16.

18. What counts as sufficient prosperity and desperate need varies. Prevailing empirical considerations have to flesh out these notions for each era.

19. One may offer Japan as a counterexample to this contention, but Japan is anomalous in several ways. Its version of democracy is no model for others.

20. Hannah Arendt, *The Human Condition* (Chicago: University of Chicago Press, 1958), 57. Hereafter cited as *HC*.

21. *HC,* 184.

22. For a report of this new policy, *New York Times* (6 November 1994): Y5.

23. Michael Walzer, *Spheres of Justice* (New York: Basic Books, 1983), 60. Hereafter cited as *SJ*.

24. *SJ,* 60–61.

25. Herbert Spiegelberg, *Steppingstones toward an Ethics for Fellow Existers* (The Hague: Martinus Nijhoff, 1986), 231–81.

26. Should a state have more than one comprehensive official language, then the candidate for naturalization ought to have to acquire only one of them.

27. See in this connection Paul Ricoeur, *Oneself as Another,* tr. Kathleen Blamey (Chicago and London: University of Chicago Press, 1992), 236–39.

Bibliography

Ackerman, Bruce. *Social Justice in the Liberal State.* New Haven: Yale University Press, 1980.

Appiah, Kwame Anthony. *In My Father's House: Africa in the Philosophy of Culture.* New York and Oxford: Oxford University Press, 1992.

Arendt, Hannah. *The Human Condition.* Chicago and London: University of Chicago Press, 1958.

———. *The Origins of Totalitarianism.* Cleveland and New York: Meridian Books, 1962.

———. "Karl Jaspers: Citizen of the World?" In *Men in Dark Times.* New York: Harcourt, Brace and World, 1968.

———. *Between Past and Future.* New York: Penguin Books, 1983.

———. "Philosophy and Politics." *Social Research* 57, no. 1 (Spring 1990): 75–103.

Aristotle. *On Rhetoric*, translated by George A. Kennedy. New York: Oxford University Press, 1991.

Aristotle. *Rhetoric*, translated by G. M. A. Grube. Indianapolis and Cambridge: Hackett, 1975.

Barber, Benjamin. *Strong Democracy.* Berkeley and Los Angeles: University of California Press, 1984.

Bardes, Barbara, Steffen Schmitt, and Mark Shelly II. *American Government and Politics Today.* New York: West Publishing, 1985.

Beardsley, Tim. "Hot Air." *Scientific American* 271, no. 3 (September 1994): 18–22.

Becker, Lawrence C. "Community, Dominion, and Membership." *Southern Journal of Philosophy* 30, no. 2 (1992): 17–43.

Bell, Daniel. *Communitarianism and Its Critics.* Oxford and New York: Oxford University Press, 1993.

Benhabib, Seyla. *Situating the Self.* New York: Routledge, 1992.

Bernstein, Richard J. *The New Constellation.* Cambridge: MIT Press, 1992.

Biskowski, Lawrence J. "Practical Foundations for Political Judgment: Arendt on Action and World." *Journal of Politics* 55, no. 4 (1993): 867–77.

Buchanan, Allen. *Secession*. Boulder: Westview Press, 1991.

———. "Self-Determination and the Right to Secede." *Journal of International Affairs* 45, no. 2 (1992): 347–65.

———. "Federalism, Secession, and the Morality of Inclusion." *Arizona Law Review* 37, no. 1 (1995): 53–64.

Christiano, Thomas. "Secession, Democracy, and Distributive Justice." *Arizona Law Review* 37, no. 1 (1995): 65–72.

Colchester, Nicholas. "Goodbye, Nation-State. Hello . . . What?" *New York Times* (17 July 1994): E17.

Connell, F. J. "Probabilism." *The New Catholic Encyclopedia* 11. New York: McGraw-Hill Book Company (1967): 814.

———. "Tutiorism." *New Catholic Encyclopedia* 14, New York: McGraw-Hill Book Company (1967): 348.

Crick, Bernard. *In Defense of Politics*. Chicago and London: University of Chicago Press, 1972.

Dahl, Robert A. *Democracy and Its Critics*. New Haven and London: Yale University Press, 1989.

Dauenhauer, Bernard P. *The Politics of Hope*. London: Routledge and Kegan Paul 1986.

———. "Ideology, Utopia, and Responsible Politics." *Man and World* 22 (1989): 25–41.

———. *Elements of Responsible Politics*. Dordrecht: Kluwer Academic Publishers, 1991.

———. "Deconstructive Politics: A Critique." *Human Studies* 14 (1991): 311–30.

———. "Ricoeur's Contribution to Contemporary Political Thought." In *Meaning in Texts and Action*, edited by David Klemm and William Schweiker. Charlottesville: University Press of Virginia, 1993.

Dietz, Mary G. " 'The Slow Boring of Hard Boards': Methodical Thinking and the Work of Politics." *American Political Science Review* 88, no. 4 (1994): 873–86.

Dworkin, Ronald. *Taking Rights Seriously*. Cambridge: Harvard University Press, 1977.

———. *A Matter of Principle*. Cambridge: Harvard University Press, 1985.

———. "Foundations of Liberal Equality." In *The Tanner Lectures on Human Values* 11. Salt Lake City: University of Utah Press (1990): 9–78.

Dye, Thomas R., and Harmon Ziegler. *The Irony of Democracy*, Belmont: Wadsworth, 1970.

Fawcett, J. E. S. "Security Council Resolutions on Rhodesia." *British Yearbook of International Law* 41, (1965–66): 103–21.

Fletcher, George P. *Loyality: An Essay on the Morality of Relationships*. New York and Oxford: Oxford University Press, 1993.

Gadamer, Hans-Georg. *Reason in the Age of Science*, translated by Frederick G. Lawrence. Cambridge: MIT Press, 1981.

Gallagher, Shawn. "Language and Imperfect Consensus: Merleau-Ponty's Contribution to the Habermas-Gadamer Debate." In *Merleau-Ponty, Hermeneutics, and Postmodernism*, edited by Thomas Busch and Shawn Gallagher. Albany: State University of New York Press, 1992.

Galston, William A. *Justice and the Common Good*. Chicago and London: University of Chicago Press, 1980.

———. *Liberal Purposes*. Cambridge: Cambridge University Press, 1991.

Geertz, Clifford. *The Interpretation of Cultures*. New York: Basic Books, 1973.

Giddens, Anthony. *Central Problems in Social Theory*. Berkeley: University of California Press, 1979.

Glendon, Mary Ann. *Rights Talk*. Toronto: Free Press, 1991.

Glenny, Misha. "The Great Fall." *New York Review of Books* 42, no. 5 (1995): 56–65.

Gomberg, Paul. "Patriotism is Like Racism." *Ethics* 101 (1990): 144–50.

Green, Melissa Fay. *Praying for Sheetrock*. Reading, Mass.: Addison-Wesley Publishing Company, 1991.

Gutmann, Amy, and Dennis Thompson. *Democratic Education*. Princeton: Princeton University Press (1987): 287.

———. "Moral Conflict and Political Consensus." *Ethics* 101 (October 1990): 64–88.

Habermas, Jurgen. *The New Conservatism*, translated by Shierry Weber Nicholsen. Cambridge: MIT Press, 1989.

———. "Discourse Ethics: Notes on a Program of Philosophical Justification." In *The Communicative Ethics Controversy*, edited by Seyla Benhabib and Fred Dallmayr. Cambridge and London: MIT Press, 1990.

———. "Further Reflections on the Public Sphere." In *Habermas and the Public Sphere*, edited by Craig Calhoun. Cambridge and London: MIT Press, 1992.

———. "Citizenship and National Identity: Some Reflections on Europe." *Praxis International* 12, no. 1 (April 1992): 1–19.

———. *Justification and Application*, translated by Ciaran Cronin. Cambridge and London: MIT Press, 1993.

———. "Three Normative Models for Democracy." *Constellations* 1, no. 1 (1994): 3–19.

———. "Reconciliation through the Public Use of Reason: Remarks on John Rawls's Political Liberalism." *Journal of Philosophy* 92, no. 3 (1995): 109–31.

Hardin, Garrett. *Living within Limits*. New York: Oxford Univesity Press, 1993.

Havel, Vaclav. *Summer Meditations*, translated by Paul Wilson. New York: Alfred A. Knopf, 1992.

Heater, Derek. *Citizenship: The Civic Ideal in World History, Politics, and Education*. London: Longmans, 1990.

Hegel, G. F. W. *The Philosophy of Right*, translated by T. M. Knox. Oxford: Clarendon Press, 1942.

Heidegger, Martin. *Being and Time*, translated by John Macquarrie and Edward Robinson. New York and Evanston: Harper and Row, 1962.

Held, David. *Models of Democracy*. Stanford: Stanford University Press, 1987.

―――. "Democracy: From City-states to a Cosmopolitan Order?" In *Prospects for Democracy*, edited by David Held. Stanford: Stanford University Press, 1993.

Hobsbawm, Eric. *The Age of Extremes*. New York: Pantheon Books, 1995.

Hoffman, Stanley. "Goodbye to a United Europe?" *New York Review of Books* 40, no. 10 (27 May 1993): 27–31.

Ignatieff, Michael. *The Needs of Strangers*. New York: Penguin Books, 1984.

Ingram, David. *Habermas and the Dialetic of Reason*. New Haven: Yale University Press, 1987.

Jonas, Hans. *The Imperative of Responsibility*. Chicago and London: University of Chicago Press, 1984.

Kant, Immanuel. "Perpetual Peace." In *Political Writings*, edited by Hans Reiss, translated by H. B. Nisbet. Cambridge: Cambridge University Press, 1991.

Kateb, George. *The Inner Ocean: Individualism and Democratic Culture*. Ithaca: Cornell University Press, 1992.

Kennan, George F. "Keeping the Faith," New York Review of Books 39, no. 15 (24 September 1992): 3–4.

―――. *Around the Cragged Hill*. New York and London: W. W. Norton and Company, 1993.

Kennedy, Paul. *Preparing for the Twenty-first Century*. New York: Random House, 1993.

Kronman, Anthony. *The Lost Lawyer*. Cambridge: Belknap Press, 1993.

Kymlicka, Will, and Wayne Norman. "Return of the Citizen: A Survey of Recent Work on Citizenship Theory," *Ethics* 104 (1994): 352–81.

LeFort, Claude. *Democracy and Political Theory*, translated By David Macey. Minneapolis: University of Minnesota Press, 1988.

Locke, John. *Two Treatises of Government*, translated by Peter Laslett. Cambridge: Cambridge University Press, 1988.

McBride, William L. *Social and Political Philosophy*. New York: Paragon House, 1994.

McCarthy, Thomas. "Practical Discourse: On the Relation of Morality to Politics." In *Habermas and the Public Sphere*, edited by Craig Calhoun. Cambridge: MIT Press, 1992.

―――. "Kantian Construction and Reconstructivism: Rawls and Habermas in Dialogue." *Ethics* 105 (October 1994): 44–63.

McDonald, John D. *One More Sunday*. New York: Alfred A. Knopf, 1984.

McIntyre, Alasdair. *After Virtue*. Notre Dame: Notre Dame University Press, 1981.

———. *Three Rival Versions of Moral Inquiry*. Notre Dame: University of Notre Dame Press, 1990.

———. *Is Patriotism a Virtue?* University of Kansas, n. d.

Melville, Keith. *Admission Decisions: Should Immigration Be Restricted?* Dayton: National Issues Forum Institute, 1994.

Merleau-Ponty, Maurice. *Phenomenology of Perception*, translated by Colin Smith. London: Routledge and Kegan Paul, 1962.

———. *Signs*, translated by Richard C. McCleary. Evanston: Northwestern University Press, 1964.

———. *Sense and Nonsense*, translated by Hubert Dreyfus and Patricia Allen Dreyfus. Evanston: Northwestern University Press, 1964.

———. *The Primacy of Perception*, edited and translated by James Edie. Evanston: Northwestern University Press, 1964.

———. *The Visible and the Invisibile*, translated by Alphonso Lingis. Evanston: Northwestern University Press, 1968.

———. *Humanism and Terror*, translated by John O'Neill. Boston: Beacon Press, 1969.

———. *Themes from the Lectures at College de France, 1952–60*, translated by John O'Neill. Evanston: Northwestern University Press, 1970.

———. *Adventures of the Dialetics*, translated by Joseph Bien. Evanston: Northwestern University Press, 1973.

Mill, John Stuart. *Utilitarianism*, edited by George Sher. Indianapolis: Hackett, 1979.

———. *On Liberty*, edited by David Spitz. New York: W. W. Norton, 1975.

Moynihan, Daniel Patrick. *Pandemonium: Ethnicity in International Affairs*. Oxford: Oxford University Press, 1993.

Murray, Alexander. *Reason and Society in the Middle Ages*. Oxford: Clarendon Press, 1985.

Nichols, Mary P. *Citizens and Statesmen: A Study of Aristotle's Politics*. Savage, Md.: Rowman & Littlefield, 1992.

Niebuhr, Reinhold. *Moral Man and Immoral Society*. New York: Charles Scribner's Sons, 1949.

Nussbaum, Martha. "Aristotlelian Social Democracy." In *Liberalism and the Good*, edited by R. Bruce Douglass, Gerald M. Mara and Henry S. Richardson. New York and London: Routledge, 1990.

———. "Human Functioning and Social Justice." *Political Theory* 20, no. 2 (1992): 202–46.

Peillon, Vincent. *La tradition de l'esprit: Itineraire de Maurice Merleau-Ponty*. Paris: Editions Grasset and Fasquelle, 1994.

Perry, Michael J. *Morality, Politics, and Law: A Bicentennial Essay*. New York: Oxford University Press, 1988.

Pitkin, Hanna F. "Justice: On Relating Public and Private." *Political Theory* 9 (1981): 327–52.

Pitkin, Hanna F. and Sara M. Schumer. "On Participation." *Kettering Review* (Summer 1994): 17–26.

Plato. *Apology.*

Pogge, Thomas. *Realizing Rawls.* Ithaca and London: Cornell University Press, 1988.

Rawls, John. *Political Liberalism.* New York: Columbia University Press, 1993.

———. "The Law of Peoples." In *On Human Rights: The Oxford Amnesty Lectures*, edited by Stephen Shute and Susan Hurley. New York: Basic Books, 1993.

Raz, Joseph. *The Morality of Freedom.* Oxford: Clarendon Press, 1986.

Ricoeur, Paul. "The Task of the Political Educator." *Philosophy Today* 17, no. 2 (1973): 142–52.

———. "Le temps raconte." *Revue de metaphysique et de morale* 89 (1984): 436–52.

———. "Ethique et politique." *Esprit* 101 (May 1985): 1–11.

———. *Lectures on Ideology and Utopia*, edited by George H. Taylor. New York: Columbia University Press, 1986.

———. "The Fragility of Political Language." *Philosophy Today* 31, no. 1 (1987): 35–44.

———. *Oneself as Another*, translated by Kathleen Blamely. Chicago and London: University of Chicago Press, 1992.

Rosenthal, A. M. "Here We Go Again." *New York Times* (13 January 1995): A15.

———. "The Nuclear Smugglers." *New York Times* (20 January 1995): A15.

Ruckelshaus, William D. "Toward a Sustainable World." *Scientific American* 261, no. 3 (September 1989): 166–70.

Sandel, Michael. *Liberalism and the Limits of Justice.* Cambridge: Cambridge University Press, 1982.

Sanger, David E. "Foreign Relations: Money Talks, Policy Walks." *New York Times* (15 January 1995): sect. 4, pp. 1, 4.

Schneider, Keith. "As Earth Day Turns 25, Life Gets Complicated." *New York Times* (26 April 1995): E6.

Sen, Amartya. "Population: Delusion and Reality." In *New York Review of Books 41*, no. 15 (22 September 1994): 62–71.

Sherover, Charles. *Time, Freedom, and the Common Good.* Albany: State University of New York Press, 1989.

Simon, Herbert. *Administrative Behavior.* New York: Macmillan, 1947.

Spiegelberg, Herbert. "Accident of Birth: A Non-Utilitarian Motif in Mill's Philosophy." *Steppingstones toward an Ethics for Fellow Existers.* Dordrecht: Martinus Nijhoff, 1986.

Spragens, Jr., Thomas A. *Reason and Democracy.* Durham: Duke University Press, 1990.

Swanson, Judith A. *The Public and the Private in Aristotle's Political Philosophy.* Ithaca and London: Cornell University Press, 1992.

Tamir, Yael. *Liberal Nationalism.* Princeton: Princeton University Press, 1993.

Taylor, Charles. "Hegel: History and Politics." In *Liberalism and Its Critics*, edited by Michael Sandel. New York: New York University Press, 1984.

———. *Human Agency and Language*. Cambridge: Harvard University Press, 1985.

———. *Philosophy and the Human Sciences*. Cambridge: Harvard University Press, 1985.

———. *Philosophy and the Human Sciences*. Cambridge: Harvard University Press, 1985.

———. "Cross-Purposes: The Liberal-Communitarian Debate." In *Liberalism and the Moral Life*, edited by Nancy L. Rosenbaum. Cambridge: Harvard University Press, 1989.

———. *Sources of the Self*. Cambridge: Harvard University Press, 1989.

———. *The Ethics of Authenticity*. Cambridge: Harvard University Press, 1991.

———. *Multiculturalism and "The Politics of Recognition."* Princeton: Princeton University Press, 1992.

Thompson, John B. *Critical Hermeneutics: A Study in the Thought of Paul Ricoeur and Jurgen Habermas*. Cambridge: Cambridge University Press, 1981.

de Tocqueville, Alexis. *Democracy in America* I, translated by Henry Reeve. New York: Alfred A. Knopf, 1976.

Walzer, Michael. *Obligations*. Cambridge and London: Harvard University Press, 1970.

———. "Philosophy and Democracy." *Political Theory* 9, no. 3, (August 1981): 379–99.

———. *Spheres of Justice*. New York: Basic Books, 1983.

———. "Citizenship." In *Political Innovation and Conceptual Change*, edited by T. Ball, J. Farr, and R. L. Hanson. Cambridge: Cambridge University Press, 1989.

———. "The Communitarian Critique of Liberalism." *Political Theory* 18, no. 1, (1990): 6–23.

———. "The Civil Society Argument." In *Dimensions of Radical Democracy*, edited by Chantal Mouffe. London: Routledge, 1992.

Weber, Max. *From Max Weber: Essays in Sociology*, translated by H. H. Gerth and C. Wright Mills. New York: Oxford University Press, 1958.

Wellmer, Albrecht. *The Persistence of Modernity*, translated by David Midgley. Cambridge: MIT Press, 1991.

Wolin, Sheldon. *Politics and Vision*. Boston: Little Brown and Co., 1968.

Index

Page numbers followed by *n* indicate notes.

About the Author

Bernard P. Dauenhauer is University Professor and Professor of Philosophy at the University of Georgia. His works in political philosophy include *The Politics of Hope* (1986), *Elements of Responsible Politics* (1991) as well as many articles published during the past fifteen years.